MULTINATIONAL INVESTMENT AND ECONOMIC STRUCTURE

Over the post-war period, the activities of multinationals (MNEs) have grown at a phenomenal rate. With global sales exceeding $4.8 trillion in 1991, the role of multinational investment in economic growth cannot be ignored. *Multinational Investment and Economic Structure* examines the relationship between industrial development and foreign direct investment (FDI) activities, and the interaction between MNE activity and economic structure, by analysing:

- the dynamics of FDI and economic growth;
- a cross-sectional test of the investment development path (IDP);
- natural and created assets as determinants of FDI;
- globalisation, homogeneity among industrialised countries and differences in FDI patterns;
- country-specific factors, trade and FDI patterns over the 1980s;
- transpacific FDI: a forty-year view of changing competitiveness.

Multinational Investment and Economic Structure explains the importance of governments in promoting economic growth through the use of FDI and examines the important role of national systems of innovation in the Triad. Connecting the theoretical approach to evolutionary economics and neo-Schumpeterian views, this book argues that globalisation has not affected multinational activity to the extent that much of the previous literature has claimed.

Rajneesh Narula is an Assistant Professor in International Business and Research Fellow at the Maastricht Economic Research Institute on Innovation and Technology (MERIT) at the University of Limburg. He has previously worked in the US, Hong Kong and Nigeria. He is also co-editor (with John Dunning) of *Foreign Direct Investment and Governments: Catalysts for Economic Restructuring.*

ROUTLEDGE STUDIES IN INTERNATIONAL BUSINESS AND THE WORLD ECONOMY

1 STATES AND FIRMS
Multinational enterprises in institutional competition
Razeen Sally

2 MULTINATIONAL RESTRUCTURING, INTERNATIONAL AND SMALL ECONOMIES
The case of Sweden
Thomas Andersson, Torbörn Freriksson, Roger Svensson

3 FOREIGN DIRECT INVESTMENT AND GOVERNMENTS
Catalysts for economic restructuring
Edited by John Dunning and Rajneesh Narula

4 MULTINATIONAL INVESTMENT AND ECONOMIC STRUCTURE
Globalisation and competitiveness
Rajneesh Narula

5 EFFECTIVE INNOVATION POLICY
A new approach
Mark Dodgson and John Bessant

MULTINATIONAL INVESTMENT AND ECONOMIC STRUCTURE

Globalisation and competitiveness

Rajneesh Narula

Routledge
Taylor & Francis Group
LONDON AND NEW YORK

First published 1996
by Routledge
2 Park Square, Milton Park, Abingdon, Oxon, OX14 4RN

Simultaneously published in the USA and Canada
by Routledge
270 Madison Ave, New York NY 10016

Transferred to Digital Printing 2010

Typeset in Garamond
by Datix International Limited, Bungay, Suffolk.

British Library Cataloguing in Publication Data
A catalogue record for this book is available from the British Library

Library of Congress Cataloging in Publication Data
A catalogue record for this book has been requested

ISBN 0-415-13013-1
ISSN 1359-7930

Publisher's Note

The publisher has gone to great lengths to ensure the quality of this reprint but points out that some imperfections in the original may be apparent.

CONTENTS

LIST OF FIGURES

LIST OF TABLES

FOREWORD

John H. Dunning

The integration of research studies on technological development and foreign direct investment (FDI) is still at a rudimentary stage. It is, however, one of the fastest growing and potentially rewarding fields of study among scholars. It is also capturing the attention of researchers from many different countries, notably the US, the UK, Italy, Sweden and Canada, and, increasingly, from an interdisciplinary perspective.

While the role of technology as a vehicle of growth and development was implicitly acknowledged throughout the nineteenth century, it was only explicitly introduced into mainstream economics by Joseph Schumpeter in the early twentieth century.[1] Work on FDI is of even more recent origin, and dates back only to the early 1960s.[2] The first intellectual twinning of the two strands of thought was attempted by Raymond Vernon,[3] who, in the 1960s, was actively involved in studying both the growth of multinational enterprises and the role of technology in international trade. His, justifiably famous, product cycle thesis attempts to show (a) why the technological advantages of multinational enterprises (MNEs) reflect the specific characteristics of their home countries, and (b) how the mode of servicing foreign markets to exploit these advantages may change over time. However, in the later 1960s and 1970s, the scholarly train of development of technology-related growth and FDI studies proceeded along very different lines. Each, indeed, spawned different explanatory models and theories, as Dr Narula details in this book. Although, periodically, bridges were built between the interests of the two groups of scholars, it was not until the 1980s that the dynamic interplay between technology and FDI was systematically examined.

The first glimpses of an integrated paradigm appeared in John Cantwell's book, *Technological Innovation and Multinational Corporations*, published in 1989.[4] *Inter alia*, Cantwell attempted to marry Nelson and Winter's evolutionary theory of growth[5] with that of the eclectic and internalisation paradigms of international production. In doing so, he proposed a developmental theory of FDI in which the competitive advantages of both firms and countries were seen to be the result of cumulative technological and organisational advances.

In the late 1980s and 1990s, further work on the interaction between technology and FDI was published. As often occurs, as a discipline develops, various different, but complementary, schools of thought emerge. Thus, today, the Sussex school and most Italian scholars are interested in technological innovation; the Swedish researchers are particularly concerned with the location of R&D; while the Reading and Canadian economists remain primarily interested in the innovatory trajectories and organisational modalities of large MNEs.

Dr Narula begins by tackling his chosen research topic from the standpoint of an international business scholar. More specifically, he is using and extending a concept developed by me in the late 1970s – namely, the investment development path – to explain the interplay between inward and outward direct investment and the changing economic structure of both host and home countries over the past thirty years or so.

However, Dr Narula does much more than identify the characteristics of this relationship. The central core of his thesis concerns the ways in which the competitive (and largely mobile) advantages of firms and competitive (but largely immobile) advantages of countries may mutually reinforce each other over time. Among other things, he shows that the interface depends on (a) the economic and political characteristics of the countries concerned, (b) the type of FDI (e.g. whether it is market, resource or asset seeking), and (c) the policies pursued by home and host governments towards both FDI and the macro-organisation of economic activity.

Dr Narula's key finding is that, as countries go through various stages of their development, the dynamics of the juxtaposition of their location bound assets with those of their own foreign MNEs changes. While both too are, to a certain extent, path dependent, as countries mature, not only do the structures of their economies tend to converge, but the uniqueness of their location bound assets becomes less based on the comparative advantage of their *natural* factor endowments, and more on their ability to *create* new assets (e.g. technology and human capital). Dr Narula also reveals a similar convergence among the leading MNEs, with their core competencies shifting from the possession of specific assets to the way a unique portfolio of assets is organised on a global or regional basis. Indeed, he suggests that part of inbound FDI in industrialised countries is not to exploit the use of existing competitive advantages of the investing firms with those of the natural resources of host countries, but rather to use the created assets of these countries to protect or upgrade their capabilities.

Another noteworthy feature of Dr Narula's monograph is that, unlike most studies of the investment development path, it pays special attention to the position of developed industrialised countries. Here, the author emphasises the growing role of national governments in organising or influencing the interface between FDI and technological development. Increasingly, as he points out, MNEs are investing abroad to acquire complementary assets to use with their own competitive advantages; and, more often than not, governments, by their education, industrial and transport and communication policies, critically influence the availability, quality and cost of these assets.

This is a brave and original study, and Dr Narula explores unchartered territory for the international business scholar. I am confident that his analysis and findings will be well received and provide the academic community with much food for thought. No less significantly, his research has considerable implications for national governments as they seek to reformulate their macro-organisational strategies in the light of the globalisation of economic activity. I congratulate him on the publication of this his first book, and look forward to reading more of his scholarly research in future years.

University of Reading
and Rutgers University
August 1995

NOTES

1 See, for example, his *Theory of Economic Development*, first published in 1912.

2 As described, for example, in Dunning, J.H. (ed.) (1992) *The Theory of Transitional Corporations*, London: Routledge.

3 See his classic article, 'International investment and international trade in the product cycle', *Quarterly Journal of Economics* 80: 190–207 (1966).

4 Basil Blackwell, Oxford.

5 Nelson, R.R. and Winter, S.G. (1982) *An Evolutionary Theory of Economic Change*, Cambridge, Mass., Belknap Press.

ACKNOWLEDGEMENTS

Unfortunately, we live in an age when too many people are gifted with the commonest of all gifts: hindsight. This may account for the large number of people (most of whom are economists) who believe they know how anything, once done, could have been done better. Regrettably, I too must stand up and be counted among these multitudes: I am painfully aware, *ex post*, of how this could be a much better book, and how to do so. Nor is this the first time: this book is based on previous work I did for my PhD thesis, completed in 1993 at Rutgers University.

There are people I must thank for their instrumental role in terminating what might possibly have been a never-ending quest. First and foremost of this group is my PhD supervisor, Professor John Dunning. Not only has he generously given of his time to hear my ideas out, he has also been pivotal in keeping my thinking focused when I have (all too often) strayed from the main issues. Chapters 2 and 7 are based largely on a paper I co-authored with Professor Dunning entitled, 'Transpacific direct investment and the investment development path: the record assessed', *Essays in International Business*, no. 10, May 1994. I am grateful for his permission to do so. I must also thank Dr Kofi Afriyie, Professor H.P. Gray, Professor Farok Contractor and Professor Terutomo Ozawa, all members of my PhD committee, for their continuous encouragement, suggestions and advice. I have always had the good fortune of being surrounded by people who are not averse to outright honesty and infinite patience. Professor John Hagedoorn of the University of Limburg is perhaps more endowed with the first of these qualities than anyone I know, and he has exercised both in no small measure since I have worked with him.

However, there are those with whom my discussions have had much the opposite effect, introducing me to new concepts that have threatened to lead me astray (and to some extent have succeeded). These individuals are too numerous to mention, although many of them are associated with the Maastricht Economic Research Institute on Innovation and Technology (MERIT) at the University of Limburg. Prior to my arrival in Maastricht, I had been blissfully unaware of more than the basics about technology, innovation and evolutionary economics. Although there are those who believe I remain so, I am nevertheless grateful to them for expanding my horizons.

Data used here have come from a variety of sources. Gratitude is expressed to MERIT for providing some of the data used, and particularly Bart Verspagen who has been very generous with his time. Other data were kindly provided by various members of the UNCTAD Program on TNCs, formerly the United Nations Center on Transnational Corporations (UNCTC). The assistance of the reference librarians at Dana Library, Rutgers University, cannot go unmentioned – especially Ka-Neng Au and Roberta Tipton, who spared no effort in discovering new treasure troves of data and information concealed in all sorts of unlikely places!

Last but by no means least, I must thank Karin Kamp, who has put up with my alternating and erratic states of panic, depression and euphoria since we first met, and continues to listen patiently to unsolicited monologues on foreign direct investment. Although she sometimes sees less of me than my Macintosh does, I urge her to keep in mind that it is quality that counts, not quantity.

A cautionary word to those who intend to read further: the subject matter herein straddles economics and international business. This is still very much a grey area, and my attempts to shed light may not meet the expectations of those with a more puritanical and rigorous persuasion. The analyses and discussion in this book follow an evolutionary process, and amply demonstrate that my knowledge of the subject at hand is incomplete, and – as must be expected from my being boundedly rational – my thinking unfortunately path-dependent. I apologise in advance for all inconsistencies and errors. On one issue, though, I am gifted with perfect information: the reader is not likely to learn as much from reading this book as I did from writing it.

Maastricht
March 1995

ABBREVIATIONS

DCMNE	developing country multinational enterprise
EC	European Community
ECU	European Currency Unit
EFTA	European Free Trade Area
EU	European Union
FDI	foreign direct investment
G-7	Group of Seven
GDP	gross domestic product
GNP	gross national product
I	internalisation
IDP	investment development path
IMF	International Monetary Fund
L	locational
M&A	mergers & acquisitions
MERIT	Maastricht Economic Research Institute on Innovation and Technology
MITI	Ministry of International Trade and Industry
MNE	multinational enterprise
NAFTA	North American Free Trade Area
NIE	newly industrialising economies
NOI	net outward investment
NSI	national systems of innovation
NTBs	non-tariff barriers
O	ownership
Oa	asset-based ownership advantages
OECD	Organisation for Economic Cooperation and Development
OLI	ownership, locational and internalisation
OPEC	Organization of Petroleum Exporting Countries
Ot	transaction-cost based ownership advantages
R&D	research & development
RCA	revealed comparative advantage

RPA	revealed patenting advantage
TPDI	transpacific direct investment
UN	United Nations
UNCTC	United Nations Centre on Transnational Corporations
Unesco	United Nations Educational, Scientific and Cultural Organisation
VCP	vicious cycle of poverty
VER	voluntary export restraints

1

INTRODUCTION

THE RESEARCH OBJECTIVES AND WHY IT MATTERS

There can be few areas of intellectual pursuit that have attracted as much interest as that of economic growth and development, as the almost infinite number of theories of economic development and learned publications on the causes of economics growth will attest to. A significant proportion of these efforts – explicitly or implicitly – regard the international economic activity of nations as being central to their economic prosperity. However, until relatively recently, international economic activity has been synonymous with trade. Over the post-war period, the activities of multinational enterprises (MNEs) have been seen to have grown at a phenomenal rate, primarily through foreign direct investment (FDI). Since 1981, FDI flows have consistently grown faster than GDP or exports on a worldwide basis. With the global sales of MNEs having exceeded $4.8 trillion in 1991, compared with world exports of goods and non-factor services in the same year of $4.5 trillion (UNCTAD 1994), this is increasingly seen as a significant phenomenon. The importance of FDI is further underscored by the growing role that MNEs play in international trade: one-third of world trade in 1991 was estimated to represent intra-firm trade.

The significance of FDI in the world economy is much less controversial than is its influence on economic growth, although an overwhelming majority of countries' economies now explicitly regard FDI as an integral and crucial part of their growth strategy. Our objective is to examine the dynamic interaction between MNE activity and economic development and restructuring in a country. The framework developed and utilised here is the dynamic version of the investment development path (IDP), originally postulated by Dunning (1981a, 1988a). Its primary thesis revolves around three issues. First, national economies undergo structural change as they grow. Second, the structure and level of development of the economy of a country are related in a systematic way to the extent and nature of the FDI activity undertaken by its domestic firms (outward FDI), as well as by those of other nationalities within its national boundaries (inward FDI). Third, the relationship between the FDI activities (both inward and outward) associated with a given country and its economic structure is a dynamic and interactive one; i.e. FDI activity is influenced by the structure of the economy, as well as vice-versa. It is not our intention to evaluate *whether* in fact FDI promotes economic development. To the extent that we assume throughout this monograph that under certain conditions this is generally so, our analysis represents a normative one.

The objectives of this book are two-fold. First, we attempt to develop an understanding of the concurrent evolution of economic development and FDI. In particular, we focus on the changing nature of competitive advantages of countries as they move from a natural asset base towards a created asset one. The balance between the level of natural and created assets essentially determines their economic structure. The nature of their comparative advantages helps determine the nature of the firm-specific assets (i.e. competitive advantages of firms or ownership (O) advantages) of the firms operating in the domestic environment. The inter-temporal dynamics that lead to shifts in the economic structure are strongly associated with both the process of technological accumulation and the development of firms' competences, as well as with the role of governments in facilitating industrial development and economic growth through policy implementation and development. The role of government is highlighted in that it is significant in determining and facilitating the efficiency with which created assets are developed and used, through infrastructural development and national systems of innovation.

The second objective of this monograph is to analyse and evaluate the nature of the relationship between FDI activities and economic structure as a result of recent profound changes in the structure of the world economy. These changes have at least two major implications for the IDP, as well as for economic policy. The first implication concerns the possible changes in the nature of the IDP among the industrialised countries. These are associated with the phenomena of 'catch-up' and convergence among these countries that are not unrelated to the process of regionalisation among the Triad countries (the EU, Japan and the US). Industrialised economies have become increasingly linked through *de facto* and *de jure* integration, as well as through an increasing extent of MNE activity between and among this group of countries which has led their economies to a high extent of interdependence. Although the intra-Triad level of FDI has grown quite rapidly over this time, the economic growth of these countries has declined. This has led to a sort of equilibrium relationship in the IDP. We introduce a fifth stage to the IDP to explain this. Countries at stage 5 no longer exhibit a direct relationship between their FDI and their income levels, since they are no longer growing in an absolute sense, but through a process of structural adjustment *within* their individual economies and *between* sectors, as well as among themselves. Indeed, it is argued here that the structural evolution of these economies is facilitated in part by the growing MNE activity associated with the Triad.

However, this process of regional integration poses serious questions as to the continuing causality of country-specific characteristics and their FDI activity among the Triad countries. The more globalised the operations of a firm, the greater the extent to which its O advantages are likely to be firm-specific, rather than determined by the economic, political and cultural conditions of its home country. Moreover, the O advantages of a firm will increasingly be dependent on its ability to acquire and develop *created* assets and on its ability to organise efficiently these assets in order to exploit the advantages arising from common governance, making the MNE less dependent on its home country's natural resources. As such, O advantages become increasingly firm-specific as MNEs become more internationalised. The consequence of this is that the outward FDI of a country's firms at stage 5 is no longer entirely dependent on the economic status and competitiveness of its home country, and is increasingly affected by the conditions in the various other countries in which they operate. Since these MNEs are increasingly involved in higher value added production activities, the ownership advantages of these firms will reflect the firm-specific assets that they have generated in other locations and countries. Therefore we should expect to see, as a country evolves from a developing country to an industrialised one, a change in the nature of the country-specific determinants of FDI activity, as well as a decline in the significance of country-specific determinants, as firm-specific factors play a more important role. Indeed, it can be argued that, as countries become increasingly integrated and homogeneous through the process of globalisation, country-specific determinants might, in the limit, become insignificant in determining the extent and nature of FDI associated with a country, and the competitive advantages of their firms might become more similar. The analysis conducted here suggests that differences between countries' MNE activity endure. On the other hand, the evidence suggests that, while countries are becoming similar in their economic structure and FDI profiles, they are by no means equivalent. A partial explanation suggested here is that there may actually be two types of country-specific characteristics. The first type concerns those that are natural-asset-based and associated with supply-side issues (e.g. natural resources) that determine the *kinds* of sectors in which firms are engaged in. This type of locational (L) advantage can be regarded as 'exogenous'. These are becoming relatively less important in determining the competitive advantages of their firms. The second type relates to those that are created-asset-based and are significantly influenced by the actions and policies of governments (e.g. infrastructure) that determine the *extent* or *level* of the competitive advantages in these sectors. This type of L advantage can be regarded as 'endogenous', and it plays an increasingly important role in determining the competitiveness of firms from the industrialised countries. The policy implications of this finding are self-evident.

The second implication is closely related to the first. The increasing dominance of the industrialised countries as a destination for outward FDI, as well as their continuing dominance as the primary source of outward FDI, is closely associated with the failure of the developing countries to catch up with the industrialised world. The industrialised countries are home to over 90% of all MNEs. In terms of outward FDI, they account for about 97% of all outflows of FDI. This state of affairs has changed only marginally during this century. What has changed is the extent to which they have been seen to increasingly dominate inward FDI: in 1914 they were host to less than 37.2% of total worldwide FDI stock, and by 1990 they accounted for 81.2% of the total (Dunning 1988a, 1993b). This has severe implications for developing countries, who have over the past decade or so moved away from import-substituting regimes towards more open and export oriented regimes. Their development strategies are (often explicitly) increasingly reliant on the inward flow of FDI, as a source of both capital and technology. Technology spillovers and capital are both necessary inputs for economic development, especially in less developed economies which are caught in the vicious cycle of poverty. With FDI increasingly flowing among the industrialised countries, this has caused a divergence, as developing countries, with the exception of the newly industrialising economies (NIEs), are experiencing slowing growth, impairing their ability to catch up with the industrialised countries. It therefore becomes increasingly germane to understand the reasons behind the growth of FDI activity among the industrialised countries, and their increasing preference to invest intra-Triad.

DYNAMIC ASPECTS OF FDI AND GROWTH: THE LINK TO 'NEW' GROWTH THEORIES

There is an increasing chasm developing within the world of international economics, between what Dosi *et al.* (1990) have referred to as the 'revisionists' and the 'heretics'. The 'revisionist' group relies on the modelling of economic activity through variants of the Heckscher–Ohlin–Samuelson framework by relaxing some of its restrictive assumptions. The 'heretic' school, on the other hand, takes a more dynamic view of international economic activity and economic development and places technology and innovation at the centre of its analysis. Differences in innovative activity determine the specialisation pattern of countries and the economic growth of countries. The process is regarded to be in a continuous state of disequilibrium, and the interaction between international economic activity, technology and economic growth is considered to be a dynamic and constantly evolving phenomenon.

There is no single unified theoretical approach to the 'heretic' school. However, although this is a field that is considerably fragmented and includes the neo-Schumpeterians, the evolutionary economists and the convergence theorists, their theoretical approaches share several fundamental features.

Much of the work in this area has focused almost exclusively on trade. Despite the growing significance of FDI, little has been done to study its relationship to economic growth and development within a dynamic and evolutionary framework, with the notable exception of Cantwell (e.g. 1989, 1991). In this monograph we utilise theoretical concepts that derive from these new growth theories, but also develop a framework of analysis that is compatible with such approaches.

Given our aim of reconciling FDI to the 'heretic' school of economics, it is therefore appropriate to summarise some of the most salient features from the perspective of our subsequent discussion. There are two facets of this body of work that are crucial in understanding our subsequent work: the nature of technology, and the convergence and catch-up theory. We provide a brief synopsis of these two issues to facilitate our subsequent discussion.

First, central to economic growth is the role of technological accumulation[1] through innovation. Some of the most important features of technology can be summarised as follows.

1 Technology is cumulative in nature and occurs on a firm-level basis. Technological capabilities are developed by the gradual accumulation of skills, information and technological effort, and firms will develop their technological capabilities in response to market, supply and demand conditions, as well as from adapting and imitating other firms in the same or similar markets. Firms are boundedly rational, and prefer to engage in innovatory activities that minimise the uncertainty of the outcome. Therefore, innovations tend to be related to a firm's existing technological competences. Given this tendency, technology is said to be path-dependent, in that current technological competences are a function of its past technological competences.
2 Although technology is primarily a firm-specific phenomenon, it is possible to speak of national technological advantages, which comprise more than the summation of technological advantages across firms in a given industry in a particular country.
3 Technology is localised in nature not only at a firm-level, because of

its path dependency, but also on a country-specific basis, since cooperation between users and producers in the innovatory process is often specific to a given location, and every location has different supply and demand conditions.

4 Technology has a partly public-good nature: although it is relatively less costly to acquire technology than to create it, because of its localised nature and its specificity to the innovating firm, there are costs to the recipient firm to utilise it efficiently in its own environment. In other words, technology is only partially appropriable by other firms, and the extent to which they can do so depends on the similarity of their environments and past technological capabilities.
5 Differences in levels of technological capabilities between countries in a particular industry determine the competitiveness of countries in that industry. Therefore they are fundamental in explaining differences in market shares between countries.
6 Technology may be said to consist of (a) ownership advantages that are generally firm-specific, both of the codifiable and non-codifiable variety, and which include knowledge pertaining to organising intra-firm transactions efficiently, and (b) the knowledge inherent in industry and the country-specific structure of markets that relate to the organisation of efficient transactions.

Throughout the rest of this book, the role of technology is taken as the primary determinant of the ownership advantages, and it is assumed that technological capabilities are endogenous to firm, MNE and economic growth. In other words, technological capabilities and the process of technological accumulation underlie the structure of economies and the competitiveness of firms and countries.

The second essential issue germane to dynamic growth, particularly with reference to the economic growth of industrialised countries, is the convergence theory. This literature[2] is aimed at explaining the recent slowdown of productivity growth among industrialised countries as well as the tendency for the per capita income levels and labour productivity to converge among these countries to the level of the leading country in the long run. Within this group, it has been demonstrated that lagging countries grow faster, exhibiting growth rates that are inversely proportional to their productivity lag. The main thesis of the convergence theory is that the level of technology embodied in a nation's capital stock is greatest for the leading country. The greater the technological gap between the lag and the lead country, the larger is the pool of technology that the lagging country may acquire, provided it possesses the capabilities to utilise it, and the greater its potential for economic growth. Logically, therefore, the smaller the difference in the capital stock between the lag and lead country, the slower its economic growth. At the same time, income levels have also been demonstrated to be growing faster within the richer economies than within the poorer ones. This divergence has occurred despite technological catch-up arising from the proliferation of the activities of MNEs, the integration of world markets and information technology, which should, theoretically, increase technological spillovers to lagging countries.

It may be argued, then, that industrialised countries have, by default, benefited the most from the integration of the world economy. For this reason, the economic growth of industrialised countries deserves special attention, not just to the reasons why their growth rates are faster than those of non-industrial countries, but to why and how their economies have evolved differently *within this group* as well as the underlying reasons for the process of convergence. Abramovitz (1990) ventures to suggest that the tendency to converge depends on the countries in question having similar *social capability* and *technological congruence.* By social capability, he refers to the political, cultural, economic and social infrastructure associated with the country. The second condition, that of technological congruence, is a function of the capability of the country to benefit from technological spillovers from leading countries, and its ability to accumulate technology. Not all countries will be equally capable of catching up in all industries, as this depends on the nature and level of a country's created and natural assets as well as the characteristics of its markets. Not every country will be able to exploit its full potential for rapid growth because of different conditions of resource supply and markets, arising from, *inter alia*, a different mix of raw materials, capital intensity, scale of operations and/or underdeveloped markets. The role of competition in an integrated economy is crucial in promoting innovation. However, this will depend on the product and industrial overlap with the leading country. As the economic distance between the lag and lead country increases, the product overlap decreases, therefore inhibiting the ability to catch up with the lead country because of reduced technological spillovers.

The simultaneous divergence of the growth in income levels between rich and poor economies, and the convergence among industrial (and rich) economies, present a paradox that can in part be explained by the vicious cycle of poverty (VCP) (Alam and Naseer 1992) prevalent in poor (and non-industrialised) countries. The inability of these countries to escape from the vicious cycle, and therefore to converge, can therefore be explained by the absence of the same conditions that underlie convergence in industrialised countries, viz. that, while technological spillovers assist productivity growth in industrialised economies, non-industrialised, poorer economies are unable to utilise such spillovers, either because they are not available to them or because the countries do not have the social and technological capability. However, the divergence trend of productivity growth is true only for the industrial sector, while in agriculture there *has* been catch-up by poorer economies. Therefore, the VCP may also be explained by the failure of non-industrialised economies to restructure their economic structure away from an agricultural base to an industrial one.

HOW THIS BOOK IS ORGANISED

Chapter 2 examines the dynamic interaction between MNE activities and economic growth, highlighting the evolutionary trends behind this symbiotic relationship and their path-dependent nature. The central theme revolves around the argument that the extent and nature of the FDI profile and the economic structure of a country at a given point in time are determined by that in previous periods. Additionally, we highlight the role of government as a prime catalyst in determining the evolution and interaction between FDI and economic development. These concepts are introduced into the investment development path, originally developed by Dunning (1981a and 1988a). Using the stages-of-growth approach taken in previous versions of the IDP, and introducing the evolutionary forces behind inter-temporal changes, we develop a dynamic version of the IDP. We introduce a fifth stage to it which reconciles the framework to structural changes in the economic structure among and between the industrialised countries which are associated with the phenomena of globalisation and economic integration.

In Chapter 3 we evaluate the proposition that there is a systematic relationship between FDI activity and economic development using a cross-sectional approach across a sample of forty countries for two periods. The variables used for our regression analysis are the extent of net outward investment (NOI) and GNP, both normalised by population for 1975 and 1988. The use of a cross-sectional approach is a proxy for a longitudinal analysis and has several limitations, primary among them being the differences between countries arising from country-specific characteristics and the difficulties associated with evaluating economic development and FDI through a two-dimensional, static approach. These problems are particularly obvious when examining the nature of the relationship for industrialised countries, owing in part to the changing structures of their economies and the process of globalisation.

The use of both NOI as a measure of FDI activity and GNP as a measure of industrial development acts as a limitation to our analysis, since both these variables are aggregative and conceal considerable differences between countries. Throughout the rest of this volume, the framework of our analysis focuses on the evolutionary process underlying our central theme rather than on the stage-wise approach *per se*. In

Chapter 4 we engage in some econometric testing by using pooled data and breaking up the sample into developing and industrialised countries. Our dependent variables are inward FDI stock and outward FDI stock, which are regressed against various measures of economic structure in order to evaluate how the extent of inward and outward FDI changes with changing economic structure as countries move from developing to industrialised, and to understand the changing significance of natural and created assets as well as the changing significance of country-specific advantages.

None the less, our results still indicate that countries are idiosyncratic, and that both the nature of their economic structure and FDI vary significantly within the broad country groupings used. We therefore narrow our analysis in Chapter 5 and subsequent chapters to the industrialised countries. We expand further on the nature of the dynamics between FDI and economic structure in the industrialised countries, given the increasing convergence among their economies. We review some of the evidence regarding the nature and pattern of FDI activity by and from industrialised countries. The evidence suggests a paradox. On the one hand, there is a trend towards regional integration and a convergence in their economic structures and the nature of their created assets. This has resulted in an increasing extent of intra-Triad FDI, while MNEs' ownership advantages are increasingly firm-specific. This argues for a declining role of country-specific factors. On the other hand, because of the path dependency of their created assets and the nature of their FDI activity and economic structure, there is a second trend, which argues that the role of country-specific factors should continue to be significant. We develop a partial explanation based on the argument that there are indeed two different types of country-specific factors at play here: 'exogenous' and 'endogenous' factors.

This theme is taken up again in Chapter 6, where we attempt to provide a theoretical justification to resolve this paradox, and evaluate this explanation using data on trade, FDI and technology variables for a sample of six industrialised countries. The results broadly confirm our hypothesis, albeit tentatively, given the poor quality of data on FDI. However, since the analyses are conducted based on exports, outward FDI and home-country-specific characteristics, it also becomes painfully clear that a comprehensive analysis of the role of country-specific factors in determining the nature and extent of FDI activity must necessarily include both home- and host-country-specific characteristics, and inward and outward FDI activity. Furthermore, the role of government is extremely difficult to proxy in a quantitative analysis.

Such an analysis also requires a longitudinal approach over a relatively long period. We attempt to do this in Chapter 7, where we conduct a bilateral study of FDI activity between Japan and the US from 1945 onwards. We evaluate the changing nature of the competitive advantages of these countries and how these have evolved as a result of, and have led to, changes in their inward and outward FDI activity. We pay special attention to the role of government, and distinguish between different motives for MNE activity, especially highlighting the use of FDI activity to acquire assets rather than to utilise them. Chapter 8 presents a summary of our findings and provides some policy implications.

2

THE DYNAMICS OF FDI AND ECONOMIC GROWTH

INTRODUCTION

It has been argued that the structure and level of development of the economy of a country are related to the extent and nature of the FDI activity undertaken by its domestic firms (outward direct investment), as well as those of other nationalities within its national boundaries (inward direct investment). Indeed, the nature of this relationship is a symbiotic one – FDI activity is influenced by the structure of the economy, and at the same time influences its development. This relationship has been formalised by John Dunning (1981a, 1988a) in his seminal work on the investment development path (IDP) using the framework of the eclectic paradigm, as well as by Ozawa (1992).

In this chapter we develop a dynamic version of the investment development path which represents the theoretical foundation for the analyses and discussion undertaken throughout the rest of this volume. The dynamic IDP differs from the original in several ways. First, it is more of an analytical framework than an economic model. It does not offer any predictions as to the extent to which countries will engage in FDI at a given point in their economic development, save for the fact that there is a systematic relationship between them. Second, it explicitly examines the concept of economic growth and its relationship to FDI, emphasising that both have an evolutionary, path-dependent nature. Third, it emphasises the role of government in acting as a catalyst in the interaction between FDI and economic development. Fourth, it introduces a *fifth* stage to the IDP, which reconciles the framework to structural changes in the economic structure among and between the industrialised countries that are associated with the phenomena of globalisation and economic integration. Fifth, it acknowledges the importance of alternative forms of international economic activity and the growing use of FDI activity by MNEs to acquire assets rather than to utilise existing ones. Indeed, the term 'investment development path' is now somewhat of a misnomer, since MNEs are increasingly engaged in non-equity forms of international economic activity.[1] Sixth, although it utilises the stages-of-growth approach of the earlier versions of the IDP, this is no longer central to its application, as subequent analyses in some of the chapters in the latter half of this volume demonstrate. By emphasising the inter-temporal processes underlying the symbiotic relationship between FDI and economic structure, its application is increasingly positive rather than normative. The novelty of the approach is in its synthesis of concepts utilised in several economics and business sub-disciplines into a single general framework.

The analytical framework used in the investment development path is that of the eclectic paradigm (Dunning 1981a, 1988a, 1993a), which will be used throughout the subsequent discussion and analysis. To facilitate this, we examine the basic tenets of the eclectic paradigm, before presenting the dynamic IDP.

THE THEORY OF INTERNATIONAL PRODUCTION

The eclectic paradigm (Dunning 1981a, 1988a, 1993a) offers a framework to explain patterns and the extent of international production undertaken by firms involved in foreign value adding activities. The theory of international production based on this approach suggests that the propensity of firms to engage in international production will depend on three main factors:

1 The extent to which they possess, or can gain access to, technology, know-how, resources or some other form of income generating asset/s which their competitors either do not possess or do not have access to; these are referred to as *ownership-specific (O) advantages;*
2 given that firms possess certain O advantages, the extent to which it is to their advantage to utilise them themselves and add value to them in a foreign location, or to sell the rights to do so to foreign firms through licensing or some other contractual arrangement. To engage in FDI the firm must consider it advantageous to own or control these value adding activities. These advantages are called *internalisation (I) advantages*;
3 the extent to which it is in the interests of firms to internalise the use of these property rights in a foreign location. This suggests that there must exist natural endowments or created assets in a foreign country that firms find beneficial to combine with or add value to their ownership advantages, rather than undertake the production in their home country. These are called *locational (L) advantages*.

The failure of neo-classical trade theory in explaining the process of international production arises, *inter alia*, because of the assumption of perfect markets. There are two types of market failure that have been identified in the literature: structural and transactional (Dunning and Rugman 1985). The first gives rise to monopoly rents and stems from the possession of, or access to, income generating assets by a firm *vis-à-vis* other firms, and gives rise to asset-type ownership advantages (Oa). The existence of structural market distortions may also influence the location decisions of MNEs. Such distortions include the actions of governments.

However, while structural market failure explains some of the activities of international investment, the picture is incomplete without examining transactional market failure. This arises from the inability of arm's-length transactions to perform efficiently, and to provide firms *vis-à-vis* external markets with the capacity to capture the transactional benefits arising from common governance. Ownership advantages that stem from transactional market failure are termed transaction-type ownership advantages (Ot) and include those based on economies of common governance, arising from economies of scale and scope.

Such market failures help explain why firms expand their operations, either vertically or horizontally, be they uninational or multinational. The difference between MNEs and uninational firms is the added dimension of international market failure where transactions result in additional considerations to do with operating across borders, and therefore, in a sense, has to deal with more than one set of market failures in each country of operation.

Therefore, the character and composition of international investment undertaken by an MNE have to deal with at least two sets of country-specific factors. The nature and value of ownership–locational–internalisation (OLI) advantages are not assumed to be constant: they will change over time. Further, their configuration will vary with, and by, country (or region), industry and firm. Thus, the propensity of firms of a particular nationality to engage in foreign production will be affected by the level of political, cultural and economic conditions of both the home and the host countries. Attributes such as government policy and attitudes, natural factor endowments, the quality of human capital, the technological and communications infrastructure and the entrepreneurial and business culture of its people are perhaps the most important. In the case of industrialised countries, the characteristics of the particular industry, such as production and transaction economies peculiar to that industry, the extent of vertical/horizontal integration and the locational limitations of resources, are examples of industry-specific advantages. At a firm level, the OLI characteristics are dependent on variables such as size, degree of international involvement, management and organisational strategies and the innovatory capabilities of firms.

It should be emphasised that, while government policy may be used as an instrument to change the OLI configuration facing a firm contemplating

FDI, over time at least, the OLI variables are interdependent of each other.[2] Thus, the successful exploitation of a country's L advantages might strengthen the investing firms' O advantages. A firm that evolves a successful strategy towards the setting up of innovatory activities in a foreign country might affect the L advantages offered by that country to other foreign firms. It follows that a policy that influences (or is designed to influence) one of the OLI variables is likely to affect the others.

Types of international production

Five main types of international production have been identified. Each might be expected to be influenced by a different configuration of OLI variables.[3]

The first type of foreign production is intended to *supply the market in the country or region* in which it is located. The belief is that the L advantages offered by the host country for the creation and exploitation of the O advantages of the investing firms are greater than those offered by other countries. The important variables likely to influence such production include the size or character of a market, relative production costs, cross-border transportation costs and barriers to exports. FDI may also be prompted by the fear of losing a particular market, or share of that market, to competitors or potential competitors.

The second type of FDI may be referred to as *trade supportive*, and it is primarily designed to support the value added activities of the investing firm by providing sales outlets and distribution facilities, or as a means of acquiring cheaper or better-quality imports for other members of the MNE system.

The third type of foreign production is intended to supply raw materials, intermediate or final products to the investing company and/or to other foreign consumers. The location of the investment is largely determined by the availability and real cost of (1) natural resources, and the cost of extracting and transporting them to their final destination, and (2) unskilled and semi-skilled labour. Thus, the host country becomes a production base through a *resource seeking or supply oriented strategy*.

The fourth type of production is of an *efficiency seeking kind* or one of *rationalised investment*. This is a form of sequential (rather than initial investment) (Kogut 1983) and is directed towards achieving economies of scale or scope through the cross-border vertical or horizontal integration of production. It is best exampled by the restructuring of US MNE activity in Western Europe since the formation of the European Economic Community (EEC) in 1958. Prior to that date, most US direct investment was of an import substituting kind designed to serve the domestic market. As a result of the past and anticipated future EC/EU integration, it is now mainly directed to supplying the EU market as a whole.

A fifth motivation for engaging in foreign production is to acquire 'created' factor endowments or intangible assets, e.g. technology and markets, with the specific purpose of protecting or advancing the global competitive position of the investing firm. We refer to this kind of MNE activity as ***strategic asset seeking investment***. It usually takes the form of mergers and acquisitions (M&A) of an existing firm, or through strategic alliances.

These five types of international production are not necessarily mutually exclusive. International production may be undertaken initially as an import substituting strategy, but as the factor endowments of the host country change (such as the availability of skilled labour) the investing firm may integrate the foreign subsidiary into a regional or global network of efficiency seeking or asset seeking investments. It is also possible that the host country possesses factor endowments or intangible assets that make it attractive as a production site not only as an efficiency- or resource-based investment, but because of its market- or government-induced barriers to trade, as a market seeking investment.

THE ANALYTICAL FRAMEWORK

The investment development path represents an attempt to relate a country's net international direct investment position to its stage of development relative to that of the rest of the world. The stage of economic development is proxied by its GNP per capita and is assumed to be an indicator of its absolute and comparative competitive advantages. Therefore changes in its OLI characteristics indicate a country's propensity to invest abroad, or to attract inward direct investment, and, as changes occur in its OLI configuration, its net outward investment position[4] will change. This presents the scholar with two questions: first, what activates these changes, and second, what are the dynamics that lead to and result from these changes? It should be noted that we assume, for the sake of simplicity of analysis, that this interaction is sequential in nature, and that the causes and effects are independent of each other.

In a developmental context, the evolution of competitive advantages derives from country-specific characteristics that determine domestic and foreign investment patterns. The capability of a country's firms to supply either a domestic or a foreign market from a foreign location depends on their ability to acquire, and/or efficiently utilise, assets not available – or not available as cheaply – to another country's firms. By 'assets' we mean resources capable of generating a future income stream

(Dunning 1993a: 77). These are of two kinds. The first are *natural* assets, which comprise natural endowments such as unskilled labour and resource endowments. The second are *created* assets, which are those that derive from the upgrading of these natural assets. These latter assets may be tangible or intangible and include capital and technology, as well as those pertaining to skilled manpower such as technological, managerial and entrepreneurial skills. When assets of either kind are available to all firms and are specific to a particular location they are considered to be L-specific advantages, whereas if they are proprietary to a particular firm irrespective of where they are used they are considered to be O-specific advantages. Natural assets are normally less mobile than created assets even though their use may be monopolised by a single firm. Trade between countries in the neo-classical sense is based entirely on the geographic distribution of natural assets. The ownership of such assets alone does not lend itself to production, and in order to derive rent from such assets it must utilise them in conjunction with both intangible (such as managerial and technical manpower) and tangible (such as capital) created assets. The evolution of the competitive advantages of both firms and countries can be said to rest on the extent to which they are able to create or acquire new assets, or more effectively to utilise existing assets.

The interactive process

We shall now consider two types of catalyst for change: those that are non-FDI-induced and those that are the direct result of FDI.

Non-FDI-induced changes

These essentially represent those changes that are exogenous to particular firms but endogenous to countries, and mainly reflect the influence of government policy and the economic system associated with the country. By economic system we mean the overall system adopted by a government to determine the way in which resources and markets are organised. Most economic systems lie somewhere along a continuum between free markets at the one extreme and central planning on the other. From a developmental perspective, there are two possible economic orientations: outward-looking, export oriented (OL–EO) and inward-looking, import substituting (IL–IS) (Ozawa 1992). Depending on the orientation of an economy, the use of either (or a hybrid of the two) will substantially affect both the structure of economic development and, hence, the nature of the investment development path taken by a particular country. Government involvement embraces specific actions taken by governments towards ensuring that the system works in a way that achieves (or comes the nearest to achieving) their objectives. These include macro-organisational policies (e.g. towards resource allocation, innovations, education, trade, FDI competition), macro-economic policies (fiscal, monetary, exchange rates, etc.) and the setting up and maintenance of an efficient legal system and commercial infrastructure. Over time, each of these variables is likely to critically affect the OLI configuration facing MNEs. However, what we wish to emphasise here is the way in which they influence the level and nature of the L advantages of a country, in so far as they determine the restructuring of an economy through the development of created assets such as new technology, better access to information, upgraded human capital and improved communications infrastructure. In other words, we hypothesise that both government policy and the economic system determine how the L-specific natural and created assets are *organised*. The investment development path in its idealised form may be applied to all countries, but it implies the assumption of a free market economy. Therefore, throughout the ensuing discussion, we shall define *government* as a variable that encompasses only government involvement as defined above.

FDI-induced changes

The activities of domestic MNEs abroad through outward direct investment, and of foreign MNEs in the domestic economy through inward direct investment, represent two ways in which the location-bound competitive advantages of particular economies may interact with each other. Such interaction may also occur through other forms of international commerce, e.g. non-equity strategic alliances, but because FDI shifts both resources and capabilities, and changes the ownership or control over the use of these resources, it is likely to exert a very specific impact.

As Figure 2.1 illustrates, it is hypothesised that these two forces at a period *t* influence the nature of OLI in that period, and lead to the dynamic evolution of OLI in consecutive periods. First, there is the static or *intra-period interaction* at a particular stage of development. During any given time frame, country-specific characteristics influence the kind of O advantages possessed by firms and the L advantages offered by countries. They also may affect the propensity of firms to internalise cross-border transactions, or, in the parlance of the eclectic paradigm, to influence the configuration of their I advantages. Some of these country-specific characteristics, such as the quantity and quality of natural and created assets, are assumed to be fixed in a single time frame, but the manner and extent to which these are utilised, and by whom, may vary according to the actions of governments. Government may influence the L advantages of a country in various ways. It may do so

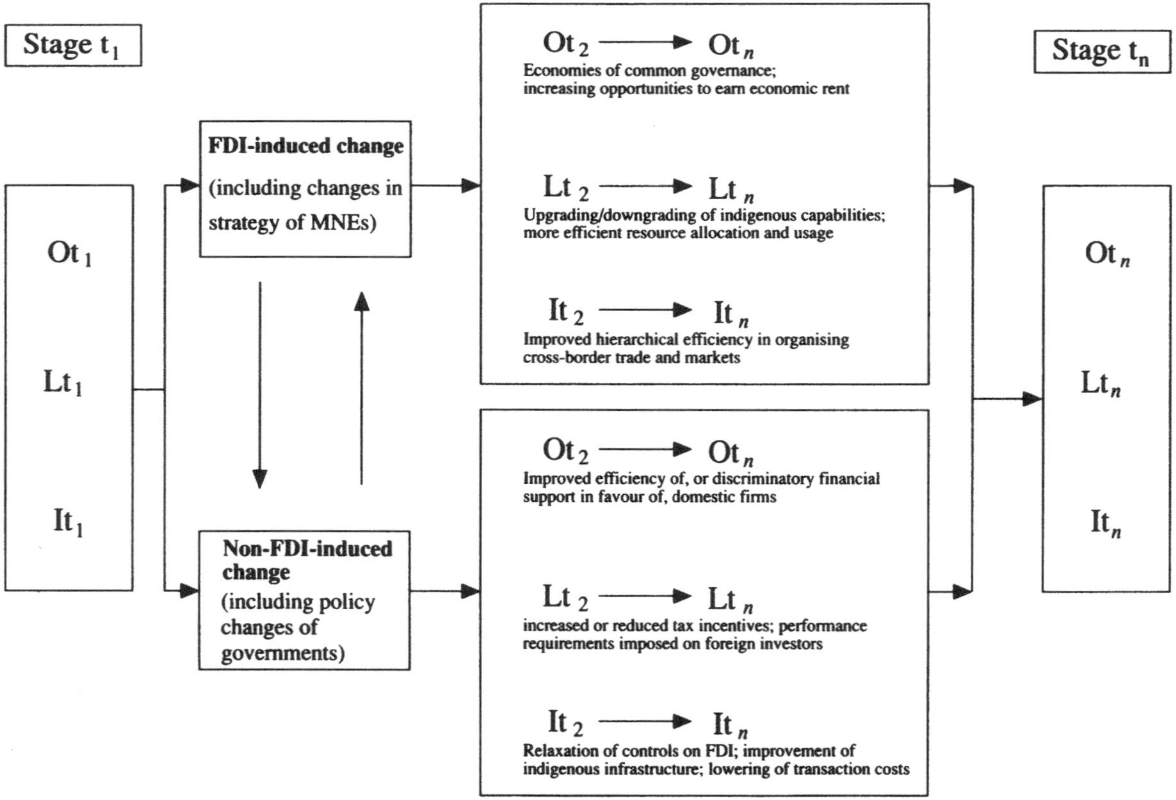

Figure 2.1 Some dynamics of the stages of growth using the eclectic paradigm
Source: Dunning, (1993a)
Note: Only two stages illustrated

directly, through the fiscal and/or regulatory framework it provides to encourage investment, and indirectly, through a wide range of policies designed to affect both the supply capabilities and the demand characteristics of a nation. Policies that influence the modality through which international business activity is undertaken, i.e. whether firms use a hierarchical, cooperative or market route to undertake cross-border activities, also create L-specific advantages. Government may further impact on the creation and development of the technology of firms operating within its jurisdiction through its policies towards property rights (patenting, trademark laws, etc.) as well as through subsidies or tax breaks it might provide for R&D. However, these government-induced L advantages are related to general or overall policies, in so far as they apply across the board and affect all firms operating within its governance. But when, for example, subsidies for exports are provided exclusively to domestic firms, they change the O advantages of these firms *vis-à-vis* foreign firms. Similarly, if foreign firms are prevented from undertaking inward direct investment in certain sectors, this affects the I advantages of these firms. This interaction may also affect the strategy of foreign and domestic firms in that period. During a single time frame, the extent of international business activity is taken as a constant and is assumed to be a consequence of the OLI configuration facing firms in that period.

Second, we are faced with the *dynamic change* associated with changes in the stage of development, or that of *inter-period interaction*. The point we wish to highlight here is that the OLI configuration in period t_1 will affect not only the strategy of firms (both foreign and domestic) in that period but also the OLI configuration in t_2. A shift in stages implies a change in the nature of the competitive advantages of firms and countries, primarily because of a change in the relative significance of their natural and created assets. Essentially, a forward inter-period interaction leads to an increasing significance of created assets, and a decreasing significance of competitive advantages arising from natural assets, and leads to economic restructuring. The nature and form of the impact of FDI-induced changes will vary according to (1) the kind of FDI undertaken, and (2) the particular stage of a country's development. The extent of the change of the OLI variables will vary across industries and firms. In a similar manner, non-FDI-induced changes will also occur. It is pertinent to note that these two types of change are themselves interrelated – and it is the configuration and interaction of these forces that will determine the OLI characteristics facing firms in t_2. It may also lead to a reorganisation of the balance between natural and created assets as well as affecting the efficiency of markets, thereby influencing the extent of international business activity in this period.

Given that the O, L and I variables are themselves interdependent, it is clear that we are faced with an exceedingly complex phenomenon (Agarwal and Ramaswami 1992). To conduct a thorough examination of all these links is outside the scope of the present work. In the current context, we shall give special attention to two kinds of interactions that are critical to the process of economic restructuring. The first is that between the O advantages of a country's firms in one period of time (Ot_1) and those of a subsequent period (Ot_2); and the second is the effect that Ot_1 will have on the L advantages of a country in subsequent periods.

The Ot_1–Lt_2 relationship occurs through the upgrading of resources, changes in the conditions of demand, and the evolution of support and related industries partly due to technological spillovers from firm (domestic and foreign owned) activity. The Ot_1–Ot_2 relationship will especially be reflected in the process of technology accumulation (i.e the development of created assets) that occurs through a gradual and cumulative process. It has been suggested by various scholars[5] that the firms of a particular nationality develop technological capability[6] (and assets) through an incremental process in which they build upon their existing and prior O advantages, which have been either acquired (in which case they will most likely be based on exclusive use of natural assets) or developed (i.e. created assets), and, through a dynamic interaction with other firms and market forces, develop and modify technologies that are idiosyncratic and more firm-specific. The development of O advantages through interaction is not limited to that involving domestic firms, but also pertains to those involving foreign firms both in the domestic economy (through inward direct investment) and in foreign economies (through outward direct investment).

The relationship between the Ot_1–Ot_2 and the Ot_1–Lt_2 interaction is self-evident: government-induced L variables affect the O advantages in the same period, and therefore Lt_2 will affect Ot_2.

This raises the issue of cumulative causation of trade, technology and production (Cantwell 1987, Dunning 1988b, Dunning and Cantwell 1989). Not only is a forward shift in a country's stage of development associated with the occurrence of a virtuous technology circle, but the ability to maintain a virtuous circle is associated with structural adjustments that may be necessitated by, among other things, wage rates rising faster than productivity in particular sectors of the economy. Here the role of government is relevant in sustaining growth in mature industries and creating and fostering innovation in nascent ones, as well as maintaining an appropriate macro-economic climate. Markets, on their own, are unlikely to respond to such shifts to the extent necessary to prevent a vicious circle.[7]

Two caveats in respect to the significance of a country's L-specific characteristics need to be noted here. The O-specific advantages of firms from countries at early stages of the investment development path are primarily a function of the economic structure of their home economies. In the context of the eclectic paradigm, this refers to the ownership advantages of other (mainly domestic) firms, which in the aggregate may be said to define the technological capability of the country, or its L advantages. The pattern and extent of the outward investment of its firms will therefore be based on their competitive advantages derived from their home country's economic structure. Likewise, inward investment will be based on these advantages *vis-à-vis* those possessed by the home country of the investing MNEs.[8] Regardless of whether the motives for investment activity are market seeking, resource seeking or strategic asset acquiring, firm-specific technological capability will grow, leading to the generation of new O advantages which are transferred back to the parent firm in the home country. Over time, and as the firm becomes increasingly internationalised, this interactive process therefore will result in the O advantages of firms of a particular nationality becoming increasingly firm-specific, i.e. less a function of the economic structure of its home country and more a function of the economic structure of the various locations of its operations. Therefore, *ceteris paribus*, the significance of country-specific characteristics in determining the extent and pattern of FDI activity and its relation to the economic structure of a country becomes increasingly complex as its extent of internationalisation increases. Therefore, the non-explanatory power of the IDP with regard to the extent and pattern of FDI activity, and its relation to the economic structure of the country with which it is associated beyond the fourth stage of IDP, is due to firm-specific rather than country-specific factors (Gray 1982). These issues are further explored in Chapters 5 and 6.

Second, the presence of a certain level of natural assets is assumed in an economy at the initial stages of the idealised investment development path. These include the presence of some extent of natural resources, unskilled labour and domestic market potential. The absence of one or more of these country-specific characteristics will lead domestic firms, *ceteris paribus*, to undertake FDI in overseas markets to acquire these assets. For the same reasons, inward investment in such an economy at an early stage will be muted. In sum, the net outward investment position of such a country is likely to be more positive at all points of the investment development path relative to the 'average' path discussed below. Likewise, a country with unique factor endowments that provide it an absolute advantage in some natural asset (for instance, a large domestic market potential such as the US, or natural resources such as in Australia) will have a net outward investment position that is more negative at all points relative to the 'average' path.[9]

FDI and economic development in a stages-of-growth framework

So much for the way in which MNE activity might interact with economic development. Let us turn to examine its role at different stages of development. The IDP framework suggests that countries tend to go through five main stages of development – and that these stages can be usefully classified according to their propensity to be outward or inward direct investors. A diagrammatic representation of these stages, not drawn to scale, is presented in Figure 2.2.

Before embarking on a discussion of the characteristics of each of the five stages, a clarification is necessary. The IDP as described here is a normative, idealised example. Although the IDP has been demonstrated here (see Chapter 3) as well as elsewhere (Dunning 1981a, 1988a, Tolentino 1993, Dunning and Narula 1995b) on a cross-sectional basis, this is merely done as a proxy for a longitudinal approach. The IDP represents a paradigm that is idosyncratic and country-specific, while in fact the shape and nature of the IDP are individual and unique for every country. Even on a general level, there are in fact several different paths that are taken by countries, and each of these possible paths can be examined in five different stages, although the extent and pattern of the FDI activity may differ from the normative one. As the various country studies undertaken in Dunning and Narula (1995b) and Chapter 7 of this

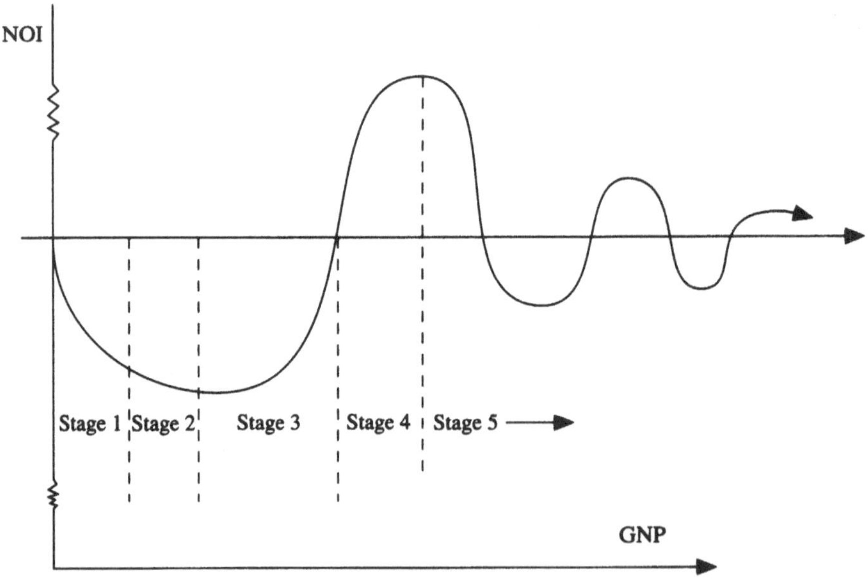

Figure 2.2 The pattern of the investment development path
Note: not drawn to scale; for illustrative purposes only.

volume show, the exact circumstance of each country is unique, and, while there are some general similarities between groups of countries, the explanatory power of the 'ideal' IDP based on cross-sectional analysis of a large group of countries is severely limited. This aggregation of countries for a given time period assumes that countries follow a broadly similar IDP, whereas, in fact, each country follows its own particular path which is determined by four main variables: (a) its resource structure, (b) its market size, (c) its strategy of economic development, and (d) the role of government in the organisation of economic activity. These factors essentially determine the nature and extent of the firm-specific assets of both foreign MNEs and domestic firms operating within its borders.

1 *Resource structure* A country may possess a significant comparative advantage, or an absolute advantage in primary commodities. Such a country is likely to spawn domestic firms that possess O advantages in exploitation of such assets. However, if such an advantage is a near absolute one, it is likely to be the recipient of considerable inward investment from MNEs that wish to internalise the supply of raw materials to their upstream activities located in other countries, and the extent of this inward investment will almost certainly continue to rise as the other L advantages associated with the host country develop. These L advantages include the availability of skilled manpower and other infrastructural facilities, and may lead to sequential vertical investment in upstream activities by both domestic firms and MNEs. As a result, an absolute or comparative advantage in a natural-resource-based industry may be sustained even where income levels rise towards a developed country standard. Such a scenario would result in a NOI position that continues to be negative, as for example in Australia. Any outward investment would also tend to be in industries that are either in or related to the primary sector, and would be dwarfed by the increasing extent of inward investment. Such countries would tend to have much greater levels of inward FDI than outward FDI, resulting in a much lower NOI at even considerably lower stages of development. This is shown in Figure 2.3.

The lack of a natural resource base (i.e. a comparative disadvantage in necessary primary commodities) would, *ceteris paribus*, result in the opposite effect. Inward investment at earlier stages would be muted, and outward investment might begin at an earlier stage to secure the availability of necessary natural resources. Such a country is also more likely to begin strategic asset seeking investment at an earlier stage (e.g. Japan). Overall, these countries would become net outward investors at considerably earlier stages of development than a country endowed with natural resources. This too is illustrated in Figure 2.3.

2 *Market size* Countries that are small in terms of market size, such as Hong Kong, Singapore, and Switzerland, are likely to have not just

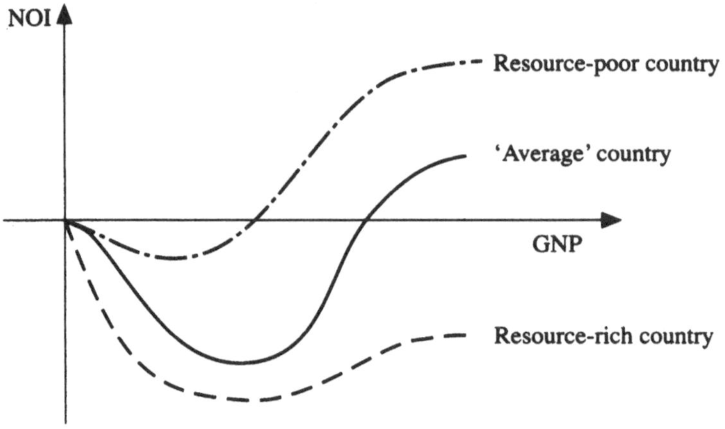

Figure 2.3 Examples of variances in individual IDPs

limited natural resources such as primary commodities, but limited attraction in terms of market size. Thus, the lack of economies of scale will inhibit foreign investment in earlier stages. As their human capital and infrastructure improve, some inward FDI may occur for export processing purposes. Small populations mean small aggregate consumption and low demand, forcing firms to engage in outward FDI or exports at an early stage to seek larger markets, which will result in a greater extent of outward FDI at earlier stages of development. As income levels rise, domestic investors that were involved in export oriented production will seek overseas locations to compensate for the shortage of low-wage human capital for labour intensive production. Such countries will reach (and remain at) a positive NOI position at a considerably earlier stage of development (e.g. Taiwan). The opposite scenario would apply for large countries; they would attract large amounts of inward FDI because of the attractions of their large markets, and their domestic firms might not have as much incentive to seek overseas markets, since economies of scale could be achieved at home (e.g. the US).

3 *Economic system* The economic orientation of a country may either be outward-looking, export oriented (OL–EO) or inward-looking, import-substituting (IL–IS) (Ozawa 1992). Depending on the orientation of an economy, the use of either (or a hybrid of the two) will substantially affect both economic development and the extent and pattern of FDI, and hence the nature of the path taken by a particular country. An OL–EO regime is likely to achieve faster growth and structural upgrading. Ozawa (1992) argues that an OL–EO regime is a necessary condition for FDI-facilitated development. We suggest here that, although it is not a

necessary condition for growth in the first two stages, the greater the extent of OL–EO policy orientation, the faster the process of structural adjustment and economic growth and the quicker a country's progress through the stages of the IDP. Our ensuing discussion of the various stages assumes an OL–EO-type policy regime beyond the second stage, but not for the first two stages.

The failure of countries that undertake an IL–IS orientation to proceed beyond the second stage is associated with the vicious cycle of poverty (VCP). This, when applied in the traditional sense, is explained as follows: low income levels in less developed countries are associated with low savings rates, which in turn result in low capital investment, thereby keeping income levels low. In the parlance of the eclectic paradigm, this is the lack of ownership advantages of domestic firms and location advantages of the country, and their inability to develop or acquire these. The O advantages referred to here include financial asset advantages, i.e. Oa and Ot type advantages, whereas the L advantages are those of infrastructure. This cycle can be broken through, *inter alia*, the infusion of capital through FDI, which allows for technological spillovers and financial capital inflows.

4 *Governments and the organisation of economic activity* Although, as we have illustrated above, the kind of economic system associated with a country broadly determines the path taken by a country, the nature of government policy associated with a particular system can vary between countries with the same economic system and at the same stage of development. There are two main areas of government strategy that directly impinge on the nature of the IDP of a country: macro-economic strategy and macro-organisational strategy (Dunning 1992c). The role of governments in determining macro-economic policy is relatively well defined, and is often associated with the economic system. On the other hand, there is considerable variance among countries in the role of governments in determining macro-organisational strategy. Macro-organisational strategy primarily influences the structure and organisation of economic activity, and the nature of the policies most appropriate at a particular stage should, in an 'ideal' situation, change as the economy evolves, reflecting the nature of market imperfections that the policy is designed to circumvent (Hamalainen 1993). Essentially, in such a best-world scenario, government plays a *market-facilitating* role in which its macro-organisational policy dynamically evolves over time. Increasing economic specialisation associated with economic development leads to a growth in market failures and increases the potential benefits of government macro-organisational policy (Durkheim 1964). However, as Hamalainen (1993) points out, governments may also fail, and society is often faced with a choice between imperfect markets and imperfect governments. Given that macro-organisational policy embraces a wide

variety of issues (see Dunning 1992c, 1993d), and that there is little agreement on what the optimal involvement of government should be, the macro-organisational policy stance varies widely among countries. The differences between the macro-organisational strategy of countries at the same stage of development influence both the structure of markets and the extent to which economic activity is efficiently conducted, thereby affecting the specialisation and economic structure of the country, as well as the extent of FDI activity associated with it.

The five stages of the IDP

We present a summary of the five stages of the IDP, in which we assume some degree of OL–EO policy regime.

Stage 1

During the first stage, the L advantages of a country are insufficient to attract inward direct investment, with the exception of those arising from the possession of natural assets. Its deficiency in created factor L advantages may reflect inadequate domestic markets – demand conditions are minimal because of the low per capita income, inappropriate economic systems or government policies, insufficient infrastructure such as transportation and communication facilities and, most important of all, a poorly educated, trained or motivated labour force. Government-induced L advantages (or disadvantages) are likely to be significant in this stage. O advantages of domestic firms are few as there is little or no indigenous technology accumulation and hence few created assets. Those that exist will be in labour intensive manufacturing and in the primary product sector (such as mining and agriculture), and may be government-influenced through infant industry protection such as import controls. Domestic firms from countries at this stage do not have the necessary O advantages to engage in outward direct investment. At the same time, there is unlikely to be much inward direct investment except for the purpose of exploiting natural resources and trade-supportive activities, as the L and I advantages of the recipient nations are too few to induce foreign investors to undertake higher value added operations. *Ceteris paribus*, they will prefer to export to and import from this market, or to conclude cooperative non-equity arrangements with indigenous firms.

Government intervention during stage 1 will normally take two forms. First, governments will attempt to reduce some of the endemic market failure that holds back development by providing basic infrastructure, and upgrading human capital via education and training. Second, they will engage in a variety of economic and social policies, which, for good or bad, will affect the structure of markets. Import protection, domestic content policies and export subsidies are examples of such intervention at this stage of development. At this stage however, there is likely to be limited government involvement in the upgrading of the country's created assets, e.g. innovatory capacity.

Stage 2

In stage 2, inward direct investment starts to rise, while outward investment remains low or negligible. Domestic markets may have grown either in size or in purchasing power, making some local production by foreign firms a viable proposition. Initially this is likely to take the form of import substituting manufacturing investment – based upon the domestic market's possession of intangible assets, e.g. technology, trademarks, managerial skills. Frequently such inward FDI is stimulated by host governments imposing tariff and non-tariff barriers. In the case of export oriented industries (at this stage of development, such inward direct investment will still be in natural resources and primary commodities with some forward vertical integration into labour intensive low technology and light manufactures) the extent to which the host country is able to offer the necessary infrastructure (transportation, communications facilities and supplies of skilled and unskilled labour) will be a decisive factor. In summary, a country must possess some desirable L characteristics to attract inward direct investment, although the extent to which foreign firms are able to exploit these will depend on its development strategy, and the extent to which it prefers to develop technological capabilities of domestic firms.

The O advantages of domestic firms will have increased from the previous stage through technology accumulation, partly as a result of the government-induced advantages that have generated a virtuous circle of technology accumulation. These O advantages will exist as a result of the development of support industries clustered around primary industries, and production will move towards semi-skilled and moderately knowledge intensive consumer goods. Outward direct investment begins to grow at this stage. This may be either of a market seeking or trade related type in adjacent territories, or of a strategic asset seeking type in developed countries. The former will be undertaken characteristically in countries that are lower in the investment development path than the home country. When the acquisition of created assets is the prime motive, these are likely to be directed towards countries higher up in the path. The extent to which outward direct investment is undertaken will be influenced by the home-country government-induced 'push' factors such as subsidies for exports and technology development or acquisition (which influence the I advantages of domestic firms), as well as by the changing (non government induced) L advantages such as relative production costs. However, the rate of outward direct investment growth is likely to be insufficient to offset the rising rate of growth of inward direct investment, and in consequence, during the second stage of development, countries will increase their net inward investment, although towards the latter part of the second stage the growth rates of outward direct investment and inward direct investment will begin to converge.

Stage 3

Countries in stage 3 are marked by a gradual decrease in the rate of growth of inward direct investment,[10] and an increase in the rate of growth of outward direct investment that result in increasing net outward investment. The technological capabilities of the country are increasingly geared towards the production of standardised goods. With rising incomes, consumers begin to demand higher-quality goods, fuelled in part by the growing competitiveness between the supporting firms. Comparative advantages in labour intensive activities will deteriorate, domestic wages will rise, and outward direct investment will be more to countries at lower stages in their investment development path. The original O advantages of foreign firms also begin to be eroded, as domestic firms acquire their own competitive advantages and compete with them in the same sectors.

The initial O advantages of foreign firms will also begin to change, as domestic firms compete directly with them in these sectors. This is supported by the growing base of created assets of the host country arising from increased expenditure on education and innovatory activities. These will be replaced by new technological, managerial or marketing innovations in an attempt to compete with domestic firms. These O advantages are likely to be based on the possession of intangible knowledge, and the public-good nature of such assets will mean that foreign firms will increasingly prefer to exploit them through cross-border hierarchies. Growing L advantages such as an enlarged market and improved domestic innovatory capacity will make for economies of scale, and with rising wage costs will encourage more technology intensive manufacturing as well as higher value added locally. The motives of inward direct investment will shift towards efficiency seeking production and away from import substituting production. In industries where domestic firms have a competitive advantage, there may be some inward direct investment directed towards strategic asset acquiring activities.

Domestic firms' O advantages will have changed too, and will be based less on government induced action. Partly because of the increase in their multinationality, the character of their O advantages will change as a result of the coordination of geographically dispersed assets. At this stage of development, their O advantages based on possession of proprietary assets will be similar to those of firms from developed countries in all except the most technology intensive sectors. There will be increased outward direct investment directed to stage 1 and 2 countries, both as market seeking investment and as export platforms, as prior domestic L advantages in resource intensive production are eroded. Outward direct investment will also occur in stage 3 and 4 countries, partly as a market seeking strategy, but also to acquire strategic assets to upgrade their O advantages.

The role of government induced O advantages will have become less significant, as those of FDI induced O advantages take on more importance. Although created factor L advantages will increase relative to natural resource L advantages, government policies will continue to be directed to reducing structural market imperfections in resource intensive industries. Thus, governments may attempt to attract inward direct investment in those sectors in which the comparative O advantages of its enterprises are the weakest but the comparative advantages of location bound assets are the strongest, while encouraging its own enterprises to invest abroad in those sectors in which its O advantages are the strongest and its comparative L advantages are the weakest. Structural adjustment will be required if the country is to move to the next stage of development, with declining industries (such as labour intensive ones) undertaking direct investment abroad.

Stage 4

Stage 4 is reached when a country's outward direct investment flows exceed or equal the inward investment flows from foreign-owned firms and the rate of growth of outward direct investment is still rising faster than that of inward direct investment. At this stage, domestic firms can now not only effectively compete with foreign-owned firms in domestic sectors in which the home country has developed a competitive advantage, but are able to penetrate foreign markets as well. Production processes and products will be state-of-the-art, using capital intensive production techniques as the cost of capital will be lower than that of labour. In other words, the L advantages will be based almost completely on created factor endowments. Inward direct investment into stage 4 countries is increasingly sequential (Kogut 1983) and directed towards rationalised and asset seeking investment by firms from other stage 4 countries. The O specific advantages of these firms tend to be more 'transaction' than 'asset' related (Dunning 1993a), and derived from their multinationality *per se*. Some inward direct investment will originate from countries in lower stages of development, and is of a market seeking, trade related and asset seeking nature.

Outward direct investment will continue to grow, as firms seek to maintain their competitive advantage by moving operations that are losing their competitiveness to offshore locations (in countries at lower stages), as well as responding to trade barriers installed both by countries at stage 4 and by those at lower stages. Firms will have an increasing propensity to internalise the market for their O advantages by producing in a foreign location rather than through exports. Since the O advantages of countries at this stage are broadly similar, intra-industry production will rise in significance, and generally will follow prior growth in intra-industry trade (Dunning 1988a). However, both intra-industry trade and production will tend to be increasingly conducted *within* MNEs.

The role of government is also likely to change in stage 4. While continuing its supervisory and regulatory function, e.g. to reduce market imperfections and maintain competition, it will give more attention to structural adjustment of the country's resources and capabilities by fostering technological accumulation in infant industries (i.e. promoting a virtuous circle) and phasing out declining industries (i.e. promoting a vicious circle). Put another way, the role of government is now moving towards reducing transaction costs of economic activity and facilitating markets to operate efficiently. At this stage too, because of the increasing competition between countries with similar structures of resources and capabilities, governments begin taking a more strategic position in their policy formation. Direct intervention is likely to be replaced by measures designed to aid the upgrading of domestic resources and capabilities, and to curb the market distorting behaviour of private economic agents.

Stage 5

As illustrated in Figure 2.2, in stage 5 net outward investment begins to fall back as outward and inward investment become more balanced. This is the situation that advanced industrial nations are approaching as the century draws to a close, and it possesses two key features. First, there is an increasing propensity for cross-border transactions not to be conducted through the market but to be internalised by and within MNEs. Second, as countries converge in the structure of their competitive advantages, and as these advantages increasingly take the form of the ability of countries to create and efficiently organise technological and human assets and to tap new markets, their international direct investment positions are likely to become more evenly balanced. It has been suggested elsewhere (Dunning 1988a) that these phenomena represent a natural and predictable progress of the internationalisation of firms and economies. Thus, the nature and scope of activity gradually shift from arm's-length trade between nations producing very different goods and services (Hecksher–Ohlin trade) to trade within hierarchies (or cooperative ventures) between countries producing very similar products.

Unlike previous stages, stage 5 in the investment development path represents a situation in which no single country has an absolute hegemony of income creating assets. Moreover, the O advantages of MNEs will be less dependent on their country's natural resources but more dependent on their ability to acquire assets and on the ability of firms efficiently to organise their advantages and to exploit the gains of cross-border common governance. Another development is that, as firms become globalised, their nationalities become blurred. As MNEs bridge geographical and political divides and practise a policy of transnational integration,[11] they no longer operate principally with the interests of their home nation in mind, as they trade, source and manufacture in various locations, exploiting created and natural assets wherever it is in their best interests to do so. Increasingly, MNEs, through their arbitraging functions, are behaving like mini-markets. Both the ownership and the territorial boundaries of firms become obscured[12] as they engage in an increasingly complex web of trans-border cooperative agreements (see Gugler 1991).

The tendency for income levels to converge among the Triad countries has been noted by, among others, Abramovitz (1986), Baumol (1986) and Dowrick and Nguyen (1989). And, indeed, during the 1970s and 1980s Japan, the EC and EFTA countries have experienced a 'catching-up' in their productivity and growth relative to the US (the 'lead' country), while a range of the newly industrialising countries began to move from stage 2 to stage 3 in their investment development path. As a result of these developments, the economic structures of many industrial economies have become increasingly similar. Countries that were once the lead countries in stage 4 now find themselves joined by others. This tends to reduce their net outward investment position and pushes them into stage 5 of the investment development path. At the same time, there has also been a 'catching-up' effect among MNEs since the 1970s (Cantwell and Sanna Randaccio 1990). Firms that have had relatively low levels of international operations have been internationalising at faster rates than their more geographically diversified counterparts. These two effects are not unrelated; firms have had to compensate for slowing economic growth in their home country by seeking new markets overseas. Given the similarity in income levels, the factors of production are broadly similar, and, as Cantwell and Sanna Randaccio (1990) have shown, firms that are trying to catch up seek to imitate competitors and develop similar O advantages as their competitors in the same industry, ***but not necessarily in the same country***.

To take this argument a step further, as income levels, economic structures and patterns of international production among the Triad countries converge, the relative attractions of a particular location will depend less on the availability, quality and price of their natural assets and more on that of their created assets. It has been noted elsewhere that the prosperity of modern industrial economies is increasingly dependent on their capacity to continually upgrade, or make better use of, their technology and human capital (Dunning and Cantwell 1991). Since many of these advantages are transferable across national boundaries, it may be predicted that, in the long run, this should lead to a more balanced international investment position, and to an increasing convergence of created asset L advantages. However, the ability of a country to upgrade its technology and human capital is a function of its country-specific characteristics and, in particular, the extent of its natural assets, demand characteristics and macro-organisational strategies of its government. We believe the role of government in affecting dynamic economic restructuring cannot be overstated. In a myriad of ways governments can promote new trajectories of economic growth which some countries are better able to cope with than others. This has been amply illustrated by the evolution of Japan's economy compared with that of the US, especially in the 1980s.

In terms of their inward and outward direct investment positions, stage 5 countries, after an initial burst of new inward direct investment (e.g. as occurred in the US in the 1980s), may be expected to settle down to a fluctuating equilibrium around a roughly equal amount of inward and outward investment. Inward investment will be of two kinds. The first will come from countries at lower stages of the investment development path and will be essentially of the market seeking and knowledge seeking type. The second will be from stage 4 (or stage 5) countries who will continue to indulge in rationalised investment among themselves, as well as making outward direct investment in less developed countries, especially in the natural resource intensive sectors. In other words, truly rationalised or efficiency seeking investment will take place as plant and product specialisation is encouraged in sectors where economies of scale and scope are important As the world economy begins to resemble a global village, strategic asset seeking investments will continue to take place, and this too will lead to increasing convergence among countries as firms seek to improve their O advantages by cross-border mergers and acquisitions (M&A) or strategic alliances. Therefore, in the shorter time frame, inward and outward investment will fluctuate depending on relative innovatory and organisational strength of the participating countries. But, as Cantwell (1989: 45) has noted,

> The sectoral pattern of innovative activity gradually changes as new industries develop and new technical linkages are forged

> between sectors. Yet this is a slow process which in general only slightly disturbed the pattern of technological advantages held by firms of the major industrialized countries in the 20 years between the early 1960's and the early 1980's.

Thus, *pro tem* at least, it is possible for one country to be a net outward investor compared with another. But over time, according to the extent and speed at which created assets are transferable,[13] the investment gap will close again, leading to a fluctuating investment position around an equilibrium level. It is within this context that the fifth stage will exist.

In other words, an equilibrium of sorts will be perpetuated, but it will not be a stable equilibrium as the relative comparative and competitive advantages of countries and firms are likely to be continually shifting. Hence, these fluctuations in relative comparative advantages, when combined with external and internal changes in the domestic economy, gradually lead to a fluctuation of the number of countries at stage 5.

The acquisition, diffusion and transfer of O advantages will be influenced by the cumulative causation in trade, production and technology, and whether the industry or sector in each of the countries at stage 5 experiences a 'vicious' or a 'virtuous' circle (Dunning 1988b, Cantwell 1989). In the former case it may serve to increase technological divergences between countries, in the latter, it may strengthen the technological linkages between them.

In summary, stage 5 is marked by a gradual convergence of industrial structures among countries and a change in the character of international transactions. MNE activity, in particular, will be directed to efficiency seeking investment with greater emphasis on cross-border alliances, mergers and acquisitions; and the governance and equity position of MNEs will become increasingly *transnational*. The success of countries in accumulating technology, as well as in inducing continued economic growth, will depend increasingly on the ability of their firms to coordinate their resources and capabilities at a regional and global level. The simultaneous trend of economic convergence of industrialised countries on one hand, and high rate of intra-Triad FDI growth on the other, will lead to an increasing economic interdependency as well as to a lessening of the role of natural assets as a country specific determinant of FDI. In stage 5, governments will increasingly assume the role of strategic oligopolists, taking into account the behaviour of other governments in the formation and execution of their own macro-organisational strategies. In this stage too, governments are likely to play an increasingly pro-active role in fostering efficient markets, and in cooperating with business enterprises to reduce structural adjustment and other transaction costs.

We conclude. Beyond a certain point in the investment development path, the absolute size of GNP is no longer a reliable guide of a country's competitiveness; neither indeed is its net outward investment position. This is for two reasons. First, the competitiveness of a country is better measured by the rate and character of growth of GNP *vis-à-vis* that of its major competitors. Second, as the motivation of FDI has evolved away from being geared primarily to the exploitation of existing O advantages to the simultaneous acquisition of new O advantages, countries that offer L advantages for the production of such advantages may increase their attractiveness to inward investment. Investments made to acquire or exploit indigenous competitive advantage, far from representing a weakness of the recipient country, could represent a strength. Certainly, recent evidence seems to suggest that, in the Triad at least, inbound and outbound FDI are increasingly complementary to each other, especially at a sectoral level (UN 1993d).

SUMMARY AND CONCLUSIONS

This chapter has examined the dynamic interaction between MNE activities and economic growth, highlighting the evolutionary trends behind this symbiotic relationship. The extent and nature of its FDI profile and the economic structure of a country at a given point in time are partly determined by that in previous periods. Additionally, we have highlighted the role of government as a prime catalyst in determining the evolution and interaction between FDI and economic development. Government represents a crucial determinant in the innovation and maintenance of 'created' assets, an issue that is highlighted by the literature on national systems of innovation (NSI) (see e.g. Lundvall 1992, and Nelson 1993). These concepts have been introduced into the investment development path, originally developed by Dunning (1981a and 1988a). Using the stages-of-growth approach taken in previous versions of the IDP, and introducing the evolutionary forces behind inter-temporal changes, we have developed a dynamic version of the IDP.

A particular feature of the 'new' IDP developed here is a clearer understanding of the changing relationship between FDI and development in industrialised countries, previously examined only briefly in the literature. Stage 5 reflects the changes in the world economy, and particularly the convergence and catch-up process that is occurring among the countries of the Triad. As countries reach stage 4 and begin to enter stage 5, the activities and growth of their MNEs are no longer a function just of the economic conditions of its home country, but of the various host countries in which it has subsidiaries. The more globalised the operations of a firm, the greater the extent to which its O advantages are likely to be firm-specific, rather than determined by the economic, political and cultural conditions of its home country. Moreover, the O advantages of firms will increasingly be dependent on its ability to acquire and develop *created* assets and on its ability to efficiently organise these assets in order to exploit the advantages arising from common governance, making the MNE less dependent on its home country's natural resources. As such, O advantages become increasingly firm-specific as MNEs become more internationalised. The consequence of this is that the outward FDI activities of a country's firms at this stage are no longer entirely dependent on the economic status and competitiveness of its home country, and increasingly affected by the conditions in the various other countries in which they operate; and therefore, after reaching a certain NOI position, a country's investment position will not necessarily be proportional to its income level or relative stage of development. To put it another way, we hypothesise that, *ceteris paribus*, a stage 5 country will continue to experience change in its FDI position regardless of whether its relative stage of development or income levels change. This is not to say that the causal relationship between FDI and economic growth will diminish to insignificance at stage 5. It is simply that the emphasis on changes in economic development as an aggregate phenomenon, and the use of per capita income as an indicator of competitiveness, are no longer appropriate. For industrialised countries, economic growth as an aggregate has slowed, but there are considerable changes taking place between sectors. This is associated with the fact that firm-specific assets and competitiveness are becoming increasingly important, and that growth takes place because of changing competitiveness and structural adjustment between sectors. It may be more appropriate, therefore, to use technological advantage as an indicator of competitiveness.[14]

Furthermore, as these countries have experienced economic convergence and *de facto* and *de jure* integration, their income levels and economic structures have become increasingly similar. They have increasingly similar factor endowments, as the competitiveness of their economies has become dependent on created assets and decreasingly a function of their natural assets. This approach explicitly relates to the neo-Schumpeterian belief that innovation is central to competitiveness (Wakelin 1995), as well as the evolutionary economics approach that technology development is endogenous and cumulative. The kind of created assets that a country possesses in this (and our) view are determined by institutional factors, which we have classified as the role of government. For this reason, we have argued that, although the competitive advantages of industrialised countries are similar, they are by no means identical, since the individual competitive advantages of a particular country are path-dependent (and therefore influenced by traditional supply conditions) and the nature of their policies idiosyncratic. This may help explain why there has been an increasing amount of FDI activity taking place among and between the countries of the Triad, often in similar sectors. This phenomenon can also be explained partly because of the increasing homogeneity in their economies, in terms of both their income levels and their consumption patterns. This explanation is reminiscent of the hypothesis proposed by Linder (1961) in reference to the increase in intra-industry trade flows among the Triad. The fact that firms and MNEs from the industrialised world are increasingly engaged in high value added activity that is knowledge intensive and of a public good nature has led to an increase in strategic asset acquiring FDI activity. The simultaneous and continuous process of asset acquiring FDI and asset exploiting FDI, together with the fact that technological leadership and competitiveness are steadily shifting, leads us to argue that countries in stage 5 will fluctuate along a kind of long-term unstable equilibrium in terms of their net outward investment position.

The issues brought up in this chapter have been several and varied. Much of the rest of this book is devoted to analysing, with the aid of both empirical and qualitative methods, some of the propositions put forward in the theoretical framework. We begin by evaluating the stage-wise approach on a cross-sectional basis in Chapter 3, to confirm that the general relationship between FDI and economic development postulated by the IDP is still valid.

3

A CROSS-SECTIONAL TEST OF THE IDP

INTRODUCTION

The purpose of this chapter is to re-examine and update the investment development path as identified and tested by Dunning (1981a). The basic premiss of the IDP is that the extent and pattern of FDI activity undertaken by a country are a function of its stage of development. As we have argued in Chapter 2, the stages-of-growth approach to the IDP is exceedingly averse to empirical testing, not least because the relationship between FDI and economic development requires the comparison of two phenomena at different levels of economic analysis. While FDI is primarily a micro-economic or firm-specific activity, economic development is a macro-economic or country-specific phenomenon (Gray 1982). The examination of FDI as a country-specific variable requires the assumption that the activities of domestic and foreign MNEs can be aggregated in terms of their motivation, both within and across industrial sectors. Such aggregation can be justified only among countries where the nature, mode and motivation of MNE activity are relatively homogeneous, and the extent of their value adding activities remains at relatively low levels, such as in the less developed countries. However, as MNEs become more globalised and engage in more complex investment activity, the importance of firm-specific factors in determining the FDI profile of a country becomes increasingly significant. This increasing complexity, taken together with the differences in measuring FDI between countries, makes any such analysis a hazardous one. The use of a cross-sectional test represents a two-dimensional, static analysis that cannot do justice to a dynamic and country-specific activity, since it requires an over-simplification of complex phenomena. Furthermore, there have been profound structural changes in the world economic structure.

A more recent attempt to confirm the IDP on a cross-sectional basis by Tolentino (1987, 1993) suggested that the relationship has become inverted since the mid 1970s. It is thus quite germane for us to investigate whether, in fact, such a relationship does exist. We shall therefore re-evaluate the relationship between NOI and GNP per capita for two time periods, 1975 and 1988, to determine whether the IDP is still valid. However, we wish to confirm merely that a causal relationship exists between development and the *extent* of FDI through a general and tentative analysis.

In particular, we intend to demonstrate that the relationship between development and FDI of the industrialised countries is fundamentally different from that of the first four stages, thereby lending support to our theoretical argument regarding the fifth stage of the IDP. Previous studies have used FDI flow data as a proxy for FDI stocks, and a novel feature of this and subsequent chapters is the use of stock data. Using these data, we intend to confirm the relationship between FDI stock levels (proxied by NOI per capita) and development (proxied by GNP per capita). However, before embarking on this exercise, we intend to briefly delve into the limitations of a cross-sectional approach as a means to analyse the IDP, which we have briefly discussed in Chapter 2.

THE LIMITATIONS OF CROSS-SECTIONAL ANALYSIS

In the previous chapter we highlighted that the IDP represents a framework that is best applied on a country-by-country basis, since broad issues including market size, policy orientation and resource availability vary considerably across countries. When examining the IDP on a cross-sectional basis, the presence of a large proportion of countries that slot into one of these groups will reduce the fit of our idealised path. For instance, countries with a natural-resource-based economy may attract an unusually large amount of inward investment which is not affected by the stage of development, and indeed may increase as their level of development increases owing to improved locational advantages such as infrastructural facilities and greater host-country-specific created assets which improve the efficient utilisation of their absolute advantages in natural assets. At the same time, some of these countries may have small populations, which do not encourage investment in manufacturing industries because of the lack of economies of scale and scope. This group of countries includes the OPEC countries of the Middle East as well as South Africa, Canada, Australia and New Zealand. Australia and Canada are particularly important outliers in that they are unlikely to become net outward investors, despite having reached a level of development that would otherwise have been associated with a growing positive NOI position, owing to the immensity of their inward FDI position; in summary, while their income levels are those of industrialised countries, the pattern and nature of their economic structure are not based on the manufacturing sector. Countries such as these represent outliers that have large negative NOI positions, and the leverage effect they have on any regression is considerable, increasing as these countries move along the IDP. Countries like Venezuela and Nigeria will have a smaller distortive effect than countries such as Australia and Canada. We shall now highlight some other issues that might have a significant impact on cross-sectional analysis.

Convergence and divergence

The structural changes in the world economy that might affect the nature of the IDP are the process of convergence of the industrialised countries and the concurrent divergence of the developing countries away from them. These structural changes have significant consequences for any cross-sectional test. We have discussed the effects of convergence among the industrialised countries at some length in Chapter 2, and have indicated that the causal relationship between NOI and GNP per capita may no longer apply. From a statistical point of view, the implications of the convergence tendency among industrialised countries are two-fold: first, it will result in the 'bunching' of these countries; and second, because of this, any attempt to estimate the true shape of the IDP based on a sample that includes a large number of stage 4 and 5 countries will cause the J curve to shift to the right, causing the second NOI = 0 point to be overestimated.

The growing divergence of at least some of the developing economies away from the industrialised economies has a similar effect. The catching-up process described earlier has not occurred among the poorer countries, which have diverged as a group from the wealthier countries and are not exhibiting a tendency to converge in relation to the world leaders (Dowrick 1992), but are in fact 'falling behind'. The effect on the FDI activities of developing countries is that less inward direct investment is coming from industrialised countries, and those developing countries that are outward investors prefer to invest in the industrialised countries wherever possible to acquire created assets. However, the 'falling behind' effect is associated primarily with stage 1 and 2 countries, while a handful of developing countries that are regarded as newly industrialising economies (NIEs) have been shown to be catching up with the industrialised economies. Indeed, data on FDI flows indicate that the four Asian NIEs account for 57.6% of total outward flows from non-oil-exporting developing countries between 1980 and 1990, and 83% over 1988–90. This would cause a second 'bunching', this time of developing countries, at the first NOI = 0 point, with relatively few countries in between. When undertaking a statistical test, these two effects would result in a significant bias that would appear as a flattening out of the IDP and, depending on the sample taken, might result in an incorrect specification of the IDP. We believe that the alternative specification found by Tolentino (1987, 1993) may be partly explained by these phenomena.

Growth of strategic investment activity

Another reason for decreasing fit may be explained by the changing motives for investment. This is compounded by the arrival of new foreign investors and government policies that embrace FDI as an integral part of their economic policy. For instance, the use of outward investment as a means of acquiring assets through strategic asset seeking investments has proliferated in recent years, and such investments are less a function of home country advantages, and more of host country advantages. This has hitherto been the domain of large internationalised firms with considerable experience in international activities, typically from industrialised countries. However, firms with limited international experience from countries (e.g. Indonesia, Philippines, Korea, Taiwan, Hong Kong, Thailand) at lower stages have also begun such activities, with active home government encouragement, in order to facilitate structural adjustment in the home country. The impact of such government-facilitated FDI activity on the home country economy is often pervasive, as has been documented by several authors including Wade (1988, 1990), Amsden (1989), UN (1993a). This symbiosis of FDI and development is not restricted to outward investment activity, but may include strategic encouragement of inward investment with the aim of developing export oriented production, as is the case of Singapore (see Mirza 1986).

FDI measurement problems

Dunning (1981a) and Tolentino (1993) both use FDI flow data for the purposes of estimating FDI stock, which, Dunning argues, represent a good proxy for stock. With the recent publication of the *World Investment Directory* by the United Nations (1992b and 1993e), however, stock figures are now available for a larger number of countries than was previously the case. Dunning (1981a) uses average flows as a proxy, whereas Tolentino (1993) uses the sum of flows. These are argued to be good substitutes for each other. Using flow data from IMF tapes, we are able to confirm that this is indeed the case. Taking the sum of flows and average flows for three periods – 1970–75, 1975–83 and 1980–88 – as proxies for stocks for 1973, 1979 and 1984, correlations were first run between average flow data and the sum of flows of inward and outward FDI for a sample of 46 countries. The R^2 was unity in all cases.

However, the relationship between stocks and flows presents a possible counterpoint to the use of flows as a proxy for stock data; for instance, if we use sum of flows for five years, they do not adequately reflect the stock at the end of the period. Using stocks and flows from the same source (the *World Investment Directory*) Malaysia's inward FDI 1970–75 is approximately half of stock, as is the case for the periods 1975–80 and 1980–85; however, outward FDI for Malaysia is exaggerated by a factor of 5 for 1970–75 although it is underestimated by one-third for 1980–85. Repeating the same procedure for US data, the sum of five-year inward flows is about half of inward stock for 1970–75, 1975–80 and 1980–85, but outward flows are about one-half, one-third and one-fourth for the same time periods.

This suggests that, while flow data provide a consistent underestimation of inward stocks, outward flows cannot be regarded as a reliable estimator for outward stock, and therefore values of NOI will be increasingly incorrect for high outward FDI growth countries, especially for those that have just begun outward investment. Therefore outward stock seems underestimated by the sum-of-flows method and the NOI position underestimated over time, causing a flattening out of the IDP, especially for countries from stage 2 onwards.

We examine this hypothesis by taking the correlation between stocks and the sum of flows for three periods: we compare flows for 1970–75, 1975–83 and 1980–88 with stock data for 1975, 1979 and 1984 respectively. Table 3.1 presents the results, calculated separately for all countries, developing countries and industrialised countries.[1]

The results indicate that for developing countries the use of sum of flows is becoming a relatively good proxy for both outward FDI and inward FDI stocks, although for 1975 the relationship was extremely weak. This may be due to several factors. First, while we would prefer to compare stocks for 1973 with 1970–75 flows or 1968–75 flows, stock data are unavailable for a large enough sample for 1975.[2] Second, it may be due to the breakdown of the system of fixed exchange rates during this period, as well as the OPEC oil crisis.

In the case of industrialised countries, the use of flows as a proxy for inward stock appears not to be a reliable indicator, and has become increasingly unreliable over the period in question. In the case of outward FDI, flows were a good proxy in the 1970s, but by 1984 their reliability had fallen. This drop may be partly attributed to the fact that 1984 was the year in which the US dollar was at its zenith *vis-à-vis* the currencies of other industrialised countries; all stock data for 1984 were converted into US dollars, and may have introduced a bias into the data.[3]

Therefore, the net result on the estimates of NOI positions indicates that the use of flow data does not provide a good indicator for stock positions for all countries; while results for developing countries suggest

Table 3.1 Correlation between sum-of-flows estimates of FDI stocks and published FDI stocks on a per capita basis, 1975–84

		All countries		*Developing countries*		*Industrialised countries*	
		N	R^2	*N*	R^2	*N*	R^2
ODI	1975	35	0.969	19	0.008	16	0.965
ODI	1979	35	0.958	19	0.097	16	0.949
ODI	1984	35	0.807	19	0.814	16	0.715
IDI	1975	35	0.036	19	0.33	16	0.327
IDI	1979	35	0.445	19	0.928	16	0.056
IDI	1984	35	0.792	19	0.976	16	0.224
NOI	1975	35	0.394	19	0.273	16	0.776
NOI	1979	35	0.009	19	0.59	16	0.429
NOI	1984	35	0.194	19	0.949	16	0.423

Notes: ODI = outward FDI; IDI = inward FDI

that the fit is improving, the opposite is the case for the industrialised countries.

TESTING THE IDP

We have argued that the effects observed by Tolentino (1987, 1993) and Dunning (1981a) may be summarised as occurring because of the combined effects due mainly to: (a) the distortions from the use of flow data, (b) distortions arising from convergence and divergence phenomena, (c) different country-specific characteristics, and (d) changing motives for investment. As we have suggested, the use of cross-sectional tests to rigorously examine the last two effects is hindered by the level of aggregation. We minimise the effects of (a) by using stock data. The limited availability of FDI data classified by motive of investment does not allow us to separate the effects of (d). The proliferation of different motives of investment is especially prevalent among industrialised countries, and is compounded by the limited sample size; the inward FDI and outward FDI curves for these countries are expected to be difficult to predict. Similar limitations prevent us from examining differences in path due to (c). These issues are the focus of Chapters 4 and 5. The effects due to (b), viz. the influence of convergence and divergence, can be examined, albeit tentatively, using a comparison of the cross-section results for 1975 and 1988.

Our earlier discussion of the increasing concentration of FDI activity within the Triad as well as the polarisation resulting from convergence and divergence suggest that the shape of the investment development path may have changed over time, but particularly among industrialised countries which have slowing economic growth but an increasing extent of inward and outward investment. Our hypothesised 'ideal' path given in the previous chapter suggests that the relationship is non-linear in nature. Because of the limitations of cross-sectional tests suggested above, we do not intend to confirm the relationship econometrically, but will confine our analysis to examining whether, and how, the nature of the path has changed between 1975 and 1988.

There are two significant difficulties associated with testing the IDP. The first is associated with sample size. While it would be optimal to examine the industrialised countries separately from developing countries, there are insufficient numbers of industrialised countries for any rigorous statistical analysis. Apart from the problems associated with aggregating both groups of countries together, net outward investment as a variable is itself an aggregation of two other variables: inward investment and outward investment. The second difficulty is associated with the specification of the relationship. Although previous work has attempted to use a quadratic expression for the relationship for NOI and GNP, there has been no prior statistical formulation for the shape of the inward and outward investment curves, although Dunning (1981a) indicates that a quadratic equation may be applicable. However, determining the statistical formulation of inward and outward investment is hindered by the small sample size of countries available. The use of a quadratic relationship allows for the fact that the dependent variable changes over time and stages, but it also assumes that the rate of change is more or less constant at all stages of the IDP.

The development of a rigorous specification of the relationship between development and investment is difficult given the complexity and is outside the scope of the present work. We shall therefore use the quadratic relationship, and, keeping in mind its limitations, we will use caution in interpreting the results.

Ideally, the data should not be examined using OLS regression because the error terms are not normally distributed, and are related to the independent variable: in other words, there is heteroskedasticity. From a visual inspection of the plot of the error terms, this would appear to be due to the aggregation of the industrial countries and developing countries which seem to exhibit very different variances. Although the optimal solution would be to use GLS, given the small sample size, the ambiguous nature of the relationship between the error terms and the independent variable,[4] and the fact that GLS estimates are only asymptotically more desirable, it may not be practical to do so. We resolve this problem by breaking the sample into two. Since the relationship is expected to be somewhat different for industrialised countries than for developing countries, the OLS regressions will be run for developing countries and industrialised countries separately. Since the sample size for industrialised countries is 17 or 18, in the absence of a strong relationship it may be that our results are inconclusive. Theoretically, dividing the sample into two groups of developing countries should be done at the second NOI = 0 point. However, because of the polarisation of countries, and the spread of industrialised countries that we have hypothesised to occur after stage 4, this point may be more to the right than is actually the case. We use the listing of GNP per capita provided in the *World Development Report*, and assume that the NOI = 0 point should occur close to the industrialised countries with the lowest GNP per capita. Since no single country is necessarily at this point, we will allow for an overlap in the two groups. This will serve to improve our sample size, as well as helping to eliminate the problems arising from convergence and divergence and the polarisation of countries.

Since we suspect that the nature of the relationship varies not just between groups of countries at different stages, but for the same countries over time owing to changing economic conditions (such as convergence and divergence), we will compare the results for two time periods 1975 and 1988 for a sample of 40 countries. GNP for these countries has been collected from various secondary sources including government publications and international organisations such as the IMF. For comparison purposes, all data were converted into US dollars. Stock data and GNP values have been normalised by population.

A COMPARISON OF THE IDP IN 1975 AND 1988

Figure 3.1 shows a plot of NOI and GNP for 1975. A quadratic equation was regressed for 1975 and gave the following equation, where Y = NOI per capita and X = GNP per capita:

$$Y = -0.1569X + 0.0000247X^2$$
$$(2.462) \qquad (2.889)$$
$$(2\%) \qquad (1\%)$$
$$N = 40 \quad F = 4.208(1\%) \quad adj.\ R^2 = 0.167$$

The plot of the estimated curve and the actual values are shown in the figure.

We repeat the procedure for the data for 1988. The hypothesised quadratic equation for 1988 gives the following summary statistics:

$$Y = -0.1131X + 0.00000709X^2$$
$$(3.4032) \qquad (4.3753)$$
$$(1\%) \qquad (1\%)$$
$$N = 40 \quad F = 14.07\ (1\%) \quad adj.\ R^2 = 0.424$$

This curve is fitted in Figure 3.2.

A casual examination of Figures 3.1 and 3.2 and their corresponding

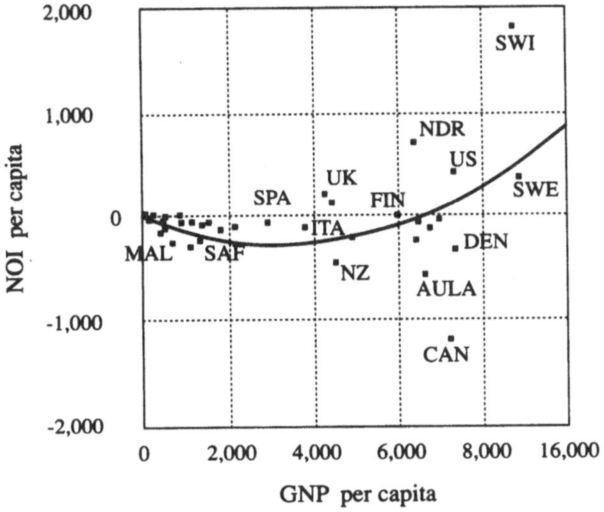

Figure 3.1 NOI and GNP for 1975

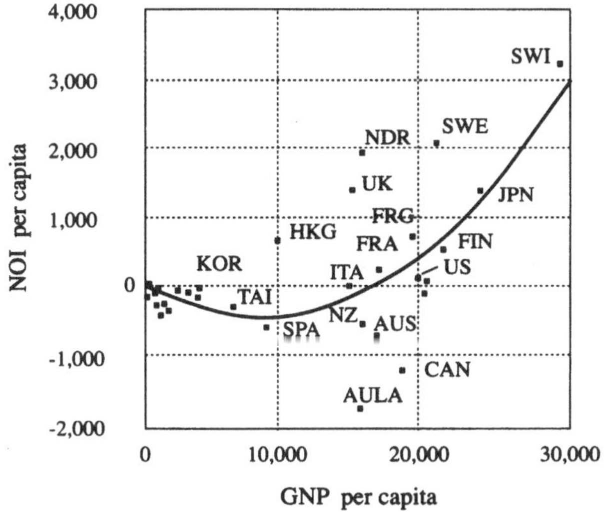

Figure 3.2 NOI and GNP for 1988

equations reveals several things. First, the industrialised countries are considerably spread out along the horizontal axis relative to the vertical axis in 1975, whereas in 1988 these countries are relatively more spread out along the vertical axis. This effect may be due to the convergence of their GNP values in 1988 and an increasing growth of their net investment

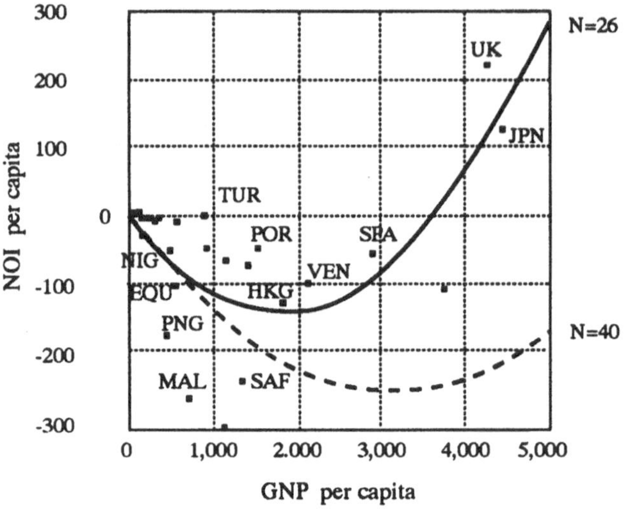

Figure 3.3 NOI and GNP for developing countries showing estimated curves, 1975

position relative to 1975. Second, the clustering of developing countries around the origin has increased over time, with only a few countries between the twin clusters of the developing countries and industrialised countries. This lends some support to the divergence argument suggested above. Therefore, although the regression results suggest that the quadratic form used above shows an increasingly better fit over time, the results are suspect because of the problems previously indicated.

However, even if the problems suggested above did not exist, the results are invalid because of the presence of heteroskedasticity. We therefore circumvent this problem by breaking the sample into two groups as earlier discussed. We first estimate the coefficients for developing countries for NOI for 1975, and then for 1988.

The relationship between NOI and GNP for developing countries

For 1975, using the equation estimated above, we find that NOI = 0 at GNP values of \$0 and \$6352.23. We repeat the regression to exclude industrialised countries. We separate stage 4 countries from stage 5 countries arbitrarily, assuming that countries with low GNP per capita among the industrialised countries as identified by the *World Development Report 1978* will more likely be close to the NOI = 0 or slightly positive. Our cutoff used is GNP $\leq$ \$4500 which includes all countries up to Japan. Figure 3.3 presents the results of this subsample. We have included the estimated curve for N = 40 and N = 26:

Table 3.2 Distribution of countries based on estimated IDP in 1975

Stage	*Country*
Stages 1 and 2 GNP per capita \$1819.35	Bangladesh, China, India, Pakistan, Indonesia, Sri Lanka, Thailand, Philippines, Papua New Guinea, Nigeria, Korea, Equador, Malaysia, Turkey, Taiwan, Brazil, Fiji
Approaching stage 3	South Africa, Mexico, Portugal, Venezuela, Hong Kong
Stage 3 \$1819.35 ≤ GNP per capita < \$3638.7	
Approaching stage 4	Spain, Italy
Stages 4 and 5 GNP per capita > \$3638.7	Italy, UK, New Zealand, Japan, Austria, Belgium, Netherlands, US, Canada, Sweden, Australia, Norway, Denmark, Finland, Germany, France

Note: Countries are listed in order of increasing GNP per capita

$$Y = -0.1549X + 0.0000426X^2$$
$$(5.8736) \qquad (5.8109)$$
$$(1\%) \qquad (1\%)$$
$$N = 26 \quad F = 17.6012\ (1\%) \quad adj.\ R^2 = 0.578$$

The NOI = 0 points are at 0 and \$3638.7. The minimum is at \$1819.4, which represents the beginning of stage 3, at NOI = −140.8. Table 3.2 classifies countries into three groups based on these observations. The divisions into the three groups were distinct, but because of the arbitrary selection of countries into developing and industrialised countries, we may have caused the turning points to be weak estimates that are biased away from the true turning points. Therefore, countries that are close to the turning point, based on the evidence in Figure 3.3, are included in separate categories.

We repeat the procedure for the 1988 data. The cutoff for non stage 5 countries for 1988 is \$15,000. The data are plotted in Figure 3.4. The results for the quadratic equation are as follows and are plotted in Figure 3.4 as a dashed line. For comparison, the quadratic equation for the case for all countries is included as a solid line. New Zealand has been excluded from the regression because of its relative dependence on natural assets, thus giving it a skewed NOI value that is negative.[5]

$$Y = -0.1074X + 0.0000109X^2$$
$$(3.1381) \qquad (3.9625)$$
$$(10\%) \qquad (1\%)$$
$$N = 25 \quad F = 9.7785\ (1\%) \quad adj.\ R^2 = 0.436$$

Table 3.3 Distribution of countries based on estimated IDP in 1988

Stage	*Country*
Stages 1 and 2 GNP per capita < $4926.61	Bangladesh, Nigeria, China, India, Sri Lanka, Pakistan, Indonesia, Philippines, Equador, Papua New Guinea, Thailand, Turkey, Fiji, Malaysia, Mexico, Brazil, South Africa, Venezuela
Approaching stage 3	Portugal, Korea
Stage 3 $4926.61 ≤ GNP per capita < $9853.21	Taiwan, Spain
Approaching stage 4	Hong Kong
Stages 4 and 5 GNP per capita > $9853.21	New Zealand, Italy, UK, Netherlands, Belgium, Australia, France, Canada, Germany, US, Denmark, Norway, Sweden, Finland, Japan, Switzerland

Note: Countries listed in order of increasing GNP per capita

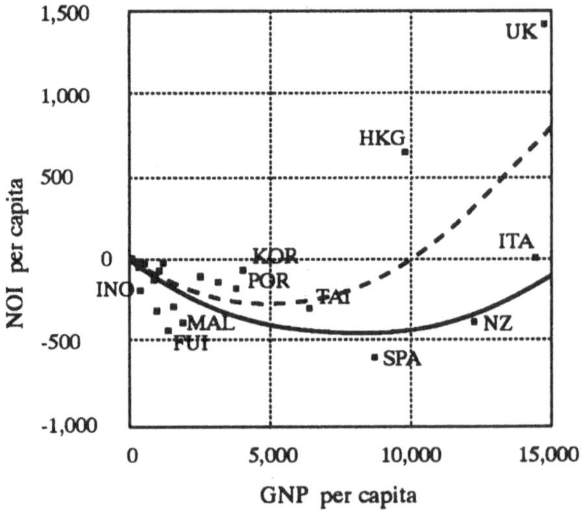

Figure 3.4 NOI and GNP for developing countries showing estimated curves, 1988

The minima for the curve are at NOI = − $264.55 and GNP = $4926.61, whereas the second NOI = 0 point is at GNP = $9853.21. However, the arbitrary selection of a cutoff for the sample may have affected the classification of the countries, especially those that are close to the turning points suggested above. Therefore, we have indicated countries that are close to the turning points separately. The classification of countries is given in Table 3.3, and is compiled on the basis of their GNP per capita and NOI figures as shown in Figure 3.4.

The evidence reviewed confirms that the IDP exists for 1975 and 1988, for developing countries. The results of Tolentino (1993) are seriously affected by the convergence and divergence process, which cause the IDP to be 'stretched', and, depending on the selection of countries, may actually lead to an appearance of an inverted U. We have allowed for the increasing spread of industrialised countries by breaking the sample into two. This has helped us to identify the true path, and confirms that the stages first identified by Dunning (1981a) still exist; casual evidence confirms that the groupings of countries are more accurate when the most industrialised countries are excluded from the regressions. For instance, for the whole sample in 1975 the UK would be classified as a stage 3 country, but by breaking the countries into groups it is classified as an industrialised country; in 1988, taking all countries together, Taiwan would be classified as a stage 2 country, while it is in reality a stage 3 country, since its outward investment has been seen to be growing faster than its inward investment.

What of the industrialised countries? We now review the evidence of the relationship between NOI and GNP for these countries for both periods.

The relationship between NOI and GNP for industrialised countries

We select the countries around the NOI = 0 point in the same manner as above, including all countries with GNP greater than the NOI = 0 level, as well as the countries whose values are close to but less than the threshold. Figures 3.5 and 3.6 show the plot of GNP against NOI for 1975 and 1988 respectively. However, because of the small sample size, we cannot run a regression for only stage 4 and stage 5 countries. None the less, visual inspection suggests that no clear pattern exists for either of these periods, although there seems to be some suggestion of an increased variance around the *X*-axis – in 1975 most countries seem to have an NOI per capita that is close to zero, with the variance increasing at higher levels of GNP per capita, whereas in 1988 this trend seems to have disappeared. The mean NOI per capita between 1975 and 1988 has increased ten-fold, from $36.1 to $378.5, while the mean GNP per capita has increased three-fold, from $6133.4 to $17,607. The standard deviation for NOI per capita has doubled from $619.7 to $1239, whereas the

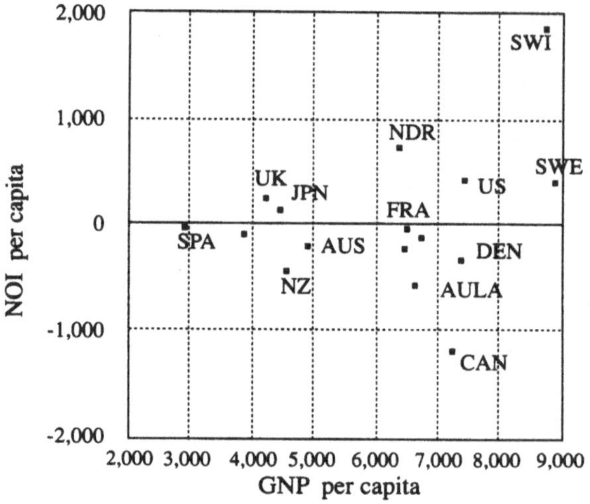

Figure 3.5 NOI and GNP for industrialised countries, 1975

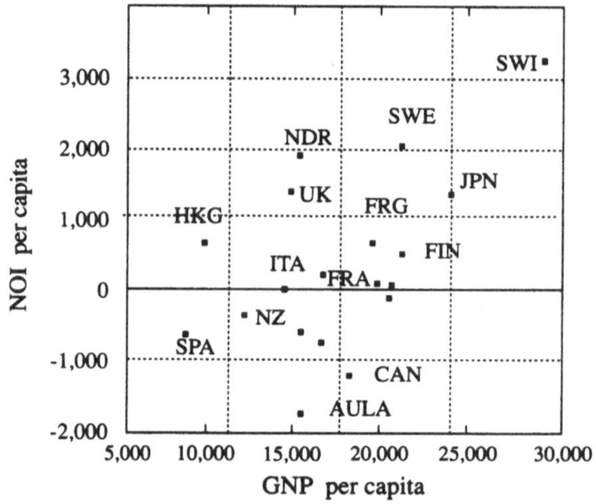

Figure 3.6 NOI and GNP for industrialised countries, 1988

standard deviation of GNP per capita has tripled, from $1650.1 to $4888.7.

This suggests that in general NOI for these countries has grown faster than GNP, and that their NOI has increasingly become larger and more positive over time. This implies that on average these countries' outward investment activities are growing faster than inward investment into these countries. The higher growth of standard deviation of GNP over

NOI suggests that disparities in GNP per capita for the industrialised countries as a group have increased relative to their NOI. Although tentative, this suggests that FDI activities of these countries are growing faster than their overall economies, but the extent of their investment activities is becoming more broadly similar across countries than are their economies.

SUMMARY AND CONCLUSIONS

This chapter has investigated the IDP on a cross-sectional basis for 1975 and 1988 by econometric analysis of net outward investment stock and GNP, both normalised by population, for a sample of 40 countries. We have found that the J relationship suggested by Dunning (1981a) continues to apply, in contrast to the results of Tolentino (1993), who found an inverted relationship. The chapter has analysed why Tolentino's results where in contrast to those of Dunning, and has suggested that this may have to do with several factors, primarily the use of flows as a proxy for stock, as well as the process of convergence and divergence, which has led to a polarisation of countries around two points. The latter problem was enhanced by Tolentino's sample. We also suggested that the shape of the path had changed, especially in the case of industrialised countries, resulting from the process associated with economic convergence (suggested in the theoretical framework outlined in Chapter 2), as countries enter a fifth stage of the IDP. That is, as countries experience economic convergence, their economies have become increasingly interdependent and their investment patterns have become increasingly similar and directed among each other as *de facto* and *de jure* economic integration takes place; their net investment position therefore tends to fluctuate around an equilibrium.

We tested this by breaking the sample of countries into two, to confirm that, for developing countries, up to the beginning of the fourth stage the original premiss of the IDP continues to hold, but as countries became industrialised, the relationship between their net investment position and development can no longer be explained without the introduction of the fifth stage.

With regards to the developing countries, the evidence suggests that there has indeed been a divergence of these countries away from industrialised countries – there has been significant increase of clustering of countries around the origin. In 1975, there seemed to be several countries that had promising growth potential and that were poised to pass beyond the second stage of the IDP, such as South Africa and Turkey. By 1988, these countries had declined economically, and, rather than demonstrating fast growth, their NOI position declined. Apart from the petroleum-based economies whose economic woes were partly a result of falling commodity prices, there has been little change in the relative positions of countries, with the exception of the Asian NIEs. With these notable exceptions, most developing countries have not shown a significant growth in their NOI positions between the two periods, even relative to the growth of their GNP.

This is certainly not the case with industrialised countries. Figures 3.5 and 3.6 dramatically illustrate the point. Their NOI positions have converged to a greater extent than has their GNP, and they have exhibited a faster growth rate. As to the question of reaching an equilibrium level, the evidence presented here is inconclusive. Apart from limitations due to the sample size, there are two other problems that make this task difficult. First, the nature of the equilibrium is not known, and even if it were, in the nature of equilibria, it is expected to be unstable. Second, the increased complexity of the motivations of FDI, and the increasing importance of firm-specific advantages in determining the extent of investments, limit the use of a cross-sectional study. What is necessary is a time series study that provides evidence on an industry level that is comparable across countries. However, with the exception of a very few countries, such data are either unavailable for a sufficiently long period, or unavailable in sufficient geographic and industrial breakdown.

Another important point must be noted here. The use of cross-sectional study such as this one is limited in scope because a cross-sectional study is merely a proxy for a longitudinal one. Each country has a different IDP, as we noted here and in Chapter 2. The economic structure of a country determines the differences in the way in which its economy develops, as well as its FDI activity. Taking the most obvious differences, as we illustrated in Chapter 2, countries with an absolute advantage in natural resources are likely to have an IDP that does not become positive, despite growth in its development – the case of Australia and New Zealand illustrate this point. Likewise, small and/or resource-poor countries are expected to be large net outward investors at a much earlier stage than countries that are not so endowed – see for example the case of Japan and Hong Kong.

We seek to address these questions throughout the rest of this volume, but, given the problems associated with the aggregate variables used here, we will no longer explicitly use a stages-of-growth approach.

4

NATURAL AND CREATED ASSETS AS DETERMINANTS OF FDI

INTRODUCTION

The previous chapter examined the changing nature of the investment development path over two time periods. Specifically, it has been demonstrated that the investment development path as initially postulated is still valid in so far as the non-industrialised countries are concerned. It has also been demonstrated that the cross-sectional approach is extremely limiting given its static nature. Furthermore, both variables used in the analysis are aggregated variables: NOI is the difference between outward and inward FDI, while GNP per capita is a general variable that precludes us from observing changes in the nature of a country's economic structure, especially in terms of the balance between created and natural assets. In this chapter we intend to overcome some of these obstacles by evaluating how the extent of inward and outward FDI individually is determined by the extent of the natural and created assets of the host and home country respectively. Ideally, we would have preferred to engage in time series analysis for several countries at various stages of the IDP, but data limitations prevent this. Instead, we pool data for several periods for the industrialised countries and developing countries separately.

As discussed in Chapter 2, the economic structure of countries evolves from a dependence on natural assets to a dependence on created assets. Likewise, the O advantages of firms move from a natural-asset, country-specific nature towards an increasingly created-asset, firm-specific nature. Since the FDI activities associated with a country are determined by the nature of the economic structure, it is reasonable to expect that the determinants of its inward and outward FDI activity will also vary with the changing economic structure as it progresses along the IDP.

However, as the relative significance of international business activity grows in an economy owing to the growing foreign value adding activities of domestic firms as well as the increasing involvement of foreign MNEs in the domestic economy, the subsequent structure and influence of such activities associated with a particular country are influenced not just by its own economic structure, but by that of the host economies in which its firms operate, as well as the home countries of foreign owned firms operating within its borders. Such extensive internationalisation is generally associated with industrialised countries. Therefore, we would also expect to see a decline in the importance of country-specific factors among the industrialised countries in determining inward and outward FDI activity relative to developing countries.

In view of the importance that FDI activity plays in influencing economic growth, it is the purpose of this chapter to examine the locational factors that influence the extent of FDI activity. What are the locational determinants of host countries that influence the extent of inward FDI? What kind of locational factors determine the extent of outward FDI by home countries? Do different factors influence the FDI activity by and from developing countries and that by and from industrialised countries? With the changes in the world economy over the last two decades, and as the production activities of MNEs from industrialised countries become increasingly globalised, has the role of country-specific determinants become minimised? These are the types of question the chapter seeks to address.

DATA AND PROPOSITIONS

Sample size and dependent variables

Our sample consists of data for forty countries[1] for four time periods: 1975, 1979, 1984 and 1988. The countries were selected on the basis of availability of FDI stock figures for those time periods. Our dependent variables are the stock of inward investment per capita (*IWPOP*) and outward investment per capita (*OWPOP*), based on FDI data published in the *World Investment Directory* (UN 1992b, 1993e), as well as various government publications. All FDI data are historical stock figures in current prices, converted into US dollars. We intend to run regressions for two groups – developing countries (DC) and industrialised countries (IC) – separately.

Although we have two different dependent variables, several of our independent variables are the same. This is because we wish to examine how economic structure is related to the *stock* of FDI. Locational advantages such as infrastructure affect not only the relative attractiveness of a country to inward investors, but also the ability of domestic firms to develop and optimally utilise their ownership advantages; they represent L advantages to inward FDI, but influence the O advantages associated with outward FDI. To give another example, the national technological capabilities are a function of the O advantages of domestic firms and influence the extent of outward investment, as well as acting as a L advantage (or disadvantage) to foreign investors seeking to invest.

However, it should be noted that country-level economic structure does not provide a complete explanation of FDI activity associated with a location. This is for several reasons. First, the O advantages of firms are increasingly firm-specific, and while these may derive from use of location-specific natural assets, through technological accumulation over time these develop into created assets which are associated with the firm. Second, FDI activity occurs as a result of the *balance* of the OLI characteristics of the host and home country: a firm will not seek to undertake international production unless there exist complementary assets to which it desires access in another location. In other words, firms will engage in outward FDI not only because of home country 'push' factors, but also because of the host country 'pull' factors. The importance of country-level economic structure is greater in the case of inward investment, especially where such investments aim to take advantage of the L advantages of the host country, such as in market seeking investments, export oriented investment and natural resource seeking investments, which are generally associated with developing countries, and in strategic asset acquiring investments, which are associated with industrialised and industrialising economies.

These two issues are compounded as the firm becomes more internationalised. The motives of production become increasingly complicated, and outward FDI from a location may take place even where the home country possesses significant L advantages relative to the host, and where the O advantages of its firms do not provide it with a competitive advantage overseas – i.e. with strategic asset acquiring investments. Also, as a firm tends towards globally rationalised production, its competitive advantages do not necessarily reflect the competitive advantages of its home country, but rather the competitive advantages associated with its operations in other locations. Such internationalisation is associated with firms from the stage 4 and 5 countries. As such, the economic structure of the industrialised home country plays a less important role, and even where the home country is in an earlier stage of the IDP the home country economic structure may only help explain the 'push' factors.

We summarise our argument in the form of propositions.

- *Proposition 1* Inward FDI to developing countries is determined by the extent of natural assets of the host country, while inward FDI to industrialised countries is determined by the created asset ('technology') variables.
- *Proposition 2* Outward FDI by developing countries is determined by

the economic structure of the host country, since it is conducted primarily to acquire assets. As such, although the O advantages of their MNEs are natural-asset-based and determined by the home country characteristics, their outward FDI is aimed at acquiring assets that are not available at home. Outward FDI by industrialised countries is a positive function of its created assets.

- *Proposition 3* Economic structure variables are more significant in explaining the inward FDI associated with countries than in explaining their outward FDI, since FDI activity is in general associated with exploiting the L advantages of the host.
- *Proposition 4* Country-specific determinants are more significant in influencing the inward and outward FDI for developing countries than for industrialised countries.

EXPLANATORY VARIABLES

Innovatory capability

Innovatory capability influences a capital exporting or importing country's ability to attract value added activity by both foreign and domestically owned MNEs (Dunning 1993a) and may be considered to be a locational advantage. Previous macro studies have used R&D expenditures (Dunning 1981a, Clegg 1987) as a proxy for innovatory capability. However, because such data are not available for a sufficiently large number of countries for the same years, we will use the ratio of patents granted in the country in question as a ratio of its R&D personnel proxied by the total number of students at the tertiary level as an indicator of a nation's technological capability (*PATPER*).[2] We hypothesise that for both groups of countries, the higher the ratio of patents granted to the skilled population (*PATPER*), the greater the attractiveness of the host country to foreign and domestic investors, and the higher the stock of both inward FDI per capita and outward FDI per capita.

Human capital: an indicator of infrastructure

Apart from the technological capability associated with firms of a particular nationality is their ability to create, acquire and organise human skills and competence, and this can be regarded as knowledge capital.[3] This is a locational advantage to foreign investors, since it implies the existence of infrastructural facilities. Papanastassiou and Pearce (1990) have used the proportion of scientists and engineers in total employment, while Dunning (1980) used a skilled employment ratio (the ratio of salaried employees to production workers). Again owing to limited data availability, we are unable to use either of these indicators. Instead, we take a ratio of total enrolment of students[4] at the tertiary level to total population of the country in question (*HCPOP*). The development and availability of post-secondary education vary widely among countries, and a large proportion of tertiary-level students as a percentage of population indicates a well developed infrastructure. In general, we hypothesise that, for both groups of countries, the higher the percentage of skilled personnel in a home country (*HCPOP*), the better the infrastructure, and the greater the extent of its inward and outward direct investment per capita.

Capital intensity

The capital intensity associated with a country is a significant determinant of the locational advantages of a host country because it is a necessary condition for the efficient exploitation of the ownership advantages of domestic or foreign firms at a particular location. We use as our proxy for capital intensity the gross fixed capital formation per capita (*GFCF-POP*) (see Alam 1992, Veugelers 1991). This variable also provides an indication of infrastructure. We hypothesise that, in the case of both developing and industrialised countries, the greater the level of capital intensity (*GFCFPOP*), the higher will be the inward and outward investment per capita.

Natural resource availability

Several studies have examined the effect of the relative abundance of natural resources in a country and how this might influence the extent and nature of its inward and outward FDI. Swedenborg (1979) and Rugman (1987) have both shown that the possession of natural resources influences the pattern of outward FDI activity by Swedish and Canadian firms respectively. Conversely, it will also affect the pattern of inward FDI – this has been demonstrated by, among others, Kumar (1990), Owen (1982) and Lecraw (1991).

A country that is well endowed in natural resources will, *ceteris paribus*, attract a larger proportion of inward investment than would a country without such an abundance at the same stage of development. Because such investments will either be in the primary sector or be related to this sector, in either related or supporting industries, the development of created assets of domestic firms will likely be in these same industries. The extent to which a country is well endowed in a natural resource may be construed from the percentage of its exports of primary commodities[5] (*XP*). For both developed and industrialised countries, we expect that, the higher the host country's primary exports as a percentage of the total exports (*XP*), the greater will be its stock of inward investment per capita.

As discussed in the theoretical section, the initial ownership advantages of firms from a less developed country will tend to be limited to the primary sector, or to industries that are related to this sector. Since a high primary export share implies a low manufacturing export share, and in the absence of significant external stimuli to encourage the growth of created-asset-based ownership advantages of firms, outward FDI would be lower given the limited scope of the ownership advantages of their domestic firms. Therefore, for developing countries as well as industrialised countries, the higher the home country's primary exports (*XP*), the smaller the extent of its outward FDI per capita.

The lack of natural resources in a country will also affect the pattern of outward investment from that country, as it will be forced either to invest abroad in primary industries to acquire supplies of necessary inputs from its domestic industries, or, in order to pay for its primary imports, to make trade-supportive and market seeking investments, and to acquire strategic assets to support its domestic manufacturing sector's international competitiveness. Therefore such a country would have a greater amount of outward investment than a country that has a better natural resource endowment at a similar stage. However, this will apply only to developing countries. An industrialised country with a relative disadvantage in resources will import about the same percentage of primary goods as it did in earlier stages, because the increased demand will be offset by high wages, resulting in an increasing preference to import (increasingly on an intra-firm basis) intermediate goods from low-wage countries, increasing the share of manufactured imports and pushing down the share of primary imports. We do not utilise this variable in our subsequent regressions to demonstrate this, because of the relatively few countries in our industrialised country sample that have an absolute disadvantage in natural resources. Therefore, for developing countries we hypothesise that, the higher a home country's imports of natural resources (*MP*), the higher its outward investment per capita.

Degree of openness

The development of a firm's ownership advantages is influenced by the extent to which it is exposed to international competition. Economies that are protected from the activities of foreign-owned enterprises by pursuing an import substituting policy not only limit the extent of their imports, but also affect the quality and quantity of their exports, owing to the limited nature of the ownership advantages of their firms. A measure of the extent to which a country participates in the international division of labour is its trade intensity (*TI*). This is measured by the sum of its exports and imports divided by its population. Countries that have an import substituting policy orientation will attract relatively less inward FDI than countries with export oriented economies which tend to have a high trade intensity. However, given the uniformly high trade intensity associated with all the industrialised countries in our sample, the use of this proxy as an explanatory variable for industrialised countries' inward FDI serves no purpose, and we examine its importance only as a determinant of inward FDI activity for developing countries: the greater a country's participation in international trade (*TI*), the larger its inward FDI per capita.

Its use as an explanatory variable for outward FDI is also limited. In the case of developing countries, as discussed earlier, developing country MNEs may undertake international production precisely because of the restrictions in international trade activity. It represents a means to acquire capital and technology for use in domestic operations and is sometimes actively encouraged by government policy. Therefore, we feel that trade intensity, as measured by our proxy, is unrelated to outward FDI of developing countries. As in the case of outward FDI, the uniformly high level of *TI* for industrialised countries negates the use of *TI* as an explanatory variable for industrialised countries also.

Market characteristics

Although demand factors can be considered as consisting of two main features – *quality* of demand and *quantity* of demand (Narula 1993) – given the complexities of measuring quality of demand in aggregate terms, we shall examine the issue of quantity of demand. By quantity of demand we refer to market size. The larger the market size of the host economy, the greater the attraction for foreign investors since the economies of large-scale production are likely to be captured. Therefore the stock of inward FDI to a country is likely to be greater when the size of the market is larger. Previous studies have proxied this with real or real lagged GNP (Culem 1988), GNP, population (Alam 1992, Kobrin 1976) or GDP (Veugelers 1991, Alam 1992). However, the market size of the host country is significantly affected by that of other countries with which it has *de facto* or *de jure* economic ties. For instance, the market size of Belgium is considerably enhanced by its membership of the EC – the market attractions of Belgium are not just its domestic market as this is increased by economic integration with the EU. This trend is particularly true of countries that have close economic ties with other countries owing to some extent of economic integration, as is the case among most countries of the Triad. Veugelers (1991) adjusts GDP for openness of the host country, to allow for countries that are small in domestic market size but have access to other markets through exports to other geographically proximate countries. Such an adjustment would not apply to a small country such as Fiji or Kuwait, which is not part of a regional economic alliance. By running separate regressions for industrialised and developing countries, we will circumvent the need to make such adjustments. We will use aggregate private consumption as our proxy for market size. However, location decisions are based not on absolute market size but on relative market size,[6] especially when economies of scale are concerned. What we suggest is that there exists an ideal or optimal market size[7] for which economies of scale are most efficient, and the closer host country markets are to this, the more FDI they will attract. We therefore normalise the aggregate private consumption figures for all countries by that of the 'ideal' market. We assume that Germany presents such an ideal market and divide the private consumption of each country by that of Germany to yield our independent variable that measures relative demand (*RELDEMD*).[8] However, given the complexities associated with identifying the real market size because of several dynamic and concurrent processes of economic integration within the industrialised world – for instance, the Netherlands is part of the EU, the Benelux and the *de facto* integration of the Triad – the use of *RELDEMD* as a determinant of industrialised countries' inward FDI is limited and therefore is not included in the regressions. However, for developing countries we expect that *RELDEMD* is positively related to inward FDI per capita.

In the case of outward FDI, large domestic markets present considerable opportunity for growth of sales. Therefore, the attraction of foreign markets, *ceteris paribus*, will be considerably less. This is especially true in the case of MNEs from industrialised countries. However, in the case of outward FDI from developing countries, investments are not normally associated with a saturation of the home market. Rather, FDI is often complementary to domestic markets – they are made to seek strategic assets (including technology and capital), and often are either encouraged by government policy or employed as a means to circumvent it. In other words, we feel that home country market size is not a determinant of outward FDI from developing countries: for industrialised countries, the greater the home country market size, the smaller the stock of outward investment per capita.

Table 4.1 summarises the expected signs and the relevant hypotheses for each of our regressions.

DISCUSSION OF RESULTS

The results of the regressions are given in Table 4.2. Equations 1 and 2 give the results for inward FDI equations, while equations 3 and 4 are the outward FDI equations. The correlation matrices for the four equations are given in Appendix 1. There may be misspecification of some of these variables, since we have assumed a linear relationship.

Table 4.1 Expected signs of hypotheses

Sample	*Ind. Var.*	GFCFPOP	TI	PATPER	HCPOP	XP	MP	RELDEMD
DC	*IWPOP*	+	+	+	+	+	N	+
IC	*IWPOP*	+	N	+	+	+	N	N
DC	*OWPOP*	+	+	+	+	−	+	N
IC	*OWPOP*	+	N	+	+	−	N	−

Note: N = not included

Table 4.2 Regression results

Eqn.	*Sample*	*Ind. var.*	*Constant*	GFCFPOP	TI	PATPER	HCPOP	XP	MP	RELDEMND	N	F *value*	*adj.* R^2
1	DC	*IWPOP*	− 47.426	− 0.155	0.178	− 928.735	0.0004	1.119		258.715	42	51.454	0.881
			(0.7535)	(2.766)***	(12.225)***	(2.806)***	(0.2259)	(1.5198)**		(1.8143)†			
2	IC	*IWPOP*	− 1244.806	0.229		1309.251	0.0279	14.435			60	9.213	0.358
			(3.3899)***	(3.3266)***		(3.5691)***	(2.8941)***	(2.950)***					
3	DC	*OWPOP*	− 2.036	0.0086		− 23.577	0.00006	− 0.0308	0.0926		42	10.167	0.528
			(0.7667)	(4.6508)***		(2.2059)*	(0.8301)	(1.1406)	(1.9477)†				
4	IC	*OWPOP*	− 1010.873	0.418		1997.776	0.0185	− 1.656		− 25.695	60	8.016	0.373
			(1.9331) +	(4.1223)***		(3.8238)***	(1.104)	(0.2258)		(0.1719)			

Notes: *** Significant at the 1% level ** Significant at the 2.5% level * Significant at the 5% level † Significant at the 10% level.

However, the results presented are of an exploratory nature, and our results and their ensuing discussion must necessarily be considered in this light. The results broadly confirm our hypotheses and propositions.

Inward FDI

As expected, variables that proxy the economic structure of the host country provide a better explanation of the extent of inward direct investment activity for developing countries than for industrialised countries: equation 2 had an R^2 of 0.358, compared with 0.881 for equation 1. There are two possible explanations for this.[9] First, a different relationship applies to explain the inward investment activity of industrialised countries; i.e. a different specification is required of existing variables. Second, it may be due to the increasing growth of intra-Triad investment, economic integration and the evolution of industrialised countries to stage 5. The inward investment into industrialised countries is increasingly of a rationalised nature, and is aimed more at seeking complementary created assets in specialised niches, and acquiring the benefits that derive from the growing efficiency in industrialised countries' organisation of economic activity arising from economic integration, than at seeking access to infrastructure or domestic markets and the utilisation of firm-specific assets. In other words, country-level economic structure plays a declining role in determining the inward FDI activity of countries as they move along the IDP.

In the case of FDI into industrialised countries, all the variables had the correct sign and were significant at the 1% level. Our regression for inward FDI into industrialised countries suggests that a high extent of outward investment is associated with home countries that have a high capital intensity, high technological capabilities and human capital. Surprisingly, inward investment is still influenced by the presence of comparative advantages in natural resources.

In the case of developing-country inward FDI, the proxies for capital intensity (*GFCFPOP*) and technological capability (*PATPER*) have the wrong sign but are significant at the 1% level. *HCPOP* was insignificant, but positive as expected. This may have to do with the extent of primary exports (*XP*), which was significant at the 1% level. The lack of created assets and infrastructure is often offset by the relatively low cost of unskilled labour and primary commodities in the host country, and much of such countries' inward FDI is aimed at exploiting these natural-asset-based advantages, through resource seeking investments. Investments into such countries are sometimes associated with export oriented intentions, whereby downstream, low value added activity is conducted within enclaves such as export processing zones and utilises a minimum of capital equipment and skilled manpower. All these investments rely on exploiting the comparative advantages of developing countries in natural assets, and the results would suggest that inward FDI into developing countries occurs *because of* the low level of created assets and capital intensity.

On the other hand, there continues to be some market seeking investment into some developing countries, especially in the NIEs. However, these countries account for less than 25% of our observations, as is suggested by the low significance of 10% (but correct sign) of the proxy for market size (*RELDEMD*).

Outward FDI

We turn now to the outward FDI regressions. It is to be noted that our aim with regard to outward investment is to identify the home country economic structural characteristics that influence the extent of this activity. In doing so, we need to emphasise that the propensity to invest overseas is greatly influenced by the host country characteristics, as we have seen in the discussion on inward FDI. Although the R^2 of developing country outward FDI is greater than that of its inward FDI (equations 1 and 3) , this is clearly not the case for the industrialised countries (equations 2 and 4), thereby only partially verifying proposition 4. However, once again, the R^2 values for outward FDI from developing countries is higher than the R^2 for that from industrialised countries, confirming proposition 3, which suggests that country-specific determinants are more relevant for developing countries.

For developing countries, capital intensity was significant at the 1% level. As for *PATPER*, it was significant at the 5% level and had the wrong sign. These seemingly paradoxical results, when taken together with the high significance of capital intensity (*GFCFPOP*), can be reconciled by the existence and growth of developing country MNEs (DCMNEs). DCMNEs tend to possess different proprietary advantages from conventional MNEs. They have acquired skills in products and processes that are standardised and are at the end of their product life cycle, which have been 'forgotten' by industrialised country MNEs, often adapting them for the small-scale labour intensive manufacturing that is more suited to the resource endowments of developing countries.[10] Low technology goods and processes emanating from the home countries of such firms are not generally patentable – the capital equipment is either purchased from industrialised countries, or is an adapted version of equipment based on such imports made by the parent firm from industrialised countries.[11] Further, patents are often difficult to obtain, or else, in the case of several countries (e.g. India), the enforcement of property rights is not permitted by law. Their proprietary advantages are therefore often based on their ability to adapt production to conditions and to a scale suitable to production in developing countries. Our proxy for technological capability does not capture the non-codifiable nature of their ownership advantages. The insignificant but positive sign of *HCPOP* provides some indication of this, but its low *T*-value is affected by the level of aggregation; the total number of engineers and scientists used as a percentage of population might provide better results, but data are not available for this proxy.

The sign for *XP* was significant at the 10% level for developing countries, but was insignificant for industrialised countries. This suggests that the role of traditional factor endowments in determining the outward investment activity is declining as created assets play an increasingly important role, and the relationship declines as countries move along the IDP.

The lack of significance of the *MP* variable (but correct sign) for developing countries is because, in the first place, there are too few countries in our sample with an absolute disadvantage in natural resources; second, the fluctuating price of most petroleum imports,[12] coupled with the fluctuation of the US dollar (as in 1984 where the US dollar was overvalued), tends to make *MP* a weak indicator of the relative importance of imports of primary goods.

The results for industrialised countries broadly suggest the increasing importance of firm-specific advantages in determining the propensity of their MNEs to invest abroad, and the declining importance of its country-specific L advantages, owing to the high level of internationalisation of its firms. The role of the home country declines as they are able to internalise the use of created asset advantages (which are generally not location-bound) from several locations as a result of their increasingly globalised operations, explaining the low significance of *HCPOP*. None the less, the bulk of their R&D facilities tends to be located in their home country, explaining the high significance of *PATPER*. The declining importance of industrialised countries' economic structure is also reflected in the correct sign but low *t*-value of *RELDEMD* and *XP*.

SUMMARY AND CONCLUSIONS

This chapter has examined the relationship between economic structure and the extent of outward and inward direct investment of countries. We have examined the relationship separately for developing countries and industrialised countries to confirm the arguments put forward in previous chapters that suggested the declining importance of economic structure in determining FDI activity as countries proceed along the IDP.

In the case of developing countries, inward investment seems to be directed towards the exploitation of natural assets and markets. Given the considerable extent of inward investment from industrialised countries and their move towards rationalised production, this is not surprising – MNEs from industrialised countries have moved the production of lower value added goods to locations where comparative advantages exist in downstream activities and sources of factor inputs.

Outward investment from developing countries seems to be associated with a high level of capital intensity but low technological capabilities of the home country, low levels of dependence on primary exports and a high level of dependence on primary imports. These results broadly confirm the conventional wisdom about DCMNEs, and lend credence to the first three stages of the IDP.

Our regression for inward and outward FDI of the industrialised countries broadly confirmed all our hypotheses. A high extent of inward investment is associated with host countries that have a high capital intensity, high technological capabilities and human capital. Inward investment is still influenced by the presence of comparative advantages in natural resources. As for outward FDI from industrialised countries, home country economic characteristics associated with high outward FDI are capital intensity and technological capability, but the presence of human capital is an insignificant (but positive) determinant. Size of the home market was also found to be an insignificant (but negative) determinant. This is partly as a result of the increasing integration among these countries, making the use of this proxy inappropriate.

In the case of both inward and outward FDI, the country-specific economic characteristics explain a decreasing proportion of the variation for industrialised countries relative to developing countries, as demonstrated by the lower R^2 in both cases. The importance of economic structure plays a less important role in determining the FDI activities associated with a country as it moves along the IDP, but there seems to be no indication that they are becoming insignificant. Further, different economic characteristics are associated with FDI activity as a country moves from being a developing country to being an industrialised one. Economic integration through supranational agreements such as the NAFTA, the EU and EFTA, and to a lesser extent the *de facto* integration of countries of the Triad through economic convergence, have led to an increase in the cross-investments between these countries, creating similar economic conditions among them. As their MNEs have developed networks that internalise the best features of each country's advantages in created assets because of the trend towards globalisation, their O advantages have become increasingly firm-specific.

However, these changes are complex in nature, and the aggregated nature of the study conducted in this chapter conceals important differences between them. Furthermore, as economic convergence takes place, differences between their economic structures are not necessarily country-specific, but associated with particular sectors and industries. We cannot explain why, despite the declining importance of country-specific characteristics, there is still a significant relationship between FDI activity and domestic economic structure, unless we examine how the process of economic convergence has affected countries' FDI patterns on a sectoral level. Ideally, this should be done using time series data for several countries across sectors. However, data are unavailable, except for a handful of countries, in sufficient detail and for a long enough time period. It is for this reason that the framework of our analysis changes for the rest of this volume, away from the IDP *per se*, towards an emphasis on the dynamics of economic structure and international business activity with an emphasis on the evolution of created assets and the role of government. Chapter 5 delves into the question of convergence and to what extent this has affected the geographical and industrial distribution of FDI activity of industrialised countries. We aim to find out what role domestic economic structure has played in determining FDI activity, the importance of country-specific characteristics in determining the evolution of natural assets to created assets, and the development of firm-specific assets. Chapter 6 seeks to identify what role traditional home-country-specific characteristics such as supply and demand conditions play relative to country-specific characteristics associated with government policies in determining the international production and trading activities of firms. We also seek to examine how the relationship has changed over the past decade for a selection of six countries.

As we pointed out earlier, it is important to remember the FDI activity is determined by the balance between the OLI characteristics of the host and home country. An analysis that explains the FDI activity of industrialised countries by examining the economic structure of the home country is incomplete, not only because of the importance of firm-specific assets, but also because it needs to take into account the type and motive of investment, and the economic structures of both countries involved. Such an analysis is conducted in Chapter 7 for Japan and the US.

5

GLOBALISATION, HOMOGENEITY AMONG INDUSTRIALISED COUNTRIES AND DIFFERENCES IN FDI PATTERNS

INTRODUCTION

The previous chapters demonstrated that a systematic relationship exists between FDI and domestic economic structure, and suggested that as countries move along the IDP the structure of the domestic economies changes, which in turn influences the nature and extent of their inward and outward foreign direct investment activities. While Chapter 4 has shown that the *extent* of their FDI activities varies with their economic structure, the use of cross-sectional data across countries as a proxy for a longitudinal study conceals potentially interesting phenomena which relate to country-specific differences. The IDP of individual countries is a function of country-specific factors such as natural resource endowments, policy orientation and domestic market characteristics. As such, it is not necessarily optimal to pool data from several countries with different characteristics, thereby concealing differences in the actual path each country might take. Such idiosyncratic differences influence the pattern and nature of investment to and from particular countries. The remainder of this volume will primarily investigate the evidence *vis-à-vis* industrialised countries, except where necessary as a means to contrast and illustrate the differences between the two groups. The focus of this study has hitherto been towards developing and verifying the stages-of-growth approach to the IDP. This and subsequent chapters concentrate on the evolutionary aspects of the growth process and their influence on FDI activities, identifying the dynamic nature of the relationship between country-specific characteristics and FDI activity, and thereby attempting to examine the differences *between* the industrialised countries. None the less, given the significance of industrialised countries as a source of FDI, and increasingly as a home for FDI from developing countries, a study such as the present one provides some policy implications for developing countries.

In the case of developing countries, natural assets may provide a country with an absolute or comparative advantage or disadvantage and are specific to a location, and as such are relatively immobile. In the sense that the presence of natural assets *per se* does not create either significant ownership advantages for domestic firms from stage 1 and 2 countries that are exploitable in overseas markets, or provide anything but the most rudimentary of locational advantages to foreign investors, the deviation from the 'general' IDP is not significant. However, as the economic structure passes the 'threshold' at stage 3 of the IDP, countries develop ownership advantages in upstream, higher value added activities, and the ownership advantages of firms become more firm-specific and created-asset-based. As a country moves along its IDP its created assets are of increasing importance, and become increasingly mobile and increasingly firm-specific.

In the case of industrialised countries, there has been a tendency for the structure of their domestic and foreign investments to converge as these countries experience *de facto* and *de jure* integration through the forces of globalisation. This trend is closely related to the growing significance of created assets. Such a scenario would, *ceteris paribus*, suggest that the nature of their FDI activities should also become increasingly similar, and less dependent on country-specific determinants. In Chapter 5 we shall examine how the country-specific determinants influence the evolution of competitive advantages from a natural asset basis to a created asset one, and how this may have affected the changing nature of FDI patterns worldwide. In doing so we hope to illustrate the growing significance of the industrialised countries both as hosts and as home countries for such investment. Although there is a broad similarity in the FDI trends of industrialised countries, there are nevertheless significant differences between them which are due to country-specific factors. These country-specific factors affect the economic structure of their domestic economy, which, in turn, determines the ownership advantages of its firms as well as its locational advantages, thereby influencing the pattern and extent of inward and outward FDI associated with that country. However, as the L advantages of countries and the O advantages of their firms evolve through economic convergence and globalisation of production towards created-asset-type advantages, the differences arising from country-specific determinants change in their role, as traditional supply conditions (such as factor endowments) are of decreasing significance, while the influence of government policy (which is also country-specific) becomes more significant.

THE LINK BETWEEN CREATED ASSETS, NATURAL ASSETS AND FDI ACTIVITY

The convergence of the economies of the Triad countries has received considerable attention in recent years. The concept of convergence is used in a general sense, in that the income levels and economic structures of these countries are becoming increasingly similar. This process has been facilitated by the growth of FDI activities and the network of MNEs that engage in international production activities and intra-firm trade. The nature of their industrial specialisation has become increasingly similar, as evidenced by the growth of intra-industry trade and the general similarity in their technological capabilities. The direction of causality between the growth of MNE activity (and specifically that of intra-Triad FDI) and the increasing homogeneity of their economies is akin to the chicken-and-egg paradox. It is not our intention to argue this issue, nor do we venture to explain whether these changes have been demand-driven or supply-driven.

The concept of comparative advantages of countries in the neo-classical sense can no longer explain much of their international economic activity, since these countries have similar factor endowments and are engaged in broadly similar sectors of production. The focus now has shifted increasingly to the issue of competitive advantages, which is similar to the argument put forward by the new growth theorists regarding the role of country-specific absolute advantages in determining the changing market shares between countries (Dosi *et al.* 1990). What we propose to analyse here is, given the convergence of these economies in terms of economic structure, why then do the competitive advantages of their MNEs differ significantly enough to result in a considerable divergence in the structure of their FDI activities? The answer lies in the role of technology, or, in the context of this volume, of created assets, and how these evolve over time. The view taken here is synonymous with that taken by the new growth theorists that technology is cumulative and path-dependent, but has a partly public-good nature given its localised nature. Because of this, even though these countries have indirect and partial access to each other's technology through the diffusion process (leading to convergence in their created assets), each country follows its own unique path depending on its own firms' innovatory activities and its national context (leading to a divergence in created assets).

Dunning (1981b, 1988a, 1993a) and Porter (1990) among others have argued that country-specific characteristics influence the kind of ownership advantages possessed by firms of a particular country as well as the location-specific advantages they offer to both domestic firms and multinationals of other nationalities. The country-specific characteristics also determine the means by which firms may seek to utilise these advantages, i.e. whether through hierarchical, cooperative or market routes.

We have hitherto used the framework of the IDP to examine the evolution of countries' relationships between their stage of development, economic structure and foreign direct investment activities. Within the rubric of the investment development path, all the industrialised countries are either in stage 4 or stage 5. Therefore, if we are successfully to analyse the reasons behind the differences in their propensity to engage in international investment activity, we need to determine how these countries differ among themselves.

The competitive advantage of a firm or a country derives from its having privileged access to assets which it is able to organise more efficiently than other firms or countries. While it is generally accepted that competitive advantage is primarily an industry- or firm-level phenomenon, it is also generally accepted that the economic prosperity of a nation is a function of the international competitive position of its industries. Two points should be noted here. First, while ownership-specific advantages such as proprietary technology (e.g. patents and process technology) and firm structure are of a firm-specific nature, there are others that are industry-specific (codifiable technology variables like capital equipment), while yet others – such as the knowledge of markets – that are location-specific (or in other words are country-level). Therefore, a firm with a given competitive advantage indulging in production at a particular location affects the competitive advantage of the industry as well as that of the country. Second, the level to which this firm can affect the national competitive advantage is a function of the nature and structure of the firms' activity relative to the national economy.

Likewise, while the evolution of ownership advantages (i.e. technology accumulation) is primarily a firm-specific phenomenon, and in the limit may be regarded as an industry-level phenomenon, through its relationship with related industries (sub-contractors, suppliers), it affects other industries, causing a 'ripple effect'. As Lall (1990) points out, national technological advantages are not simply the summation of the technological advantages of its firms, but are due to a *synergy* between individual technological advantages[1] (Narula 1993).

What determines the competitive advantages of firms and, more importantly, why do these differ across countries? Given that demand conditions in the industrialised countries are increasingly homogeneous, the answer must lie in the nature of their supply conditions. However, these countries have similar capital–labour ratios, and their endowments in a neo-classical sense (i.e. natural assets) are similar. Since the nature of their natural assets is essentially god-given and constant over time, we refer to these assets as 'exogenous' factors. The exogenous issues affect the development of competitive advantages through the path-dependent nature of the development of created assets, since these originally derive from natural assets. On the other hand, the development of these created assets is also determined by a second set of country-specific factors, which constrain the 'trajectory' taken by firms and are due directly and indirectly to institutional factors such as government policy, now more fashionably called national systems of innovation (NSI). These factors vary over both the short and long term, and are therefore considered to be 'endogenous' factors. We offer some general comments on their role in determining FDI activities.

Exogenous influences: the path-dependent nature of economic structure and FDI

The extent and nature of a country's created assets (or technological advantages) are a decreasing function of its natural assets over development stages. As Krugman (1992) points out, competitive and technological advantages of industrialised countries are not necessarily the result of underlying differences in primary resources, because of the process by which advantages are often created through a dynamic interaction of various forces described as a process of positive feedback. The evolution of the competitive advantages of a particular location derive from the development of created assets through the interaction and development of its supply and demand conditions. Figure 5.1, based on Krugman (1992), illustrates the nature of this relationship.

It is necessary to clarify the difference between created and natural assets. The term 'assets' is based on Dunnings (1993a) definition of them as 'resources capable of generating a future income stream'. Natural assets refer to natural endowments that are tangible, such as unskilled labour and resource endowments, whereas created assets are those that derive from the development of these natural assets and may be tangible or intangible; they include capital and technology, as well as those assets pertaining to skilled manpower such as technological, managerial and entrepreneurial skills. When assets of either kind are available to all firms and are specific to a particular location they are considered to be L advantages, whereas if they can be utilised only by a single firm they are considered to be ownership advantages. Natural assets can be regarded as being immobile and therefore, although their use may be monopolised by a single firm, they are location-bound ownership advantages. Trade in the neo-classical sense is conducted on the basis of comparative advantages in natural-asset-based goods. Ownership of natural assets alone does not lend itself to production: in order to derive rent from such assets, both intangible (such as managerial and technical manpower) and tangible (such as capital) created assets which are not immobile must be utilised. Assuming that the country in question is at an early stage of development and has limited created assets of its own, it may do this either by using the appropriate created assets that are available locally and supplementing such location-bound O advantages through arm's-length acquisition from overseas firms, or by providing its location-bound natural assets through an equity or non-equity arrange-

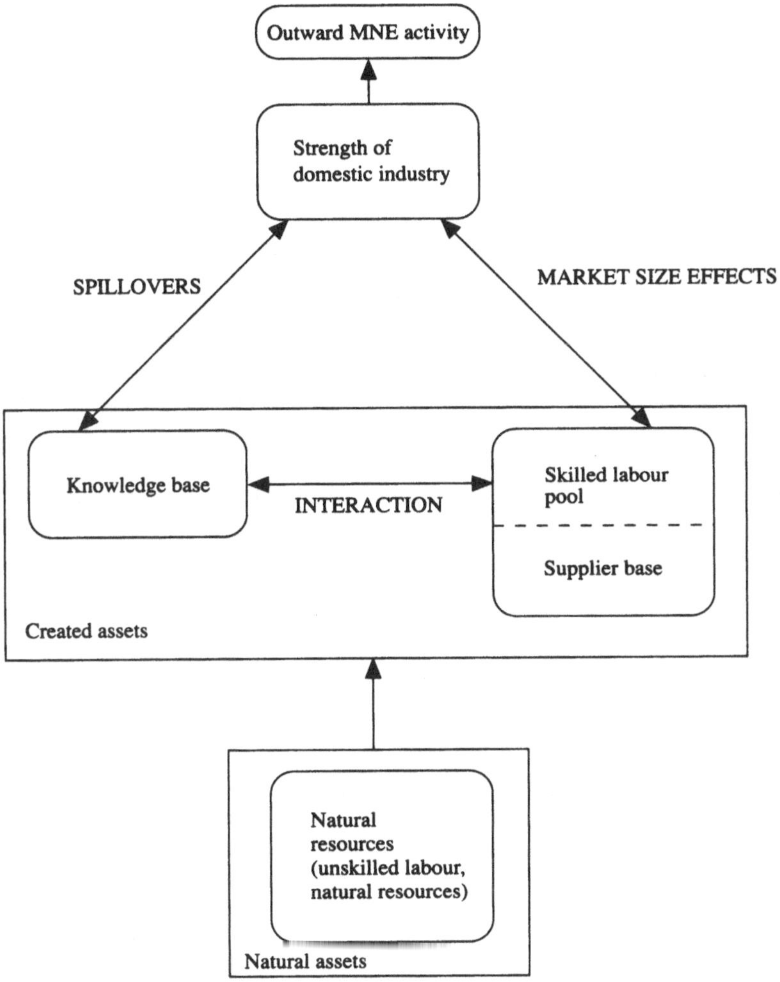

Figure 5.1 The interdependency of created and natural assets on competitive advantage
Source: adapted from Krugman (1992)

ment to a foreign enterprise which possesses the necessary created assets to utilise these advantages efficiently. If the domestic firm acquires the created assets via equity (such as a joint venture), this results in inward direct investment, and if through the market (e.g. through licensing), it results in domestic-owned production.

Let us assume for the purposes of discussion that the firm wishes to internalise the use its initial O advantages through acquiring the appropriate created assets through the market. *Ceteris paribus*, the use of such resources will lead to the accumulation of technology through learning-by-doing in created assets relevant to the exploitation of their initial O advantage and eventually will lead to the development of peripheral technologies. As Nelson and Winter (1982) have explained, given that the rationality of decision makers is bounded, and given the uncertainty associated with engaging in R&D in a new area, firms are more likely to engage in a 'local search'. That is to say, innovations tend to be linked to current activities of the firm in question. These may take the form of management or marketing skills, or improved production techniques. Furthermore, because of market failure, such O advantages become specific to the firm that develops them (Dunning 1981b). Therefore, a firm that initially began with an advantage in (say) privileged access to a source of crude oil is likely to develop subsequent (created-asset-type) ownership advantages in the management and extraction of crude petroleum and, over time, *vertical expansion* forwards into petroleum processing.

As the ownership advantages of firms develop in exploiting and utilising its natural assets, forward vertical expansion into overseas markets may occur to serve markets. At the same time, *horizontal expansion* may occur into other countries where similar natural assets exist, especially where its created assets provide it with an advantage over *de novo* firms.[2]

Inward direct investors into a country that possesses a comparative advantage in natural resources, but where such natural assets are location-specific (as opposed to firm-specific), will seek to internalise their use; therefore, where the property rights of the natural resource are not internalised, these same resources are L advantages which can be used by the MNEs in conjunction with their complementary O advantages. Such investment is often undertaken as backward integration by MNEs that require the use of natural resources as an input for their secondary sector operations in other locations that possess a comparative disadvantage in that resource.

It should be noted that privileged access to natural assets will not give firms the same ownership advantages at all points of the stages of the investment development path, as the comparative advantages change owing to changes in the factor costs of the natural assets, or, in the case of created-asset-type ownership advantages, as the product or process becomes standardised,[3] thereby diminishing its ownership advantage. It then becomes increasingly profitable for the domestic firm to exploit these ownership advantages through outward direct investment or, in the case of inward direct investors, to relocate that portion of its operations to another location which might be at a lower stage of the IDP that has the appropriate L advantages.

The domestic structure of a country is expected to change with the changing nature of the O and L advantages of the firms operating within its boundaries. However, the nature of its assets (both natural and created) at period t + n will be a function of its assets in period t. Likewise, the competitive advantages of domestic firms at $t + n$ will be a function of the country's competitive advantages at t, as will be the case with its inward and outward direct investment activities. The greater the value of n, the less the influence of the comparative and competitive advantages in t on the structure of domestic and international investment activity. In other words, although there is a path dependency, as a country evolves from a natural-asset-based economy, its industrial structure will reflect that dependency decreasingly over time.

However, there are two provisos that must be noted to such a general statement. The first pertains to the increasing extent of internationalisation of its economy as a country moves along the IDP to higher stages. As technologies become more mature and diffused, firms increasingly engage in value added activities in overseas locations. The motivation of their FDI activities becomes increasingly complex as the breadth of their ownership advantages expands away from natural assets towards created assets (and towards higher value added activities) and thus towards specialisation within the secondary and tertiary industries. Furthermore, from the fourth stage of development onwards, the extent of firms' international production activities is such that the O advantages of the firm are decreasingly a function of the home country characteristics, and are increasingly affected by the characteristics of the host countries. Likewise, the L advantages of a country will be influenced by the home country characteristics of foreign multinationals. As such, these exogenous country-specific characteristics will become increasingly less significant as globalisation occurs.

The second provisio pertains to the nature of the natural assets. It may be that a country possesses 'unique' factor endowments which are found only in a few countries, thereby providing it with an absolute advantage in such resources. In such a case, the tendency will be for the domestic structure of production, as well as the structure of its international investment activity, to show a continued bias towards those industries related to the exploitation of this resource. A similar but opposite scenario applies for natural-asset-deficient economies.

The role of country-specific demand conditions in determining the structure and extent of international investment activity is more ambiguous than that of supply characteristics. Although demand conditions cannot strictly be regarded as exogenous, to the extent that they are determined by natural assets of a country and do not vary except in the long term, they can be considered to be so. The development of created assets is often a direct result either of demand for a particular product for a particular function, or of demand for a product of particular price. However, while demand conditions affect the way in which the technology accumulation takes place, it does not affect national technological advantage *per se*: instead it does so on the firm level. Demand conditions are specific to a particular industry in a particular country but are not country-specific in and of themselves. There is clearly a significant role for factors such as the size of a country as a market, as well as for overall consumption patterns which can be referred to as *market size effects*. In the sense that these represent a locational advantage to firms in terms of the opportunities for achieving economies of scale and scope, they thereby help determine where production might be optimally undertaken. Such market characteristics represent a natural asset that is a locational advantage,[4] and can be regarded as exogenous and country-specific. The role of market characteristics such as these is exogenous to the firm, and the development of technological accumulation and their significance need to be examined separately.

A country at an earlier stage of the IDP will by definition have a low income per capita, and will have a comparative advantage in resource intensive sectors, with a gradual shift towards production of manufactured goods. However, the extent to which domestic and foreign firms undertake the production of manufactured goods locally will depend on the size of the market and the level of their consumption, as well as the availability of inputs for the production process. *Ceteris paribus*, a country with a small population (such as Niger) presents less of a locational advantage to a manufacturer of, say, detergents than another country with a larger population (such as Ghana), assuming the same per capita income. This is because the market size and hence potential demand do not make for economies of scale. Therefore, unless there are barriers to imports, local demand will be satisfied by exports from another location. Unless production in such a country is undertaken to supply other markets, domestic production of goods that have a relatively high minimum efficient scale is less likely to be undertaken. By the same token, though, firms from such countries have an increased incentive relative to larger countries to undertake outward investment that is trade-supportive (in the first instance) in order to increase their *de facto* market size. As the comparative advantage of such countries changes at later stages and firms develop corresponding competitive advantages, they may seek to relocate production to other locations at earlier stages of the IDP. The argument we wish to emphasise here is that smaller market size, *ceteris paribus*, will be associated with a greater propensity to seek export markets and hence will lead to a greater extent of outward investment per capita at later stages than for countries with larger markets and at the same stage. This greater tendency towards internationalisation also implies that the role of home-country-specific influences on the characteristics of its created assets will decrease faster than would otherwise be the case, thereby reaching a greater extent of interdependency since the size and extent of the firms' overseas activities will be greater than their domestic activities.[5,6]

Inward investment per capita will be muted for the same reasons, unless these are made to utilise other L advantages such as the availability of created assets, or where the location of production in such a location provides access not just to the country's domestic market but to its extended *de facto* or *de jure*[7] market. For instance, the L advantages of the Netherlands in terms of market size are enhanced by that country's membership of the EU. Because of the trend towards regionalisation, and as a country's L advantages and its firms' O advantages are increasingly based on created assets (and less on natural assets and related production), the importance of its market size becomes insignificant. This is generally true for most of the industrialised countries.

What of the behaviour and evolution of these factors among industrialised countries? In the limit, market characteristics become homogeneous as economic convergence takes place and individual economies become increasingly internationalised. This is a direct consequence of the importance and mobility of created assets as well as the increasing propensity to internalise the use of such assets by firms. The greater the firm-specific nature and the less the country-specific nature of these assets, therefore, the greater the extent of international production and the stronger the trend towards regionalisation. As such, despite (and perhaps, *because* of) the trend for slowing economic growth among industrialised countries, the growth of foreign direct investment is expected to continue unabated, as firms increasingly seek similar markets and privileged access to created assets, leading to a continuous and dynamic process of economic restructuring of the countries in which they operate.

Endogenous factors: the role of government in national systems of innovation

On a macro level, it is not possible to examine the evolution of created assets or the 'how' of technology accumulation from a purely 'exogenous' supply and demand perspective. The discussion so far has not taken into account the role of government policy. Although innovation is generally regarded as a firm-specific process, governments are able to influence firms' technological trajectories by influencing supply and demand conditions, as well as by affecting the extent and level of diffusion taking place within sectors. It is by now axiomatic that the structure of a country's economy may be influenced by policy that affects the rate and kind of created assets that firms develop through R&D subsidies and other forms of industrial targeting, which may change the character of their O advantages as well as the country's L advantages.[8] A government's influence on the locational advantages of the country can be through educational policies and the development of other forms of infrastructure. Policies on property rights can also influence the extent to which firms may internalise the use of both created and natural assets. In addition, subsidies and other government policy tools can be used to encourage outward investment as a means to restructure the domestic economy, as well as affecting the internalisation advantages of foreign firms by restricting entry into certain sectors, ostensibly to protect these sectors from competition. The result of government activity through NSIs can therefore influence the technological specialisation of its firms, the competitiveness of its products, the propensity of the country to engage in international economic activity and, indeed, the mode (FDI or strategic alliances) by which it does so. Endogenous factors, unlike exogenous ones, have remained exceedingly idiosyncratic (see for instance Guerrieri 1991, Archibuigi and Pianta 1992, 1993, Lundvall 1992, Nelson 1993).

Government policy is an important country-specific determinant of FDI activity, but if differs from country-specific demand and supply conditions in that *it can be regarded as a created asset itself*. It is able to influence not just the extent and nature of the economic activity associated with a country, through affecting the country-specific supply and demand conditions by influencing the kind of created assets that are associated with that location, but also the extent to which these are firm-specific, and the efficiency with which they are utilised. In other words, government policy influences not only the comparative advantage of countries, but also the competitive advantages of firms operating within its borders.

INTROSPECTION WITHIN THE TRIAD: GENERAL FDI TRENDS

In this section we review some general data on FDI activities in the Triad. We wish to highlight the increasing introspection of FDI activities among these countries, and the effect, if any, that the process of economic convergence has had on the extent and pattern of FDI.

One of the most interesting features of the changing patterns of international production over the last two decades or so has been the continued domination of the developed market economies as the primary source of outward direct investment. As Table 5.1 shows, their share of total world outward investment has remained at about 97% since 1967. However, it is interesting to note that the US, UK and Netherlands, which together accounted for almost 75% of all outward stock in 1967, accounted for just over half of total stock by 1988, with only the UK showing a marginal increase in its share. The most rapid decline has been that of US firms, from just over 50% to 30.5%, whereas the most marked growth has been by Japanese and German multinationals, which have grown from 1.34% and 2.67% in 1967 to 9.78% and 9.12% in 1988 respectively. On the surface, it might be argued that such a shift reflects the economic resurgence of Western Europe and Japan after the Second World War and the gradual decline of the hegemony of the US. Such an argument would suggest that the share of the US in total world GNP would experience a decline and that there would be a corresponding increase in the share of those countries that have increased their prominence as outward investors. This is in fact not the case: the US continues to account for about 28% of world GNP over the same period and Germany for about 7%, although Japan's GNP as a percentage of the total has increased by a factor of 2.5.

Table 5.1 also gives the growth rates of GNP and outward FDI over the period 1973–80[9] and 1980–88. FDI growth rates for both industrialised countries and developing countries as groups are 1.9 and 3.4 that of GNP growth rates for 1980–88 respectively.[10] However, for the earlier period, these same figures are 1.3 and 1.1. Several countries experienced a negative FDI growth rate relative to GNP growth between 1973 and 1980 including Japan, Sweden, France, Italy and the Netherlands, with the UK showing the highest growth, by a factor of two. This is an especially interesting observation because the UK also had the worst economic growth in real terms among the major industrialised countries (with the exception of Switzerland), and Japan the best over the same period. These results are underscored by the data for the period 1980–88, where the two highest FDI/GNP growth ratios are those of Sweden (8.3) and the UK (4.0), which also had among the slowest real economic growth of the industrialised countries, as did the US, which has a negative ratio for the same period. This casual examination of the data would suggest that there is no apparent causality between FDI and GNP growth.

These facts can be examined with reference to the economic convergence argument, which postulates that economic (and productivity) growth among lagging countries is inversely related to their initial economic (and productivity) levels. The argument is based on the logic that the lead country possesses the largest pool of technology, and that the greater the lag, the greater the technological difference with the lead country, and subsequently the greater the potential for growth, *provided* they possess the potential capability to assimilate technology spillovers.[11] This condition is met by all the industrialised countries in our sample. Soete and Verspagen (1992) demonstrated that there has also been a catching-up in the field of international trade; they have shown that the growth rate of export market share over the 1970–85 period is inversely

Table 5.1 Outward stock of FDI by major home countries and regions, 1967–88 (US$bn)

Countries and regions	1967				1973				1980				1988				1973–80 (annual average)		1980–88 (annual average)	
	Value	Value as % of total	GDP as % of total	Value as % of GDP	Value	Value as % of total	GDP as % of total	Value as % of GDP	Value	Value as % of total	GDP as % of total	Value as % of GDP	Value	Value as % of total	GDP as % of total	Value as % of GDP	GDP growth	FDI growth	GDP growth	FDI growth
Developed market economies	109.30	97.33	82.08	4.75	205.00	97.11	79.99	5.07	505.00	97.43	80.73	5.91	1101.80	97.20	81.15	7.98	0.16	0.21	0.08	0.15
US	56.60	50.40	28.42	7.11	101.30	47.99	25.89	7.73	220.00	42.45	24.42	8.50	345.40	30.47	28.48	7.13	0.14	0.17	0.11	0.07
UK	15.80	14.07	3.89	14.50	15.80	7.48	3.44	9.08	79.20	15.28	4.94	15.15	183.60	16.20	4.13	26.14	0.29	0.57	0.04	0.16
Japan	1.50	1.34	6.21	0.86	10.30	4.88	8.26	2.46	19.60	3.78	9.82	1.88	110.80	9.78	16.71	3.90	0.21	0.13	0.22	0.58
Germany	3.00	2.67	6.78	1.58	11.90	5.64	6.90	3.41	43.10	8.32	7.73	5.26	103.40	9.12	7.06	8.60	0.19	0.37	0.06	0.17
Switzerland	2.50	2.23	0.89	10.04	7.10	3.36	0.87	16.21	22.40	4.32	0.96	22.08	44.10	3.89	1.09	23.86	0.19	0.31	0.10	0.12
Netherlands	11.00	9.80	1.19	33.13	15.80	7.48	1.21	25.77	42.40	8.18	1.58	25.29	77.50	6.84	1.34	33.95	0.25	0.24	0.05	0.10
Canada	3.70	3.29	2.47	5.34	7.80	3.69	2.51	6.14	21.60	4.17	2.39	8.53	50.70	4.47	2.56	11.63	0.14	0.25	0.09	0.17
France	6.00	5.34	4.43	4.84	8.80	4.17	4.60	3.78	20.80	4.01	6.15	3.19	56.20	4.96	5.58	5.92	0.26	0.19	0.06	0.21
Italy	2.10	1.87	2.67	2.80	3.20	1.52	2.61	2.42	7.00	1.35	3.72	1.78	39.90	3.52	4.87	4.81	0.28	0.17	0.14	0.59
Sweden	1.70	1.51	1.06	5.72	3.00	1.42	0.97	6.13	7.20	1.39	1.16	5.87	26.20	2.31	0.94	16.39	0.22	0.20	0.04	0.33
Other*	5.40	4.81	24.06	0.80	20.00	9.47	22.73	1.74	21.70	4.19	17.85	1.15	64.00	5.65	8.39	4.48	0.09	0.01	0.03	0.24
Developing countries	3.00	2.67	17.92	0.60	6.10	2.89	20.01	0.60	13.30	2.57	19.27	0.65	31.70	2.80	17.04	1.09	0.15	0.17	0.05	0.17
Total	112.30	100.00	100.00	4.01	211.10	100.00	100.00	4.17	518.30		100.00	4.89	1133.50	100.00		6.66		0.21	0.08	0.15

Source: adapted from Dunning (1993a)
Note: * Australia, Canada, Japan, New Zealand, South Africa

related to the initial level of per capita income, and positively associated with the growth rate of GNP per capita in the same period.

Although we are unable to test econometrically whether catching-up has occurred in FDI, the evidence presented here suggests that if such an effect were occurring countries such as Japan and Germany, which experienced the highest real GNP growth rate, would have the highest FDI growth rates and the countries with the slowest GNP growth rates, such as the UK and the US, would have the slowest FDI growth rates. Instead, we find that there is no clear pattern, leading us tentatively to conclude that there is no evidence of a catching-up in outward FDI similar to that occurring in trade and economic growth.

However, one fact is clear – that outward FDI activity is growing faster overall than the domestic economies of both industrial and developing countries, and that the difference between the two growth rates has continued to increase with time, growing twice as fast as the domestic economic activity for industrialised countries and three times as fast for developing economies over the 1980–88 period.[12]

This overall higher growth rate of FDI over GNP has none the less resulted in an increasing significance of outward direct investment activity to the respective home economies, almost doubling from 4.8% of GNP in 1967 to 8% in 1988 for industrialised economies as a whole. However, the importance of foreign activities varies widely among industrialised countries, with smaller countries such as Sweden, Switzerland and the Netherlands having the highest percentages, and larger market economies such as Germany, the US, Japan and Italy recording the lowest shares,[13] typically less than 10%.

Although inward direct investment is not as concentrated as outward investment, as Table 5.2 shows, there has nevertheless been a tendency for an increasing percentage to be directed towards industrialised countries; investment into these countries has grown between 1967 and 1988 from 69.4% of the total to 78.9%. This represents a growth factor of 13, whereas that to developing countries has experienced an eight-fold increase, decreasing in percentage terms from 30.6% to 21.3% The share of investment to host countries in Africa and Latin America declined, whereas that to Asian economies grew. However, once again, such aggregation hides the concentrated nature of FDI inflows to just a few countries – it has been estimated (UN 1992a) that ten developing economies accounted for 68% of the total inflows of FDI to developing countries over the period 1980–90.[14]

The single largest host for inward investments by 1988 was the US, accounting for 27% of all inward stock, with the UK coming second at 9.8%. Indeed, the growth in the share of industrialised countries is accounted for in large part by the growth of inward FDI to the US and UK, which increased by factors of 18 and 15.1 respectively between 1967

Table 5.2 Inward stock of FDI by major host countries and regions, 1967–88 (US$bn)

	1967				1973				1980				1988				1973–80 (annual average)		1980–88 (annual average)	
	Value	*% of total*	*GDP as % of total*	*Value as % of GDP*	*Value*	*& of total*	*GDP as % of total*	*Value as % of GDP*	*Value*	*% of total*	*GDP as % of total*	*Value as % of GDP*	*Value*	*% of total*	*GDP as % of total*	*Value as % of GDP*	*GDP growth*	*FDI growth*	*GDP growth*	*FDI growth*
Developed market economies	73.2	69.38	82.08	3.18	153.7	73.86	79.99	3.80	403.4	78.53	80.73	4.72	959.5	78.69	81.15	6.95	0.16	0.23	0.08	0.17
Western Europe	31.4	29.76	26.66	4.21	73.8	35.46	26.17	5.57	186.9	36.38	41.77	4.22	444.5	36.46	30.91	8.45	0.33	0.22	0.02	0.17
UK	7.9	7.49	3.89	7.25	24.1	11.58	3.44	13.85	63	12.26	4.94	12.05	119.6	9.81	4.13	17.03	0.29	0.23	0.04	0.11
Germany	3.6	3.41	6.78	1.89	13.1	6.30	6.90	3.75	47.9	9.32	7.73	5.85	83.5	6.85	7.06	6.95	0.19	0.38	0.06	0.09
Switzerland	2.1	1.99	0.89	8.43	4.3	2.07	0.87	9.82	14.3	2.78	0.96	14.09	23.2	1.90	1.09	12.55	0.19	0.33	0.10	0.08
US	9.9	9.38	28.42	1.24	20.6	9.90	25.89	1.57	83	16.16	24.42	3.21	328.9	26.97	28.48	6.79	0.14	0.43	0.11	0.37
Other*	31.9	30.24	27.00	4.22	59.3	28.50	27.93	4.20	133.5	25.99	14.53	8.67	175.7	14.41	21.68	4.76	0.01	0.18	0.17	0.04
Japan	0.6	0.57	6.21	0.34	1.6	0.77	8.26	0.38	3.3	0.64	9.82	0.32	10.4	0.85	16.71	0.37	0.21	0.15	0.22	0.27
Developing countries	32.3	30.62	17.92	6.44	54.7	26.29	20.01	5.40	110.3	21.47	19.27	5.40	259.8	21.31	17.04	8.96	0.15	0.15	0.05	0.17
Africa	5.6	5.31	2.22	8.99	10.2	4.90	2.33	8.67	13.1	2.55	2.98	4.15	30.9	2.53	1.87	9.70	0.24	0.04	0.00	0.17
Asia	8.3	7.87	7.61	3.89	15.3	7.35	8.29	3.65	34.9	6.79	6.56	5.02	114.0	9.35	7.49	8.95	0.09	0.18	0.10	0.28
Latin America and the Caribbean	18.5	17.54	4.18	15.80	28.9	13.89	4.65	12.28	62.3	12.13	6.98	8.42	114.9	9.42	4.75	14.21	0.31	0.17	0.01	0.11
Other	n.a.	n.a.	3.90	n.a.	0.3	0.14	4.74	0.13	n.a.	n.a.	2.75	n.a.	n.a.	n.a.	2.93	n.a.	0.03	n.a.	0.09	n.a.
Total	105.5	100.00	100.00	3.77	208.1	100.00	100.00	4.11	513.7	100.00	100.00	4.85	1219	100.00	100.00	7.16	0.16	0.21	0.08	0.17

Source: adapted from Dunning (1993a)

Note: *Other developed market economies: Australia, Canada, Japan, New Zealand, South Africa

and 1988, compared with an average of 9.2 for the rest of the industrialised world. Table 5.2 also gives details of the FDI and GNP growth rates over the periods 1973–80 and 1980–88. Inward FDI stocks in the US grew at a rate 3.1 times that of its domestic economy between 1973 and 1980, and at 3.4 times the domestic growth rate in the subsequent period. Once again, results do not indicate any particular relationship between FDI growth rates and GNP growth rates except that there is a clear acceleration of inward investment activity in the 1980s compared with the 1970s, relative to domestic economic growth for all countries and regions. Slow growth countries (such as the UK, US, Switzerland and the African countries) did not exhibit uniformly a high FDI growth trend, nor did the high growth countries (such as Japan and Germany) have a clear tendency to high or low growth in inward FDI activity.

The significance of inward investment to host countries has risen among almost all industrialised countries except Japan, where inward stock as a percentage of GNP has remained less than 1% over the entire period. Overall, the significance of inward FDI in domestic activity among industrialised countries is lower than that among developing countries.

Let us sum up the discussion thus far. With the slowing of domestic economic growth among the Triad countries, the significance of the activities of multinational firms to their domestic economies has grown. This implies that their economies are more dependent on both the overseas activities of their MNEs and the domestic activities of foreign-owned multinationals than they were at the beginning of the period in question. The performance of their overseas subsidiaries, assuming that they possessed the same level of competitive advantage (i.e. firm-specific advantages) over the period in question, would be a function of the economic performance (i.e. the country-specific factors) of the various host countries in which they were located. In other words, as the home country's economy becomes more internationalised, the subsequent economic performances of its MNEs will be increasingly influenced by the economic changes in the host countries. To examine the same issue from an opposing viewpoint, the performance of a foreign affiliate, assuming the economic performance of the host country remained on par, would be a function of its firm-specific advantages, which in turn would be determined by the country-specific factors of its home country as well as by those of those of the other host countries in which its parent firm has subsidiaries.[15]

It might be argued that, as the industrial economies become more dependent on the international activities of their firms, as market characteristics become increasingly homogeneous and as ownership advantages of their firms become more firm-specific and therefore increasingly mobile, the nature of their competitive advantages and inward and

Table 5.3 GNP, net outward investment (NOI), inward FDI and outward FDI, 1988

Country	*GNP*	*NOI*	*Inward FDI*	*Outward FDI*
New Zealand	12,217.95	−368.67	963.13	594.46
Italy	14,503.39	0.40	642.12	642.52
UK	14,727.53	1401.44	2121.18	3522.61
Netherlands	15,335.25	1939.14	3031.92	4971.06
Belgium	15,517.48	−549.09	2016.00	1468.00
Australia	15,656.50	−1769.14	3307.49	1538.35
Austria	16,527.29	−717.98	896.89	178.91
France	16,676.00	245.03	693.85	938.89
Canada	18,329.16	−1227.98	3563.49	2335.51
Germany	19,674.11	725.75	1046.68	1772.42
US	19,888.59	128.44	1284.45	1412.89
Denmark	20,470.51	−97.38	1069.26	971.88
Norway	20,765.72	72.92	582.04	654.96
Sweden	21,133.33	2078.32	865.97	2944.28
Finland	21,325.00	558.52	614.10	1172.63
Japan	23,775.13	1415.56	104.35	1519.91
Switzerland	29,347.27	3315.39	3839.03	7154.42

Note: All figures in US$, market values, and normalised by population

outward activities will be broadly similar. However, the data presented thus far suggest that there are significant differences in the propensity of firms from different countries to engage in foreign production, despite their being at similar stages of the IDP. Table 5.3 provides details of the extent of direct investment activities associated with all the industrialised countries. The UK and Italy, for example, have similar income levels but a completely different investment profile, with the UK's outward stake almost six times as much as that of Italy's and its inward investment three times as large. Sweden and Japan both have similar income levels as well as considerable outward investment per capita, but they have vastly different levels of inward investment.

Earlier tables have revealed that there has been an increasing diversification of the country of origin of outward stock, away from a domination by 'traditional' home countries such as the US, UK, France and the Netherlands: these accounted for 79.5% of all outward stock in 1967 and only 58.5% in 1988. Overall, the evidence indicates that not only do the industrialised countries continue to account for a majority of the outward stock outstanding, they also account for an increasing share of the total worldwide inward direct investment stock. Although the geographical investment patterns of the leading outward investors are similar, there are also some differences in the pattern of clustering (Dunning 1993a). As Dunning notes, there are two main types of clustering. The first is associated with MNEs that operate in global industries and/or are highly internationalised and are consolidating their established international production facilities in such a way as to achieve gains from common governance and economies of scale and scope. The second reflects historical and current political, cultural and social ties which result in lower 'psychic' distance and/or similar market characteristics. These two kinds of clustering have tended to overlap in recent times, especially in the case of industrialised countries, owing to various levels of economic integration agreements such as NAFTA and the EU. Clustering arising from globalisation is particularly closely associated with industrialised countries' firms since these also tend to be the best established and most internationalised MNEs.

As seen in Table 5.4, there is an overall trend for the industrialised countries to seek markets in other industrialised countries, the exception being the US, whose share of investment directed towards other industrialised countries has dropped from 78.8% in 1976 to 74.9% in 1990. Within this pattern, there is another interesting trend that has drawn considerable attention – that of the development of the Triad countries, the EU, Japan and the US (UNCTC 1991, UN 1992a, Dunning 1993a). Investment to each of these three main markets has increased, not only by industrialised countries, but also by some of the leading outward investors in the Third World, which have traditionally preferred to invest in neighbouring countries with which they have had close cultural and economic ties and similar market characteristics. Although some of the firms of these countries may have made investments as part of an efficiency-seeking strategy, there is some evidence to suggest that these investments are aimed at servicing local markets and strengthening their competitive positions (see e.g. UN 1993a, Lecraw 1993).

Table 5.5 illustrates some of the changing geographical patterns associated with inward direct investment. Although these are broadly similar to those discussed with respect to outward investment, they serve to highlight several important differences. First, they highlight the decreasing importance of the US as a home country *vis-à-vis* Western Europe. This is especially significant when one notes that even Canada and the UK, which have traditionally received the lion's share of their inward investment from the US, have become considerably less dependent on the US for inward investment. The data also illustrate the rising share of Japanese inward FDI among both developing and industrialised countries, and especially in the US. None the less, the source of inward FDI varies considerably among host countries, and the change in geographic distribution partly reflects the changing competitive advantages of the home country, as well as the changing locational characteristics of the host country relative to the home country. As has been discussed elsewhere (Dunning 1988a, 1993a, Ozawa 1989), the motives

Table 5.4 Geographical distribution of FDI outward stock by home country/region, various years (% of total stock)

	Industrialised countries					*Developing Countries*					
Home country	*Total*	*Western Europe*	*North America*	*Japan*	*Others*	*Total*	*Asian NICs*	*Latin America*	*Africa*	*Others*	*Eastern Europe*
Industrialised countries											
France											
1982	77.81	44.10	32.10	0.71	−1.30	21.67	0.67	8.52	0.56	11.91	0.53
1989	88.20	55.60	31.51	0.35	2.70	11.59	0.74	2.52	0.50	7.83	0.22
Germany											
1976	74.33					25.65					0.02
1980	77.41	48.88	24.35	1.18	5.74	22.49	1.99	12.31	2.22	5.96	0.10
1989	83.90	49.69	29.74	1.93	5.22	16.06	2.34	7.05	0.88	5.80	0.04
UK											
1974	79.15					20.85					
1981	78.12	23.07	34.63	0.66	26.45	21.88	8.34	6.00	6.70	0.85	0.00
1989	85.86	26.77	47.18	1.10	16.10	14.14	4.89	6.99	1.78	0.48	0.01
Italy											
1975	66.87					33.13					
1980	66.90	58.31	8.59	0.00	0.00	33.10	0.00	0.00	0.00	33.10	0.00
1989	80.68	66.88	10.69	1.26	2.99	19.15	0.00	12.00	1.03	6.12	0.01
Netherlands											
1975	82.25					17.75					0.00
1984	84.87	36.36	46.73	0.79	5.32	15.13	3.14	8.97	1.65	1.36	0.00
1989	88.40	49.12	37.11	0.89	4.96	11.60	3.16	6.34	0.80	1.30	0.17
Sweden											
1980	82.20	59.87	22.33	0.00	1.70	17.36	0.57	11.36	0.26	5.17	0.44
1988	90.20	71.90	18.30	0.00	0.00	9.80	0.00	3.27	0.00	6.54	0.00
Spain											
1975	54.47					44.59					0.94
1984	45.85	6.71	3.81	0.05	35.29	54.15	0.00	6.31	0.29	47.54	0.00
1989	67.89	45.63	11.95	0.08	10.74	31.55	0.10	17.12	0.81	13.52	0.56
US											
1976	78.82					21.18					0.56
1980	73.84	43.63	22.31	2.83	27.38	26.16	3.86	19.79	1.72	0.80	0.00
1990	74.79	48.11	17.02	4.96	21.72	25.21	5.79	17.52	0.89	1.00	0.00
Canada											
1975	77.04					22.96					
1980	84.20	18.14	62.23	0.40	3.43	15.80	3.92	11.37	0.51	0.00	0.00
1989	85.78	19.61	62.71	0.49	2.96	14.22	3.71	10.18	0.25	0.08	0.00
Japan											
1976	38.75					61.25					
1980	44.84	11.72	26.85	0.00	8.80	54.63	26.93	16.90	3.96	6.83	0.53
1990	65.71	17.56	42.93	0.00	7.03	34.20	15.94	14.52	2.08	1.67	0.09
Australia											
1975	51.25					48.75					
1980	44.04	14.11	15.26	0.00	14.68	55.96	8.20	0.00	0.00	47.75	0.00
1989	79.10	30.94	33.70	0.43	17.09	20.90	6.84	7.49	0.09	6.48	0.00
Developing countries											
Korea											
1976	25.352					74.65					
1980	31.777	2.72	20.59	7.40	1.19	68.22	28.79	4.83	17.59	17.01	0.00
1988	55.473	3.67	43.83	2.66	13.56	44.53	22.73	2.32	1.14	18.33	0.00
China											
1981	34.498					65.50					
1984	57.781	6.70	48.96	0.14	2.56	42.26	26.19	4.50	10.05	1.51	0.00
1987	66.734	6.47	14.76	43.86	2.62	33.18	21.88	3.52	5.45	2.33	0.09
Brazil											
1983	57.99	11.47	45.70	0.82	0.02	42.01	1.34	38.19	1.32	1.15	0.00
1989	53.292	13.47	39.33	0.49	0.01	46.71	.80	44.43	0.79	0.69	0.00
Taiwan											
1980	56.517	0.00	43.37	0.00	13.14	43.48	33.37	0.00	0.00	10.11	0.00
1988	71.251	0.00	60.50	0.00	10.75	28.75	24.41	0.00	0.00	4.34	0.00

Source: UN (1992b, 1993e), and government sources

for investments vary with the extent of multinationality of MNEs as well as with the stage of the investment development path of both the home and host country. For instance, Japanese outward investment in the 1960s and 1970s was concentrated in the developing world, with particular emphasis on countries that had implemented import substituting programmes and on neighbouring countries in Asia, to seek

Table 5.5 Geographical distribution of FDI inward stock by host country/region, various years (% of total stock)

	Industrialised countries					*Developing countries*					
Home country	*Total*	*Western Europe*	*North America*	*Japan*	*Others*	*Total*	*Asian NICs*	*Latin America*	*Africa*	*Other*	*Eastern Europe*
Industrialised countries											
France											
1982	90.13	74.96	13.37	1.67	0.43	9.43	0.00	1.13	0.02	8.28	0.44
1989	92.58	74.15	14.70	3.67	1.56	7.13	0.16	0.54	0.08	6.35	0.29
Germany											
1976	96.71					2.96					0.33
1980	94.97	49.68	41.96	3.30	0.79	4.77	0.35	1.42	0.01	3.00	0.51
1989	95.19	54.53	32.95	7.39	1.41	4.18	0.47	1.08	0.02	2.61	0.63
UK											
1974	95.24					4.76					
1981	95.10	26.69	61.62	1.91	10.14	4.90	3.09	1.22	0.00	0.59	0.00
1989	95.38	39.06	44.10	4.17	13.00	4.62	2.10	1.77	0.07	0.68	0.00
Italy											
1975	92.79					7.21					
1980	99.67	81.16	18.52	0.00	0.00	0.33	0.00	0.00	0.00	0.33	0.00
1989	94.35	77.76	15.35	1.16	0.52	5.59	0.00	1.87	0.28	3.43	0.06
Netherlands											
1975	90.55					9.43					0.03
1984	86.49	47.57	36.37	2.34	0.48	13.48	0.34	12.43	0.17	0.54	0.02
1989	86.83	57.11	25.82	3.67	0.69	13.15	0.41	11.86	0.07	0.82	0.02
Sweden											
1980	97.77	68.60	27.24	0.00	3.00	0.36	0.00	0.00	2.50	−2.14	0.34
1988	99.11	82.97	15.65	0.00	0.59	0.89	0.00	0.00	0.17	0.72	0.04
Spain											
1975	97.48					2.51					0.01
1983	93.31	66.74	26.03	0.53	1.17	6.68	0.02	2.88	0.28	3.50	0.01
1989	93.74	80.45	10.80	2.48	0.82	6.25	0.13	4.43	0.29	1.40	0.01
US											
1976	89.07					10.93					
1980	86.99	65.75	14.64	5.69	15.55	12.96	0.34	11.65	0.21	0.76	0.06
1990	93.38	63.50	6.87	20.68	9.19	6.61	0.74	4.87	0.12	0.88	0.01
Canada											
1975	98.60					1.40					
1980	98.14	17.91	78.90	0.98	0.35	1.86	0.17	1.69	0.00	0.00	0.00
1989	97.17	26.27	64.00	3.95	2.95	2.83	1.13	1.52	0.00	0.18	0.00
Japan											
1976	98.35					1.65					
1980	94.26	23.26	56.67	0.00	16.90	5.74	3.09	0.58	0.00	2.07	0.00
1990	86.79	23.24	51.72	0.00	13.02	13.21	2.89	0.00	0.00	10.32	0.00
Australia											
1975	90.28					9.72					
1980	92.53	42.83	42.65	6.26	3.28	7.23	2.62	2.68	0.06	1.93	0.23
1989	87.11	41.66	30.51	12.07	6.86	12.73	3.18	2.83	0.01	6.71	0.16
Developing countries											
Korea											
1976	90.10					9.90					
1980	91.63	9.80	20.05	61.70	0.14	8.37	2.18	5.47	0.00	0.72	0.00
1988	94.13	13.02	28.15	52.80	0.19	5.87	3.90	1.54	0.00	0.42	0.00
China											
1984	[illegible]	[illegible]	[illegible]	[illegible]	[illegible]	[illegible]	[illegible]	[illegible]	0.17	0.28	0.00
1987	34.96	9.51	17.04	7.15	2.52	65.01	63.92	0.46	0.19	0.44	0.03
Thailand											
1975	82.92					17.28					
1980	80.18	18.06	32.45	29.02	0.31	20.32	20.29	−0.09	0.00	0.12	−0.50
1988	77.26	15.40	24.46	36.70	0.96	22.83	21.33	1.00	0.15	0.35	−0.09
Malaysia											
1980	58.62	28.94	6.75	17.57	5.72	41.38	38.17	1.45	0.00	1.77	0.00
1988	59.23	27.30	7.34	20.10	5.70	40.77	37.94	0.80	0.00	2.04	0.00
Mexico											
1980	99.50	23.10	70.50	5.90	1.50	0.50	0.00	0.00	0.00	0.50	0.00
1990	94.37	25.24	64.33	4.80	1.38	5.64	0.00	0.00	0.00	5.64	0.00
Venezuela											
1980	82.60	17.36	64.60	0.59	7.73	17.37	0.02	16.72	0.10	0.54	0.03
1989	89.43	30.39	55.14	3.87	2.14	10.52	0.00	7.54	0.02	2.96	0.05
Taiwan											
1980	63.23	9.67	35.00	18.56	0.00	36.77	26.33	0.00	0.00	10.43	0.00
1988	72.31	13.36	32.10	26.85	0.00	27.69	17.14	0.00	0.00	10.55	0.00
Brazil											
1975	92.12	41.96	38.42	11.52	5.85	7.88	0.38	6.91	0.58	0.01	0.01
1983	88.45	42.35	36.83	9.13	4.69	11.60	0.42	8.04	2.14	0.99	0.00
1989	91.79	47.33	35.09	9.17	5.46	8.20	0.26	5.48	1.46	1.01	0.01

Source: as for Table 5.4

low-cost labour for relatively low technology intensive goods. As the competitive advantage of Japanese firms moved to higher technology intensive production and also towards differentiated goods for which markets were located in the industrialised world, and as the relative cost of manufacturing these goods in Japan rose so as to make domestic production less attractive, the emphasis of their FDI shifted towards local production in Western Europe and North America. Similarly, as the relative costs of Japanese production in Korea began to rise in the 1970s owing to changes in the locational advantages of Korea, production shifted to other neighbouring countries such as Thailand and Taiwan where the factor costs were lower.

Because certain countries possess an absolute advantage in certain natural assets, they are likely to receive a larger amount of inward investment from home countries that require the use of such immobile assets as input for higher value added production in other locations including their home country. Examples of these are natural-resource-rich countries such as Norway and Australia. The opposite would be true for resource-poor countries, which would be forced to seek strategic control of such assets through outward direct investment, e.g. Japan. On the other hand, investments may be made to seek markets, either because of restrictions on non-equity forms of investment or import restrictions (such as voluntary export restrictions, e.g. the US, or as a part of economic policy) or because the nature of the ownership advantage of the investing firm has a public-good nature, and therefore its use needs to be internalised if economic rent is to be made (as is the case in service investments).

In other words, the extent and pattern of inward direct investment reflect the differences in industrial structure, the extent to which the competitive advantages of the home and host country complement each other, and the nature of the locational advantage of the host country that the investing firm seeks to utilise. Within the industrialised countries, which we have seen to have similar investment trends and an increasing tendency towards cross-investment among themselves, and are at the same stage of development, there is an increasing trend towards specialisation. In general, their firms tend to be more highly internationalised, and, as they become more global in their production and marketing strategies, the structure of their domestic and foreign investments tends to complement, and converge with, each other (Dunning 1993a). There is therefore an increasing degree of specialisation, and this tends to mirror the competitive advantages of their domestic economy, which, although increasingly firm-specific, will reflect the country-specific characteristics (primarily the locational advantages) of its home country. For instance, resource rich countries with an absolute or near-absolute advantage in a natural asset such as mining will foster domestic firms with ownership advantages, and will attract inward investment that is related to the exploitation of these resources. As their economies develop, the domestic firms may develop competitive advantages in higher value added activities, i.e. *vertical* specialisation. At some stage, these firms may seek to exploit these same advantages through direct investment in other locations in similar or related industries, which may lead to *horizontal* specialisation.

Tables 5.6 and 5.7 provide details of the industrial distribution of outward and inward FDI stock for several industrialised countries. These data provide some evidence of the differences in industrial specialisation within this group. Countries such as Austria, Japan and Germany, which are poorly endowed with primary resources, have negligible amounts of inward investment in this industrial sector. However, the propensity of their firms to invest overseas in primary products is inhibited by a corresponding lack of ownership advantages in this sector, in stark contrast to resource rich countries such as Australia (mining), Norway and the UK (petroleum), whose firms possess a competitive advantage in these industries and hence have a significant overseas presence. Similarly, they attract a proportionally large amount of inward investment in these industries.

Bellak (1993a) has shown that since the mid 1970s there has been a clear trend towards tertiarisation of domestic economies among developed countries and a subsequent (i.e. time-lagged) trend towards tertiarisation of their inward and outward investments. However, the extent to which tertiarisation of FDI has occurred varies between countries and its growth rate is not necessarily related to the rate of growth of its domestic tertiary sector. Tables 5.6 and 5.7 confirm that service sector FDI has begun to take on an increasingly significant role, accounting for almost half of the outward stock on average by the end of the 1980s. While the growth of the domestic tertiary sector is undoubtedly an important factor, service sector firms, whose ownership advantages are of a public-good or intangible nature, are more likely to use FDI as a means to service foreign markets (UN 1993c). Governments have tended to discourage inward FDI in the service sector, especially among developing countries, where a considerable share of the service sector (such as financial services and communications) may be dominated by parastatals. Interestingly enough, outward investment in services by industrialised countries is directed primarily towards the industrialised world; the share of outward tertiary investment stock of Germany, the UK and France in the late 1980s to the developing countries was 13.7%, 22.8% and 8.9% of their total tertiary stock outstanding.[16] Corresponding figures for their inward investment were: 3.8%, 11.5% and 9.7%. This trend is mirrored for almost all industrialised countries, leading us to suggest that the phenomenal growth of intra-industrialised country FDI may be accounted for in part by the growth of their service sectors.

Table 5.6 Industrial distribution of outward FDI stock of major home countries (%)

	US *(1990)*	*UK* *(1987)*	*Canada* *(1989)*	*Germany* *(1989)*	*Australia* *(1989)*	*Japan* *(1989)*	*Austria* *(1988)*	*Norway* *(1988)*
Primary	8.28	26.99	6.48	2.68	19.93	6.73	0.00	11.57
Agriculture	0.14	1.02	0.00	0.44	0.28	0.74	0.00	0.00
Mining	1.22	0.00	6.48	0.47	19.66	5.99	0.00	0.00
Petroleum	6.92	25.97	0.00	1.77	0.00	0.00	0.00	11.57
Secondary	44.28	34.43	51.59	41.74	18.90	26.05	53.51	33.51
Food, drink, etc.	4.55	6.84	6.11	0.64	0.00	1.29	1.65	0.57
Textiles, leather	0.48	0.00	0.00	0.95	0.00	1.26	1.36	0.28
Paper	2.74	2.89	11.66	0.87	7.94	1.05	3.31	2.24
Chemicals	9.16	9.42	7.16	15.61	0.96	3.41	0.00	21.93
Rubber	1.66	0.00	0.00	1.34	0.00	0.00	0.00	0.00
Non-metallic	0.65	0.00	0.00	1.27	1.28	0.00	0.00	0.17
Metals	2.31	0.73	16.09	2.31	3.87	3.65	15.96	3.43
Mech. eqpt.	6.80	1.63	3.53	4.03	1.83	3.65	0.00	4.33
Elect. eqpt.	3.22	3.80	0.00	6.90	0.00	2.55	0.96	0.00
Motor vehicles	5.29	1.05	0.00	6.09	0.06	5.78	0.00	0.00
Other transport	0.39	0.00	0.00	0.52	0.00	0.00	0.00	0.04
Other mfg.	2.51	8.07	3.53	1.16	2.98	3.52	14.08	0.53
Tertiary	47.43	38.58	41.93	55.48	61.16	66.99	46.49	54.92
Construction	0.25	1.82	0.00	0.44	2.09	0.82	0.00	0.32
Distrib. trade	13.71	9.00	4.79	19.59	5.45	9.91	4.95	1.60
Transports	0.53	2.07	2.06	0.85	3.59	6.01	0.00	10.52
Communic.	0.73	0.00	0.00	0.00	0.00	0.00	0.00	0.00
Finance and invest.	27.83	13.44	27.63	17.94	49.30	22.56	26.61	40.76
Real estate	0.59	0.00	0.00	9.64	0.00	13.68	0.00	0.00
Other	3.78	12.25	7.44	7.12	0.73	14.00	14.93	1.73
Total	100	100	100	100	100	100	100	100

Source: as for Table 5.4

Table 5.7 Industrial distribution of inward FDI stock of major host countries (%)

	US (1990)	*UK (1987)*	*Canada (1989)*	*Germany (1989)*	*Australia (1989)*	*Japan (1989)*	*Sweden (1988)*	*Austria (1988)*	*Norway (1988)*
Primary	3.48	29.13	4.76	0.20	15.05	0.00	0.20	0.00	13.19
Agriculture	0.28	0.24	0.00	0.08	1.38	0.00	0.00	0.00	0.00
Mining	2.55	0.00	4.76	0.09	6.60	0.00	0.00	0.00	0.00
Petroleum	0.64	28.88	0.00	0.03	7.07	0.00	0.00	0.00	13.19
Secondary	46.82	36.20	61.01	39.29	30.50	65.17	75.80	56.32	28.58
Food, drink, etc.	5.67	5.69	6.95	2.89	5.96	1.81	0.00	1.57	1.11
Textiles, leather	0.62	0.00	0.68	0.53	0.60	0.33	0.00	2.85	0.11
Paper	3.23	2.42	7.45	0.91	1.99	0.00	11.00	1.91	1.57
Chemicals	10.32	7.75	7.27	8.04	6.09	17.39	7.00	14.08	13.42
Coal and petroleum products				3.98					
Rubber	0.96	0.00	0.00	1.56	0.00	0.49	0.00	0.00	0.00
Non-metallic	2.39	0.00	2.10	0.63	0.19	0.90	0.00	0.00	0.75
Metals	4.36	2.03	18.44	2.58	3.86	3.17	0.00	12.04	2.87
Mech. eqpt.	3.22	4.63	0.00	7.36	2.31	3.17	47.00	0.00	8.57
Elect. eqpt.	4.13	5.97	0.00	4.98	0.00	34.30	0.00	5.32	0.00
Motor vehicles	0.68	4.17	0.00	4.48	0.49	0.00	0.00	0.00	0.00
Other transport	0.21	0.00	0.00	0.20	0.00	0.00	0.00	0.00	0.15
Other mfg.	3.85	3.56	1.01	1.13	9.02	2.36	10.80	18.56	0.04
Tertiary	49.70	34.67	34.23	60.51	51.63	34.83	24.00	43.68	58.23
Construction	0.52	0.27	0.00	0.19	0.96	0.52	0.00	0.00	1.52
Distrib. trade	16.72	9.82	7.52	16.35	18.15	14.14	4.00	18.42	21.48
Transport	0.64	0.33	0.00	0.70	0.88	0.81	2.00	4.95	2.86
Communic.	0.47	0.00	0.00	0.00	0.00	0.81	0.00	0.00	0.00
Finance and invest.	14.47	17.99	20.93	9.74	30.41	3.65	16.00	13.04	30.81
Real estate	8.58	0.00	0.00	30.72	0.00	5.07	2.00	0.00	0.00
Other	8.31	6.24	5.78	2.81	1.23	9.82	0.00	7.27	1.57
Total	100	100	100	100	100	100	100	100	100

A significant country-specific determinant is that of policy orientation, which can influence the pattern and extent of direct investment activity. This can be through direct means, for example overall economic policy stances such as an import substituting and/or protectionist economic policy that specifically discourages inward foreign direct investment from particular countries or particular industries, as was alluded to in the above discussion regarding the service sector. Indeed, Japanese industrial policy until the early 1980s discouraged FDI in almost all sectors, accounting for its extremely low inward direct investment per capita (Table 5.3). Inward investment in Norway, on the other hand, has been inhibited by the indirect influence of economic policy, viz. the overvalued exchange rates.

SUMMARY AND CONCLUSIONS

The central thesis of this chapter revolves around the changes in the world economy resulting from a convergence of the economies of the Triad owing to the process of globalisation. Specifically, we have tried to develop an understanding of how the increasing homogeneity of the Triad countries, in terms of economic structure, has influenced the nature of their inward and outward FDI. The role of created assets in these economies has become increasingly significant, and we have highlighted the evolution of created assets over time as well as the ownership advantages of firms from these countries. We have also examined to what extent the increasing similarity of their economic structures has resulted in a convergence in the nature and pattern of their FDI activities.

The evidence presented in this chapter suggests several important trends regarding the international investment activities of industrialised countries. Some of the most important ones are as follows:

1 Outward and inward direct investment activities of the industrialised countries are growing faster than their domestic economies, which suggests that, while domestic economic growth is slowing, growth of FDI has been gathering pace.
2 Multinationals from industrialised countries are increasingly concentrating their outward investment activity on other industrialised countries, and subsequently a larger percentage of the inward investment into these countries is from other industrialised countries.
3 There is both an increasing tertiarisation of their domestic economies and a growth in the share of FDI in the tertiary sector.
4 The outward and inward investment activities associated with individual industrialised countries still reflect their country-specific characteristics and advantages, although these differences may be decreasing as they become increasingly interdependent.

The continuing significance of industrialised countries as home countries for investment into developing countries has policy implications for the developing countries. With the domestic policy changes that encourage FDI flows as a source of capital (Julius 1991), the demand for such investments is on the rise. The evidence presented here suggests that, with the exception of a handful of NIEs, outward investment from industrialised countries is being directed to other countries in the Triad. These countries in turn are directing an increasing proportion of *their* outward investment in industrialised countries. This has severe implications for the economic growth of developing countries, since the opportunities for technology spillovers and capital will lessen. This has the potential to create a vicious circle, leading to an increasing divergence between industrialised and developing countries, promoting even further the vicious cycle of poverty.

As we have seen from the discussion in this chapter, there are two clear and seemingly irreconcilable trends in the FDI activity associated with industrialised countries. First, there is a trend towards regional integration and convergence of economic activity as their economies become increasingly intertwined, interdependent and homogeneous, a trend that is further enhanced by agreements such as NAFTA and the EU. This is associated with the increased importance of created assets in these economies as well as the increased propensity to internalise the use of these assets by their firms. The complex investment and trade patterns of these countries among themselves are due in part to their convergence as well as to the mobility of created assets and the increasing importance of firm-specific factors. This trend argues for a diminishing role of country-specific factors in determining the FDI patterns associated with a given country as the economies of the industrialised countries continue to converge.

Second, the kind of created assets that are associated with a given country, and the nature of economic activity of domestic and foreign firms both at home and overseas, are a function of country-specific endowments and natural assets that are inherently country-specific. If they are path-dependent, then this second trend argues that the role of country-specific factors should remain significant as determinants of FDI activity, suggesting a continued divergence among countries' competitive advantages.

We have argued that the pattern of FDI activity will reflect these 'exogenous' supply and demand conditions that are country-specific, as well as their 'endogenous' country-specific determinants such as government policy. We have argued that this paradox is associated with the changing role of 'exogenous' versus 'endogenous' factors.

The next chapter seeks to examine this paradox, by evaluating how the specialisation of countries of a sample of industrialised countries has changed over the 1980s in both their domestic and international production, as well as how and to what extent their exports and outward direct investment in the manufacturing sector are influenced by country-specific determinants.

6

COUNTRY-SPECIFIC FACTORS, TRADE AND FDI PATTERNS OVER THE 1980s

INTRODUCTION

We have seen from Chapter 5 that the outward direct investment of countries reflects their traditional comparative advantages in that the competitive advantages of these countries are associated with their natural asset advantages. In this chapter we shall compare the extent and industrial distribution of international economic activity across the manufacturing sector between a sample of countries of different sizes and endowments in natural resources, so that we can evaluate whether or not these differences are reflected in the created assets of their MNEs if we exclude the sectors in which competitive advantages derive directly from access to natural assets. We intend to examine the importance of country-specific determinants in influencing the outward investment activity of firms from these countries, as well as their exports.

We have suggested in the previous chapter that there are two types of country-specific determinants: the 'exogenous' kind, which derive from characteristics such as market size and natural resource endowments, and the 'endogenous' kind, which derive from the use of government policy. We argue that, while the role of the former is declining as countries move along the IDP, the significance of the latter is increasing. Through this process, we intend to reconcile the paradox suggested by the last chapter that, although convergence among these countries is taking place, the competitive advantages of their firms continue to reflect biases owing to country-specific advantages, such as country size and natural asset endowments, as well as government policy.

Is there an increasing extent of specialisation of the comparative advantages of countries and the competitive advantages of their firms? What, if any, is the effect of one on the other? To what extent do the country-specific advantages influence the competitive advantages of their firms in international and domestic production? How does the increasing role of international production activities of firms affect the export activity associated with their home country? With the growth of intra-firm exports, are exports and FDI complements or substitutes? What is the net effect of the increasing significance of 'endogenous' determinants and the declining role of 'exogenous' determinants on the outward investment activity and exports of their firms? These are the kinds of question that this chapter seeks to answer.

EXPLAINING THE PARADOX

As MNEs become regionally and internationally integrated, trade and investment activity moves from being based on natural assets to being based on created assets. Such regional and global integration of MNE activity is a characteristic of firms from countries in the fifth stage. Dunning and Cantwell (1991) have argued that the competitiveness of industrial economies is increasingly dependent on their capacity to upgrade their technology and human capital. Since created assets are transferable across national boundaries, we can argue that over time, and as the process of integration takes place among the stage 5 countries, there will be an increasing similarity among these countries concerning their created asset L advantages. The same is true for the asset-based O advantages (Oa) of their firms, as these too are increasingly a function of created assets. As firms become more multinational in their operations, the character of their O advantages will reflect not just the comparative advantages of their home country, but those of the various host countries in which they operate. As the created asset L advantages of the industrialised countries become similar, it is logical to expect that the Oa advantages of firms from these countries will become broadly similar with other firms in the same industry but not necessarily in the same country (Cantwell and Sanna Randaccio 1990). This is not to argue that the role of asset-type Oa advantages will diminish to insignificance over time for stage 5 countries, since the extent of individual technological advantages of firms is a function not just of the spillovers from various national systems of innovation, but of their own R&D efforts as well. Several studies[1] have confirmed that firm size (and, by implication, the competitiveness of firms) is highly positively correlated with innovative activities. What we wish to stress here is that a similarity of O advantages does not imply that they will be identical. However, the accumulation of technology through R&D efforts and the consequent Oa advantages therefrom presume an initial O advantage on which the firm has built its subsequent technological effort, and, *ceteris paribus*, at an earlier period this advantage would have been a function of its home-country-specific endowments. For instance, a Japanese firm is unlikely to develop competitive advantages in petroleum products because Japan has an absolute disadvantage in petroleum production.[2]

The demand conditions also restrain the sectors and kinds of Oa advantages that firms of a particular nationality develop. Small market size constitutes a disadvantage in the development of process technology as the economies of scale are not present, but it may provide a competitive advantage in product innovation (Walsh 1988). This applies to the kind of created asset L advantages that small countries can provide,[3] since they have fewer resources,[4] and must either spread resources more thinly over the various disciplines, or must select areas as priorities, and these areas often (but not always) are those in which they have a natural asset advantage and lead to a specialisation of domestic firms in particular niche sectors (Soete 1987, 1988, Archibuigi and Pianta 1992). Needless to say, they tend to attract inward investment in these same sectors. On the other hand, small country economies tend to be more highly internationalised because of the limited economies of scale the home market provides, and their firms tend to be more highly internationalised, and often are involved in rationalised production owing to the limited resources of their home economies. Blomstrom (1984) has found that small Swedish firms are more export oriented and are more likely to invest abroad than similar size US firms.

Furthermore, it is important to point out that, while the created assets of industrialised countries are becoming similar, this does not imply that locations will become substitutes for each other in the long run. As we have already mentioned, small countries may choose to concentrate their international and domestic economic activity in a few sectors; although they may possess created assets in other sectors, they may not have a competitive advantage in these sectors. The point here is that, though there may be a similarity in the *kind* of created assets, all countries will not have the same *extent* of created assets in the same sectors. The case of the small countries illustrates our point, but at the same time suggests that 'exogenous' country-specific determinants can be influenced by 'endogenous' determinants such as government policy.

The role of government has played a dual and conflicting role in the evolution of created assets. On the one hand, were it not for the astute use of government policy, the process of economic convergence and 'catch-up' might not have occurred among the industrialised countries; almost all of these countries have targeted sectors for growth and have created the infrastructure and industrial policies to develop technological advantages in particular sectors over the post-war era,[5] and this accounts for the general similarity in the nature of their created assets.[6] On the other hand, the difference in the L advantages of these countries and the O advantages of their firms – in particular, the created-asset-based sectors between these countries – increasingly depends on the relative success or failure of these policies in individual countries. Government policy has become all the more important as the 'exogenous' determinants have declined in significance in determining their L advantages, partly as a result of globalisation of firms (Chesnais 1992). Indeed, the increasing trend towards rationalised international production activities can be said to have been accelerated by the process of specialisation of technological advantage of countries in particular sectors as a result of different national systems of innovation. The influence of government policy remains significant on other L advantages too. Even though there has been a convergence among these countries, there remain considerable differences in the organisation of economic activity: markets are more efficient in some locations than in others.

What we are trying to emphasise here is that the created asset advantages of firms and countries may become broadly similar among industrialised countries as their economies and firms integrate through international investment activities, but the range of sectors and industries and the extent to which this occurs are still affected by the country-specific determinants of every individual country. *'Exogenous' factors may determine the kinds of sectors in which they have a comparative advantage, but it is increasingly the 'endogenous' factors that determine whether they have a competitive advantage in these sectors.*

Our discussion hitherto would suggest that, although the kinds of created asset associated with industrialised locations are converging, the degree of specialisation (i.e. the extent of their advantages) of individual countries shows no signs of convergence and is less a function of the country-specific 'exogenous' determinants and more likely to be increasingly dependent on the countries' national systems of innovation and their government policy in general (Dalum 1992) – what we have termed the 'endogenous' country-specific determinants. Furthermore, this trend seems to be independent of increasing internationalisation and may even be said to be occurring *because* of the trend towards globalisation.

What of the growth of MNEs? Our discussion would suggest that the L advantages of countries continue to show patterns of specialisation that are country-specific but not natural-asset-specific. This might bring one wrongly to conclude that, because the O advantages of firms are becoming less country-specific and increasingly firm-specific, MNEs will not benefit as much from this trend. This is not the case. As Cantwell (1989) has noted, because of this differentiation of national systems of innovation, MNEs have an incentive to disperse their R&D facilities so that they can exploit the complementary areas of technological specialisation to their advantage and integrate these at the corporate level.

Let us now turn to the other side of the paradox: the evolution of the O advantages of MNEs from industrialised countries. Since the Oa advantages of MNEs from industrialised countries are becoming similar because of similar country-specific determinants, why then are they experiencing high growth? There are at least two reasons for this. First, it is important to emphasise that similarity of technological advantages across firms does not mean that they will become identical, since technology accumulation is a localised process. Since every firm is engaged in its own search procedures and is boundedly rational, and the NSI of countries is heteregeneous, it is not reasonable to expect that the Oa advantages will become identical.

Second, as has been argued elsewhere (Cantwell 1989, Narula 1993), technological competitiveness in the form of a firms accumulated experience and knowledge determines its opportunities for growth, and this accumulated learning is not just a function of technological innovation that lowers the unit costs of production or allows entry into a new or related field, and derives from the composition of its internal resources,[7] but also includes firm-specific advantages that derive from the firm's position in the market and its knowledge of how it can most efficiently internalise them.

Were Oa-type advantages of MNEs to become similar, their competitive advantages would then depend increasingly on the transaction-cost-based O advantages (Ot), which are firm-specific and depend on the comparative efficiency of markets and hierarchies, and thus remain different between MNEs. The growth of Ot advantages is associated with development of integrated technological systems and is partly a natural result of the growth and internationalisation of such firms and the process of innovation, which is enhanced both through experience and through the internalisation of various external alliances (Dunning and Cantwell 1991). Essentially, the organisation of technology has become an increasingly important source of competitive advantage, and a significant factor in the evolution of firms from the triad countries. This source of competitive advantage represents just one facet of the firm-specific advantages that derive from multinationality (i.e. transaction type O advantages).[8] This, once again varies between countries and is determined by their NSI.

THE RELATIONSHIP BETWEEN FDI AND TRADE

The exact nature of the relationship between FDI and trade is a controversial issue in international economics and business, although the literature is unanimous on the importance of this link. It is clear that FDI and trade are interrelated, in that MNE activity has a distinctive affect on the structure of trade of both home and host countries because of their ability and willingness to internalise cross-border transactions, thereby affecting the value added activity both within a country and between countries (Dunning 1993a).

However, depending on the circumstances, the *net* effect of MNE activity could be positive or negative depending upon the nature and extent of its activities relative to the structural characteristics of its home and host markets. By 'nature' of activities we mean the motives of its international production activities and the kind of output that the MNE generates. FDI can be *trade substituting* when direct investment occurs in import substituting activities aimed at supplying a domestic market; it can be *trade promoting* when FDI is aimed at acquiring offshore production facilities to supply other markets; it can be *trade complementing* if the investment is directed towards rationalised production and provides backup and intra-industry support facilities in export markets; and it can be *trade diverting* where foreign investment is aimed at taking advantage of unfilled quotas under preferential arrangements (Ariff 1989). This simple taxonomy is complicated by at least three other factors. First, as industrialised economies have become internationalised and their firms have globalised, the motivations for production are complex and investment may be undertaken for more than one reason. Second, the forces of both *de facto* and *de jure* regional economic integration among and between these countries and their relative positions in the various regional groupings may affect the type of FDI undertaken by their firms, and hence the nature and extent of trade (Dunning 1993a, UNCTC 1990). Third, the task is complicated by the growth of intra-firm trade, as firms replace markets with hierarchies.

It is germane to study the influence of FDI on trade in a study such as the present one because of the considerable importance of international trade in the international economic activity of nations. Almost without exception, the share of exports to GDP is much higher than that of outward direct investment to GDP, even among industrialised countries. Furthermore, the significance of world manufacturing exports as a proportion of total world exports of goods has continued to rise – from 61.1% in 1978 to 73.1% in 1988, with the exports of technology intensive exports growing at twice the rate of other manufactures (Daniels 1993). This growth is important from two perspectives. First, with the growth of MNE activity, a considerable (and often increasing) share of international trade is being conducted through MNEs rather than through the market. For example, in the US in 1988, about 50% of all imports and exports were conducted by multinationals, and almost a third of exports and 40% of imports are believed to be intra-firm (UNCTC 1991). Second, it indicates the growing importance of created assets relative to natural assets.

In most neo-classical theories of trade, factor inputs are assumed to be immobile. Foreign markets are always supplied by domestic firms (which are uninational, since international production is presumed not to exist), and trade is considered to be a reflection of the country-specific endowments rather than of the ownership advantages of the exporting firms. In this view, therefore, the extent of trade would be strongly related to country-specific advantages. In light of the increasing extent of foreign direct investment, especially by the industrialised countries, this may no longer be the case. First, FDI may either be trade enhancing, or trade replacing. A country's exports may decline not because it no longer has a comparative advantage in the factor inputs necessary, but because its firms now supply the foreign market through overseas production.[9] Second, since MNEs are able to transfer inputs across national boundaries but within their enterprise, they may be able to influence the comparative advantages of countries engaged in trade. This is germane in technology intensive industries where the inputs require created assets, which are mobile. Thus, the competitive advantage of a country's exporters will reflect not just their home-country-specific endowments, but, as in the case of FDI, the endowments of the various host countries in which they operate. In other words, a country's exports may increasingly reflect the firm-specific advantages of the firms that are engaged in production within its boundaries, which may or may not reflect country-specific endowments depending on their level of internationalisation.[10] None the less, it should be said that the pattern and nature of exports of a nation's firms provide a better indicator of, and better reflect, the country-specific comparative advantages than do the pattern and nature of the FDI activity of its firms. It is for this reason that in studies contrasting FDI and trade there is often an attempt to distinguish between the export performance of MNEs and that of domestic firms (Dunning and Buckley 1977, Cantwell 1989).

THE ANALYTICAL FRAMEWORK

Although the data analysed in Chapter 5 suggested that there are differences in the patterns of international production that are due to country-specific characteristics, these broad differences are indicative only of the presence or absence of fundamental differences and to some extent can be considered as exogenous. For instance, the presence of natural assets such as natural resources explains the extent of FDI activity in the primary sector in a particular country. Policy orientation such as restrictions on service sector foreign investments and the changes in the extent of inward and outward direct investment in the tertiary sector can be considered to be exogenous. FDI activity in primary and tertiary sectors only provides ambiguous evidence of a country's competitive advantages, since these may be based not on firm-specific O advantages, but on OLI advantages that are either non-FDI-induced or natural-asset-based and are therefore location-specific endowments. Therefore, if we are to examine the relationship between the competitive advantages of a country and its comparative advantage, we must necessarily restrict ourselves to advantages that are associated with created assets. The important point to note here is that created asset advantages of firms may originate from the location-specific endowments, but the *use* of these advantages is not so confined (Dunning 1981b). We shall therefore concentrate our ensuing analysis on the manufacturing sector.

We have already argued that, while 'exogenous' country-specific determinants are declining in importance, 'endogenous' country-specific endowments are becoming increasingly important in determining the differences between the L advantages of industrialised countries in the manufacturing sector. That is, these countries will continue to show a tendency to specialise in certain sectors, but these sectors will not necessarily be those in which they have traditional comparative advantages but rather those in which their national systems of innovation and organisation of economic activity have been strongest.

What does this mean to the overseas production activities of firms from the industrialised countries, given the relatively high extent of internationalisation of their firms and the firm-specific nature of their O advantages? What then will be the net effect of the two types of home-country-specific determinants on international production and trade? Cantwell (1989) has argued that as internationalisation proceeds the L advantages of countries will become an increasingly significant determinant. Ideally, we need to examine outward FDI *to a specific location*. This would help identify the advantages of one location over another and would reveal the nature and extent of the investment, the kinds of complementary assets in question and the peculiar features of the government policies of the home and host countries. Such a study would require a detailed breakdown of outward FDI by industrial sector and geographical destination, as well as detailed information on the nature of the government policy of each of its major host countries, and is outside the scope of this chapter.[11]

Another difficulty we are faced with is identifying a reliable means to measure the influence of government policy on the L advantages of a country: separating the 'endogenous' factors from the 'exogenous' ones is an extremely complex (and, one might argue, futile) exercise. We resolve this by identifying a group of countries with significant differences arising from 'exogenous' factors. Then, when examining the relationship between our proxies for country-specific variables and dependent variables, differences resulting from exogenous factors should reveal themselves as differences between groups of countries.

What we wish to demonstrate in this chapter is the importance of 'endogenous' country-specific characteristics as determinants of outward FDI and exporting activity among the industrialised countries in the 1980s as increasing regionalisation occurs among countries of the Triad. The economies of these countries have become increasingly interdependent, in part because of the increasing internationalisation of their econo-

Table 6.1 Groups of industrialised countries based on a cluster analysis in 1988

Market size	*Low resource intensity*	*Medium resource intensity*	*High resource intensity*
Small markets	Belgium	Netherlands	New Zealand
	Austria	Canada	Australia
	Sweden	Denmark	Norway
	Finland		
	Switzerland		
Medium markets	Italy		
	France		
	Germany		
	UK		
Large markets	Japan	US	

mies and their firms. While the structure of foreign production and exports are still influenced by the endowments specific to the country in which they operate, as well as by those of their home country, there is an increasing similarity in both the created asset type O and L advantages among these countries, and this trend is associated with the internationalisation of their economies. Indeed, the extent to which countries of the Triad are linked to each other's economy, and thereby the extent to which they have become relatively homogeneous in the nature of their created assets, differentiates stage 4 and stage 5 countries. We hope to show that there exists a relationship between the competitive advantages of a country's firms and those of the country itself, but that the structure of its FDI and trading activity is decreasingly a function of its 'exogenous' country-specific factors as a country becomes regionally integrated through FDI activity, implying that this relationship is due to the increasing importance of 'endogenous' country-specific determinants.

Sample selection and variables

Figure 6.1 presents a graphical analysis of possible clusters of the industrialised countries in 1988. The *x*-axis variable is the difference between the share of primary exports and share of primary imports (*DIFPRI*), and provides a measure of the extent of natural resource dependency, whereas the *y*-axis is population (*POP*) as an indicator of market size. Visual inspection suggests six distinct groups, and this is confirmed through a cluster analysis[12] of market characteristics and natural resource intensity for the industrialised countries in 1988. Market characteristics are proxied by the aggregate consumption and population, whereas resource intensity is proxied by the share of primary exports and share of primary imports. The cluster membership is identical to

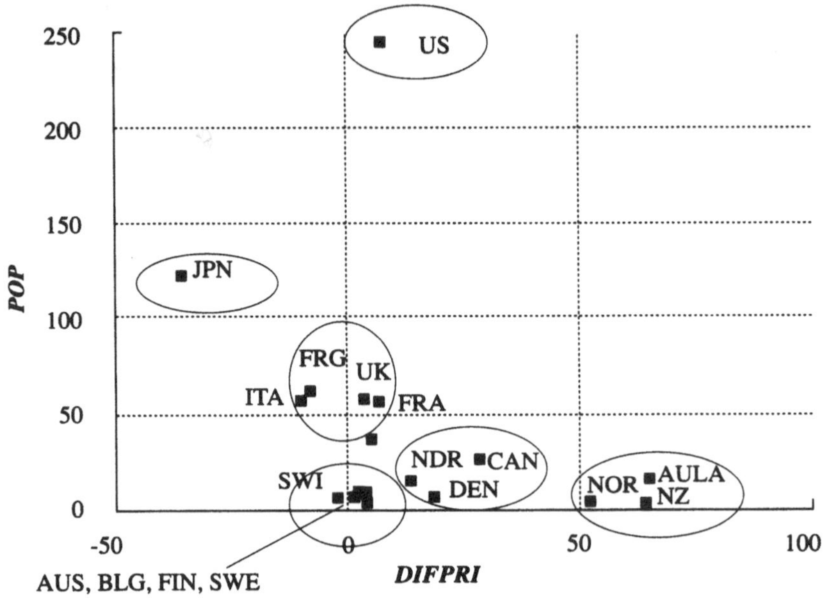

Figure 6.1 Market size versus resource dependency, 1988

that suggested by Figure 6.1 and is re-interpreted into a 3 × 3 matrix in Table 6.1.

In order to illustrate the contrasts and similarities between countries and to provide us with an objective sample so that we do not bias our results by selecting similar countries, we select one country from each group. The countries selected are: Australia, Austria, Canada, US, Germany and Japan. Table 6.2 gives some summary statistics regarding the inward and outward manufacturing investment associated with these countries.

The indicators used in our analysis are described below.[13] The industrial breakdown is limited by the availability of FDI data, and the classification used is based on that in the *World Investment Directory*. Appendix 2 provides details of the industrial breakdown and is based on ISIC revision 2.

We wish to examine the evolution of the sample countries over the 1980s, and in order to do so, ideally, we should compare data between two years from the beginning and the end of the decade. Although the various other statistics used here are available for all the years during the decade, FDI statistics are available only on a comparable basis on the level of breakdown we need for two years for each country. Data on outward FDI are available for all countries for 1980 except Austria, for which data are available for 1982. Data for the end of the decade are available for Australia, Canada, Germany and Japan for 1989, for the US for 1990 and for Austria for 1988.

1 Revealed comparative advantage of outward direct investment (RCA(I))

RCA(I) is defined as follows:

$$RCA_{ij}(I) = (ODI_{ij}/\Sigma_j ODI_{ij})/(\Sigma_i ODI_{ij}/\Sigma_i\Sigma_j ODI_{ij}).$$

The revealed comparative advantage for an industry i for a country j is denoted by $RCA_{ij}(I)$, while the value of outward FDI of industry i from country j is denoted by ODI_{ij}. A value greater than one indicates that the firms of a country are advantaged in that industry, and less than one that the firms of the country are disadvantaged in the sector in question.

The data used to calculate this are from the *World Investment Directory* (UN 1992b, 1993e) as well as various other unpublished data from secondary sources. All figures have been converted from their various domestic currencies into US dollars using year-end exchange rates from the *IMF International Financial Statistics*. Because 97% of all outward FDI is from industrialised countries, the RCA(I) calculated can be said to be either relative to the world, or relative to the total OECD value of outward FDI.

2 Revealed comparative advantage of exports (RCA(X))

RCA(X) is defined as follows:

$$RCA_{ij}(X) = (X_{ij}/\Sigma_j X_{ij})/(\Sigma_i X_{ij}/\Sigma_i\Sigma_j X_{ij}).$$

The revealed comparative advantage for an industry i for a country j is denoted by $RCA_{ij}(X)$, while the value of exports of industry i from country j is denoted by X_{ij}. A value greater than one indicates that a country is advantaged in that industry, and less than one that the country is disadvantaged in the sector in question. These are calculated from OECD data, and the totals are for OECD countries; therefore all the RCA(X) calculated here are relative to the OECD countries.

3 Revealed patenting advantage (RPA)

RPA is defined as follows:

$$RPA_{ij} = (P_{ij}/\Sigma_j P_{ij})/(\Sigma_i P_{ij}/\Sigma_i\Sigma_j P_{ij}).$$

The revealed comparative advantage for an industry i for a country j is denoted by $RPA_{ij}(X)$, while the value of patents of industry i from country j is denoted by P_{ij}. A value greater than one indicates that a country is advantaged in that industry, and less than one that the country is disadvantaged in the sector in question. These are calculated based on US patent data, using the patents granted, fractional count method.

4 Labour productivity (*LP*)

These figures are in 1980 US dollars for the years used, and are calculated by dividing the value added in any sector by the total number of persons employed in that sector in the country in question, and are based on OECD data.

5 Trade ratio (*TRAT*)

This is the ratio of exports in an industry divided by its imports in the same industry. It should be noted that the trade ratio is often used as an indicator of comparative advantage of exports, and is often used in place of *RCA*(*X*).

6 Share of OECD's outward FDI

The data source for these figures is the same as for that of *RCA*(*I*).

7 Share of OECD's exports

The data source for these figures is the same as for that of *RCA*(*X*).

THE EXTENT OF SPECIALISATION OF COUNTRIES AND FIRMS

We examine some general indicators of the countries in our sample in Tables 6.2–6.8 to confirm the extent of differences between the countries in our sample and for casual evidence of the differences that are due to size and resource intensity.

The 'small' countries in our sample (Canada, Australia and Austria) differ from the 'larger' countries in terms of their international economic activity by the relative importance of such activity to their economies (Table 6.2). None the less, the ratio of total international economic activity to GDP for Germany is almost the same as for that of Austria. This has to do with Germany's traditional reluctance to engage in outward direct investment, preferring to export goods and services instead – Germany's exports as a proportion of GDP are twice that of Japan, a country with a similar lack of resources and size, and three times that of the US (Table 6.2).

Table 6.2 Extent of international economic activity for six industrialised countries, 1980 and 1989

Country	*Exports as % of GDP*	*Imports as % of GDP*	*IDI as % of GDP*	*ODI as % of GDP*	*Total internat. econ. activity as % of GDP*	*Share of world mfg. ODI*	*Share of world mfg. exports*	*Share of IDI from IC countries*	*Share of ODI from IC countries*
Germany									
1980	23.79	23.19	4.52	5.33	56.84	9.37	14.00	94.7	77.4
1989	28.88	22.82	6.23	10.31	68.24	10.38	15.22	95.2	83.9
Japan									
1980	12.25	13.34	0.28	3.45	29.33	5.74	8.61	94.3	44.8
1989	9.57	7.83	0.55	8.86	26.3	13.51	7.32	86.8	65.7
US									
1980	8.4	9.57	3.09	8.2	29.27	49.24	12.48	87	73
1989	7.04	9.54	7.23	7.32	31.16	38.3	11.74	92.8	74.1
Canada									
1980	25.56	23.61	19.48	8.52	77.17	6.61	5.14	98.1	84.2
1989	21.85	21.77	18.59	12.54	74.75	7.28	5.81	97.2	85.8
Austria									
1980	22.74	31.75	4.11	0.69	59.29	0.15	2.18	77	52
1988	24.46	28.4	5.38	1.07	59.32	0.19	2.25	36.7	49.9
Australia									
1980	14.65	14.93	8.78	1.51	39.86	0.34	2.26	92.5	44
1989	13.26	15.81	22.41	9.29	60.78	0.99	1.73	87.1	79.1

Source: IMF, *International Financial Statistics*, MERIT Data Base, UN (1992b, 1993e)

Table 6.3 Indicators of domestic and international production for the US, 1980 and 1990

	RCA(I)	*RCA(X)*	*Trade ratio*	*RPA*	*Labour product.*	*Share of OECD*	
						Exports	*ODI*
(*a*) *1980*							
Less technology intensive	0.74	0.96	0.77	1.03	359.45	12.00	32.94
Food, beverages & tobacco	0.80	1.20	1.02	1.00	510.53	14.97	35.33
Textiles, leather & clothing	0.71	0.93	0.63	0.82	206.22	11.56	31.63
Paper, printing	1.02	1.16	0.98	n.a.	388.38	14.42	45.15
Non-metallic mineral products	1.57	0.67	0.75	0.97	391.19	8.31	69.68
Metals & metal products	0.51	0.78	0.66	1.05	385.19	9.75	22.46
More technology intensive	1.34	1.42	1.25	0.92	459.99	17.68	59.53
Petroleum products	1.79	0.42	0.17	1.24	1723.49	5.24	79.57
Rubber & plastics	1.48	0.75	0.51	0.97	321.05	9.36	65.62
Non-electrical eqpt	1.58	1.85	2.61	0.91	408.59	23.04	70.20
Motor vehicles	1.56	1.04	0.60	0.82	n.a.	12.93	69.40
Other transportation eqpt	0.89	2.60	2.86	0.88	n.a.	32.42	39.62
Chemicals	1.00	1.49	2.64	0.87	791.18	18.65	44.50
Electrical eqpt	1.01	1.21	0.84	0.96	377.08	15.05	44.82
Other manufactures	0.95	1.29	0.89	0.99	318.19	16.06	42.33

Table 6.3 (cont.)

	RCA(I)	RCA(X)	Trade ratio	RPA	Labour product.	Share of OECD	
						Exports	ODI
*(b) 1990**							
Less technology intensive	0.82	0.94	0.57	1.01	566.03	10.98	29.65
Food, beverages & tobacco	1.00	1.31	1.19	0.70	891.25	15.25	36.39
Textiles, leather & clothing	0.76	0.70	0.24	0.91	363.32	8.17	27.45
Paper, printing	1.03	1.18	0.89	n.a.	501.42	13.74	37.50
Non-metallic mineral products	1.21	0.69	0.51	0.91	583.54	8.02	43.96
Metals & metal products	0.48	0.72	0.51	1.06	566.60	8.33	17.57
More technology intensity	1.27	1.42	0.85	0.87	610.47	16.50	46.22
Petroleum products	2.11	1.19	0.36	1.27	2318.73	13.81	76.63
Rubber & plastics	2.02	0.89	0.38	0.94	355.68	10.36	73.20
Non-electrical eqpt	1.30	1.54	1.10	0.86	465.18	17.98	47.30
Motor vehicles	1.41	0.91	0.41	0.71	n.a.	10.61	51.11
Other transportation eqpt	2.53	2.98	2.81	0.86	n.a.	34.65	71.09
Chemicals	1.09	1.35	1.59	0.87	1241.77	15.71	39.60
Electrical eqpt	0.83	1.51	0.69	0.85	521.34	17.56	30.01
Other manufactures	0.56	1.31	0.60	1.00	456.56	15.25	20.46

Source: MERIT data base, OECD data and UN *World Investment Directory*
Note: * RPA is for 1989. Labour productivity is in 1980 prices

Table 6.4 Indicators of domestic and international production for Japan, 1980 and 1990

	RCA(I)	*RCA(X)*	*Trade ratio*	*RPA*	*Labour product.*	*Share of OECD*	
						Exports	*ODI*
(*a*) *1980*							
Less technology intensive	1.45	1.03	1.38	0.73	305.63	8.88	7.52
Food, beverages & tobacco	0.41	0.19	0.18	0.98	290.44	1.68	2.12
Textiles, leather & clothing	5.43	0.91	1.01	1.26	174.77	7.83	28.10
Paper, printing	1.54	0.30	0.59	n.a.	348.41	2.58	7.96
Non-metallic mineral products	0.00	1.11	5.79	0.94	344.72	9.54	0.00
Metals & metal products	1.80	1.80	3.37	0.67	414.97	15.48	9.30
More technology intensive	0.91	1.57	3.46	1.05	376.19	13.50	4.73
Petroleum products	0.00	0.14	0.05	0.32	1707.29	1.18	0.00
Rubber & plastics	0.00	1.26	4.97	0.91	300.17	10.82	0.00
Non-electrical eqpt	0.75	1.17	4.88	0.86	346.29	10.07	3.90
Motor vehicles	0.00	2.47	39.48	1.46	n.a.	21.27	0.00
Other transportation eqpt	10.97	2.03	4.59	1.21	n.a.	17.49	56.80
Chemicals	1.20	0.80	1.53	1.01	708.96	6.87	6.20
Electrical eqpt	1.88	2.84	9.31	1.37	295.58	24.42	9.74
Other manufactures	1.90	0.82	0.95	1.15	225.87	7.03	5.64

Table 6.4 (cont.)

	RCA(I)	RCA(X)	Trade ratio	RPA	Labour product.	Share of OECD	
						Exports	ODI
*(b) 1990**							
Less technology intensive	0.94	0.83	0.52	0.73	371.31	5.33	12.01
Food, beverages & tobacco	0.48	0.16	0.07	0.61	374.80	1.00	6.18
Textiles, leather & clothing	3.37	0.71	0.35	1.06	0.00	4.56	43.20
Paper, printing	0.67	0.42	0.63	n.a.	407.40	2.70	8.60
Non-metallic mineral products	0.00	1.35	1.67	1.19	487.91	8.67	0.00
Metals & metal products	1.30	1.60	1.21	0.72	508.08	10.23	16.65
More technology intensive	1.07	2.52	3.28	1.21	353.54	16.14	13.65
Petroleum products	0.00	0.43	0.18	0.38	1678.06	2.77	0.00
Rubber & plastics	0.00	1.58	1.98	1.08	296.63	10.11	0.00
Non-electrical eqpt	0.83	2.53	4.54	1.10	307.07	16.22	10.65
Motor vehicles	1.61	3.42	8.95	1.71	n.a.	21.86	20.60
Other transportation eqpt	0.00	1.52	2.21	1.19	n.a.	9.71	0.00
Chemicals	0.69	1.25	1.41	0.87	962.23	7.98	8.84
Electrical eqpt	2.52	4.15	5.62	1.55	157.44	26.56	32.30
Other manufactures	1.34	1.58	0.83	1.11	311.49	10.11	17.20

Source: as for Table 6.3
Note: * RPA is for 1989. Labour productivity i in 1980 prices

Table 6.5 Indicators of domestic and international production for Germany, 1980 and 1990

	RCA(I)	*RCA(X)*	*Trade ratio*	*RPA*	*Labour product.*	*Share of OECD*	
						Exports	*ODI*
(*a*) *1980**							
Less technology intensive	0.58	1.01	0.89	1.02	355.38	14.13	4.88
Food, beverages & tobacco	0.19	0.77	0.73	0.61	650.32	10.72	1.64
Textiles, leather & clothing	0.94	0.97	0.51	1.72	224.60	13.58	7.94
Paper, printing	0.35	0.74	0.81	n.a.	320.47	10.37	2.98
Non-metallic mineral products	2.85	1.21	1.20	1.08	399.07	16.96	24.07
Metals & metal products	0.69	1.25	1.45	1.01	312.43	17.49	5.86
More technology intensive	1.50	1.33	1.80	1.32	378.27	18.56	12.70
Petroleum products	0.05	0.71	0.39	0.46	4596.19	9.92	0.45
Rubber & plastics	0.92	1.32	1.20	1.30	298.90	18.50	7.73
Non-electrical eqpt	1.08	1.44	2.70	1.45	313.19	20.09	9.09
Motor vehicles	2.11	1.65	3.45	1.78	n.a.	23.05	17.80
Other transportation eqpt	0.00	0.66	1.09	1.37	n.a.	9.21	0.00
Chemicals	2.13	1.39	1.78	1.55	385.04	19.49	17.96
Electrical eqpt	2.26	1.29	1.63	0.96	329.74	17.99	19.09
Other manufactures	0.41	0.89	0.88	0.98	347.62	12.53	3.50

Table 6.5 (cont.)

	RCA(I)	*RCA(X)*	*Trade ratio*	*RPA*	*Labour product.*	*Share of OECD*	
						Exports	*ODI*
*(b) 1990**							
Less technology intensive	0.49	1.01	0.94	1.15	566.62	15.35	4.80
Food, beverages & tobacco	0.15	0.73	0.83	0.51	826.02	11.09	1.47
Textiles, leather & clothing	1.59	1.03	0.61	1.57	491.09	15.75	15.65
Paper, printing	0.35	0.85	1.02	n.a.	453.75	12.93	3.43
Non-metallic mineral products	2.50	1.17	1.35	1.43	672.23	17.74	24.60
Metals & metal products	0.51	1.26	1.32	1.21	518.02	19.13	5.05
More technology intensive	1.50	1.23	1.77	1.47	557.70	18.67	14.79
Petroleum products	0.03	0.59	0.46	0.49	9886.82	9.00	0.32
Rubber & plastics	1.73	1.29	1.30	1.34	372.66	19.59	16.98
Non-electrical eqpt	0.82	1.26	2.13	1.69	485.13	19.21	8.06
Motor vehicles	1.72	1.51	2.92	1.95	n.a.	23.04	16.91
Other transportation eqpt	3.63	0.79	1.03	1.61	n.a.	11.95	27.58
Chemicals	1.98	1.29	1.68	1.87	807.46	19.65	19.42
Electrical eqpt	1.88	1.03	1.38	1.02	417.87	15.61	18.47
Other manufactures	0.28	0.92	1.21	0.89	477.22	14.03	2.70

Source: as for Table 6.3
Note: * RPA is for 1989. Labour productivity ≅ in 1980 prices

Table 6.6 Indicators of domestic and international production for Canada, 1980 and 1989

	RCA(I)	RCA(X)	Trade ratio	RPA	Labour product.	Share of OECD	
						Exports	ODI
(a) 1980							
Less technology intensive	1.87	1.00	1.71	1.10	316.77	5.14	11.16
Food, beverages & tobacco	1.18	0.64	1.10	1.21	340.76	3.32	7.06
Textiles, leather & clothing	0.00	0.17	0.25	0.45	206.66	0.85	0.00
Paper, printing	3.07	3.55	5.61	n.a.	371.53	18.24	18.29
Non-metallic mineral products	0.00	0.29	0.39	0.56	343.70	1.47	0.00
Metals & metal products	2.75	0.89	1.68	1.14	334.14	4.59	16.38
More technology intensive	0.71	0.68	0.70	0.75	361.01	3.52	4.22
Petroleum products	3.35	0.76	2.93	1.28	746.56	3.93	19.98
Rubber & plastics	0.00	0.36	0.38	0.69	281.46	1.86	0.00
Non-electrical eqpt	0.00	0.50	0.44	0.92	323.94	2.56	0.00
Motor vehicles	0.00	1.42	0.78	0.83	n.a.	7.29	0.00
Other transportation eqpt	0.00	0.72	0.94	0.97	n.a.	3.71	0.00
Chemicals	0.31	0.53	1.01	0.56	521.04	2.75	1.85
Electrical eqpt	0.00	0.32	0.42	0.65	307.96	1.65	0.00
Other manufactures	0.78	1.21	1.32	0.99	245.05	6.22	4.66

Table 6.6 (cont.)

	RCA(I)	*RCA(X)*	*Trade ratio*	*RPA*	*Labour product.*	*Share of OECD*	
						Exports	*ODI*
(*b*) 1989*							
Less technology intensive	2.22	1.02	1.43	1.07	535.30	5.95	15.27
Food, beverages & tobacco	1.16	0.59	1.11	0.48	663.49	3.40	7.98
Textiles, leather & clothing	0.oo	0.14	0.16	0.76	321.72	0.81	0.00
Paper, printing	3.78	2.95	4.19	n.a.	604.28	17.11	26.04
Non-metallic mineral products	0.00	0.38	0.40	0.72	593.95	2.20	0.00
Metals & metal products	2.90	1.04	1.36	1.17	512.48	6.06	19.97
More technology intensive	0.50	0.76	0.72	0.82	454.98	4.39	3.45
Petroleum products	2.82	1.00	1.47	1.48	836.30	5.79	19.42
Rubber & plastics	0.00	0.66	0.55	0.94	278.17	3.82	0.00
Non-electrical eqpt	0.00	0.36	0.36	1.00	314.34	2.12	0.00
Motor vehicles	0.00	1.83	1.08	0.82	n.a.	10.62	0.00
Other transportation eqpt	0.00	0.64	0.91	1.05	n.a.	3.70	0.00
Chemicals	0.73	0.47	0.81	0.63	815.10	2.71	5.05
Electrical eqpt	0.00	0.38	0.36	0.71	414.22	2.19	0.00
Other manufactures	0.68	1.06	1.34	0.99	319.74	6.14	4.69

Source: as for Table 6.3
Note: * Labour productivity is in 1980 prices

Table 6.7 Indicators of domestic and international production for Austria, 1981 and 1988

	*RCA(I)**	*RCA(X)*	*Trade ratio*	*RPA*	*Labour product.*	*Share of OECD*	
						Exports	*ODI*
(*a*) *1981**							
Less technology intensive	2.44	0.94	1.15	0.81	239.60	1.99	0.32
Food, beverages & tobacco	0.48	0.30	0.60	0.78	316.82	0.63	0.06
Textiles, leather & clothing	0.46	1.44	0.93	0.44	179.19	3.03	0.06
Paper, printing	0.82	1.28	1.58	n.a.	260.57	2.69	0.11
Non-metallic mineral products	0.00	1.60	1.50	0.98	299.62	3.38	0.00
Metals & metal products	5.63	1.04	1.49	0.84	224.22	2.18	0.74
More technology intensive	0.41	0.52	0.74	0.94	259.25	1.10	0.05
Petroleum products	0.00	0.07	0.08	0.27	564.10	0.16	0.00
Rubber & plastics	0.00	1.14	1.04	0.65	234.12	2.41	0.00
Non-electrical eqpt	0.00	0.61	0.86	1.61	288.61	1.28	0.00
Motor vehicles	0.00	0.25	0.41	1.23	n.a.	0.52	0.00
Other transportation eqpt	0.00	0.00	0.58	1.21	n.a.	0.26	0.00
Chemicals	1.14	0.60	0.77	0.64	282.63	1.26	0.15
Electrical eqpt	0.28	0.74	0.99	0.37	217.65	1.57	0.04
Other manufactures	0.50	1.10	1.40	1.10	193.70	2.31	0.07

Table 6.7 (cont.)

	RCA(I)*	RCA(X)	Trade ratio	RPA	Labour product.	Share of OECD	
						Exports	ODI
*(b) 1988***							
Less technology intensive	1.41	0.99	1.05	1.06	321.82	2.27	0.25
Food, beverages & tobacco	0.30	0.28	0.61	0.39	416.09	0.65	0.05
Textiles, leather & clothing	1.77	1.20	0.75	0.44	282.49	2.76	0.31
Paper, printing	1.03	1.39	1.55	n.a.	252.41	3.20	0.18
Non-metallic mineral products	0.00	1.39	1.35	1.34	480.16	3.19	0.00
Metals & metal products	2.77	1.22	1.30	1.17	304.48	2.80	0.49
More technology intensive	0.58	0.61	0.80	0.95	336.89	1.41	0.10
Petroleum products	0.00	0.17	0.16	0.28	1043.91	0.38	0.00
Rubber & plastics	0.00	1.18	0.99	1.29	282.19	2.72	0.00
Non-electrical eqpt	0.00	0.64	0.83	1.39	352.95	1.47	0.00
Motor vehicles	0.00	0.41	0.57	1.09	n.a.	0.94	0.00
Other transportation eqpt	0.00	0.23	1.12	1.08	n.a.	0.54	0.00
Chemicals	1.60	0.63	0.80	0.72	436.05	1.46	0.28
Electrical eqpt	0.20	0.84	0.97	0.53	230.64	1.93	0.04
Other manufactures	2.62	0.96	1.10	0.94	276.53	2.20	0.46

Source: as for Table 6.3
Notes: * $RCA(I)$ is for 1982; labour productivity is in 1980 prices
** Labour productivity is in 1980 prices

Table 6.8 Indicators of domestic and international production for Australia, 1980 and 1989

	RCA(I)	*RCA(X)*	*Trade ratio*	*RPA*	*Labour product.*	*Share of OECD*	
						Exports	*ODI*
(*a*) *1980*							
Less technology intensive	2.29	1.20	2.06	0.91	260.15	2.70	0.71
Food, beverages & tobacco	0.60	2.60	6.49	0.70	273.16	5.88	0.19
Textiles, leather & clothing	0.59	0.39	0.38	0.42	191.55	0.88	0.18
Paper, printing	2.12	0.12	0.12	n.a.	256.15	0.27	0.66
Non-metallic mineral products	12.40	0.12	0.15	0.85	327.77	0.28	3.84
Metals & metal products	3.20	1.04	2.85	0.96	291.54	2.36	0.99
More technology intensive	0.50	0.15	0.20	0.68	261.49	0.34	0.16
Petroleum products	0.00	0.48	0.39	0.24	588.46	1.09	0.00
Rubber & plastics	0.00	0.11	0.10	0.55	249.36	0.24	0.00
Non-electrical eqpt	1.18	0.13	0.14	0.95	227.30	0.28	0.37
Motor vehicles	0.40	0.07	0.12	1.14	n.a.	0.16	0.12
Other transportation eqpt	0.00	0.29	0.59	1.05	n.a.	0.65	0.00
Chemicals	0.73	0.15	0.23	0.46	399.06	0.34	0.23
Electrical eqpt	0.00	0.09	0.11	0.45	221.44	0.19	0.00
Other manufactures	0.46	0.30	0.37	1.07	219.84	0.67	0.14

Table 6.8 (cont.)

	RCA(I)	RCA(X)	Trade ratio	RPA	Labour product.	Share of OECD	
						Exports	ODI
*(b) 1989**							
Less technology intensive	2.34	1.25	1.32	1.28	573.81	2.16	2.18
Food, beverages & tobacco	0.00	2.40	3.56	1.64	581.79	4.15	0.00
Textiles, leather & clothing	0.00	0.72	0.52	0.51	544.76	1.25	0.00
Paper, printing	7.02	0.16	0.12	n.a.	436.69	0.27	6.56
Non-metallic mineral products	5.56	0.16	0.12	0.78	620.31	0.28	5.20
Metals & metal products	1.90	1.19	1.62	1.28	670.26	2.06	1.78
More technology intensive	0.27	0.17	0.14	0.75	0.00	0.29	0.26
Petroleum products	0.00	1.26	0.72	0.83	811.72	2.18	0.00
Rubber & plastics	0.00	0.16	0.08	0.60	0.00	0.27	0.00
Non-electrical eqpt	0.82	0.12	0.09	1.17	484.89	0.21	0.77
Motor vehicles	0.03	0.10	0.11	0.79	n.a.	0.18	0.03
Other transportation eqpt	0.00	0.15	0.09	0.83	n.a.	0.27	0.00
Chemicals	0.27	0.19	0.20	0.57	795.33	0.33	0.25
Electrical eqpt	0.00	0.10	0.10	0.47	650.52	0.18	0.00
Other manufactures	1.57	0.18	0.14	0.89	487.52	0.31	1.46

Source: as for Table 6.3
Note: * Labour productivity is in 1980 prices

Tables 6.3–6.8 provide some general indicators of the competitive position and economic activity of the sample countries in the manufacturing sector. We can see that, compared with total exports and outward FDI of all industrialised countries, the small countries' international economic activity is concentrated in relatively fewer sectors than that of the larger countries. There is also a clear propensity for their production activities to be in the less technology intensive sectors. Their *RPA* and *RCA* indices confirm this observation. There do not seem to be any tangible differences between the resource intensive countries and the resource poor countries in these indices except in the case of petroleum products and non-metallic mineral products.

Let us examine the hypothesis that small countries have specialised more rigorously in fewer industrial sectors than have large countries. Pavitt (1988) tests this by taking the standard deviation of *RPA* across sectors for various countries. He finds that small countries have a high standard deviation of *RPA* across industrial sectors while large countries have a relatively low standard deviation for the same index. The rationale behind this is that, since small countries are specialised in relatively few industries where their *RPA* will be high, industries other than these will have a low *RPA* index, thereby leading to a wide standard deviation.

We examine this hypothesis in Table 6.9, which gives the standard deviation for both periods for *RPA* , *RCA*(*X*) and *RCA*(*I*), since the same argument can be extended to these other two indicators. Although the evidence from Tables 6.3–6.8 provides some suggestion that this hypothesis may be valid – Austria, Canada and Australia have zero or insignificant share of total exports and outward investment in several sectors as well as a zero *RCA*(*I*), Japan and Germany have a share of export and outward FDI share in many more sectors, while the US has a considerable presence in almost all sectors – the use of standard deviations does not bear out this hypothesis. Indeed, there seems to be no pattern suggested by the results. This may be because of the high level of aggregation of our industrial breakdown.

None the less, the data in Table 6.9 provide some tentative evidence of several other interesting phenomena. As several scholars have confirmed,[14] a majority of the R&D associated with MNEs is conducted in their home country, even where these firms are highly internationalised. Therefore the *RPA* index can be said to be a good indicator of country-specific advantages. On the other hand, *RCA*(*X*) is a less perfect indicator of home-country-specific advantages for reasons discussed above, whereas *RCA*(*I*) is the indicator that may most reflect firm-specific advantages. Without exception, the dispersion of *RCA*(*I*) is much greater than the standard deviation of *RPA* . Likewise, with the exception of Germany, the standard deviation of *RCA*(*X*) is greater than *RPA* for each country for either period. And finally, except for the US (both periods) and Japan (in 1989) the standard deviation of *RCA*(*I*)

Table 6.9 Standard deviation of revealed advantages, six countries, 1980 and 1989

	RCA(I)		*RCA(X)*		*RPA*	
	1980	*1989*	*1980*	*1989*	*1980*	*1989*
US**	0.4020	0.6206	0.5653	0.5989	0.1148	0.1516
Japan	3.0820	1.0411	0.8509	1.1722	0.4106	0.3705
Germany	0.9525	1.0739	0.3425	0.2695	0.4135	0.4895
Canada	1.2987	1.3474	0.8807	0.7598	0.2756	0.2686
Austria*	1.5213	1.0518	0.5276	0.4469	0.4000	0.3994
Australia	3.3584	2.3155	0.6971	0.6984	0.3040	0.3485

Notes: * Data for Austria is 1982 and 1988
** Data for the US is for 1980 and 1990

was greater than *RCA*(*X*). In other words, $\sigma(RCA(I)) > \sigma(RCA(X)) > \sigma(RPA)$. If we are to assume that the relative extent of specialisation of a country or firms of a particular nationality can be estimated by its standard deviation, we may hypothesise that, if a country's comparative advantage in exports or outward FDI is a function of its home country advantages, the standard deviation of these indicators should be roughly the same, since the industrial specialisation would be the same. We conclude from the evidence that this not the case. Since the standard deviation of *RCA*(*X*) and *RCA*(*I*) are both higher than that of *RPA* , we must conclude that their advantages in exporting and outward investment are not in the same industrial sectors as their home country advantages. However, what is also evident is that in general the industrial specialisation of their outward investment is narrower than the industrial specialisation of their exports, which in turn is more specialised than the industrial specialisation of their country-specific advantages. This is an intuitive observation, since firms of a country are likely to export or engage in FDI only in industries in which they possess considerable O advantages (i.e. industries in which they are most competitive), and these industries are fewer than those in which it has a general technological competence or engages in domestic production. Also, the extent of O advantages must, *ceteris paribus*, be higher than in exports for the country to engage in FDI. The exception helps confirm the rule: the activities of US MNEs were more industrially diversified than US exports in 1980, as US MNEs are among the most internationalised, and are likely to exhibit a wider variety of O advantages which they have acquired through their overseas operations. However, as the competitiveness of MNEs from other industrialised countries has risen and those of the US have declined, their operations have become more specialised in fewer industries. The reverse is true for Japan, where the standard deviation of exports shows that these have become more specialised, but their FDI is dispersed in a greater number of industries.

THE STABILITY OF OUTWARD FDI, EXPORTS AND TECHNOLOGICAL ADVANTAGE OVER THE 1980s

We now seek to confirm more rigorously the extent to which the industrial pattern of activity has been stable over the 1980s for our sample of countries by examining the relationship between the industrial distribution of shares of international production and exports between the early 1980s and the late 1980s using the following regressions:

$$SHODI_{it} = \alpha + \beta SHODI_{it-1} + \varepsilon_i,$$

$$SHX_{it} = \alpha + \beta SHX_{it-1} + \varepsilon_i,$$

where $SHODI_{it}$ is the share of outward FDI of firms from a country in industry i for period t (1989) and $t-1$ is the previous period (1980), and SHX_{it} is the share of exports from a country in industry i for a period t. This analysis is based on that of Cantwell (1989).[15] Essentially, the t-statistic of β measures the degree of positive correlation between the two distributions, and R is the value of the Pearson correlation coefficient. The relative absolute value of β and R indicate whether the degree of specialisation has risen or fallen. If $|\beta| > |R|$, the degree of specialisation has risen, whereas if $|\beta| < |R|$ then the degree of specialisation has fallen. The results are given in Tables 6.10 and 6.11.

We also test the stability of the industrial pattern of the technological advantages of countries by conducting a similar test for the revealed patenting advantage of countries (RPA) in order to compare the pattern of stability with that of exports and outward FDI:

$$RPA_{it} = \alpha + \beta RPA_{it-1} + \varepsilon_i.$$

The results are given in Table 6.12. They indicate that the industrial distribution of technological advantages has remained relatively stable for all countries except Australia and, to a lesser extent, Canada. The extent of specialisation has risen for Japan, Germany and the US. In the case of international production, there is a significant correlation between the two periods for Canada, Austria, Australia and the US, although the latter was significant only at the 10% level. For these countries, then, the structural pattern of international production has remained stable over the 1980s. These are the countries that have shown the least amount of growth in their manufacturing outward FDI and exports over the period in question (Table 6.2). The degree of specialisation has risen in the case of the US, Germany, Canada and

Table 6.10 Regression of national firms' share of international production over the 1980s

	α	β	tα	tβ	R
US	11.7083	0.6676	0.6793	2.0769*	0.5310 $\lvert B\rvert > \lvert R\rvert$
Japan	11.5898	0.1044	2.5328**	0.4175	0.1250
Germany	7.7834	0.5716	1.8312*	1.6030	0.4350 $\lvert B\rvert > \lvert R\rvert$
Canada	0.2466	1.1719	0.3554	15.3713***	0.9780 $\lvert B\rvert > \lvert R\rvert$
Austria	0.0784	0.6434	1.8247*	3.2083***	0.6950
Australia	0.5053	1.4109	0.9737	3.0590**	0.6780 $\lvert B\rvert > \lvert R\rvert$

Notes: * Coefficient significantly different from zero at 10% level
** Coefficient significantly different from zero at 5% level
*** Coefficient significantly different from zero at 1% level
$N = 13$

Table 6.11 Regression of national shares of exports over the 1980s

	α	β	tα	tβ	R
US	1.7226	0.8711	0.7548	6.1968***	0.8820
Japan	0.7222	0.9033	0.3939	6.2216***	0.8820 $\lvert B\rvert > \lvert R\rvert$
Germany	2.9375	0.8531	2.0613*	9.5693***	0.9450
Canada	0.9104	0.9384	1.8498*	11.9303***	0.9630
Austria	0.3266	0.9226	2.3357**	12.9564***	0.9690
Australia	0.1847	0.7170	1.2505	8.8692***	0.6780 $\lvert B\rvert > \lvert R\rvert$

Notes: * Coefficient significantly different from zero at 10% level
** Coefficient significantly different from zero at 5% level
*** Coefficient significantly different from zero at 1% level
$N = 13$

Australia, but has fallen in the case of Austria and Japan. With regard to Japan and Germany, we must conclude that there have been significant changes in the industrial distribution of their international production.

The data given in Tables 6.3–6.8 certainly help to confirm this. As one might expect from 'small' countries such as Canada, Australia and Austria, their industrial pattern of specialisation is in fewer sectors than for the 'larger' countries. There has been no significant change in the distribution of their advantages among the industries in which they are specialised.

The changes in Japan's high growth rate of outward direct investment in manufacturing – from 5.74% to 13.51% between 1980 and 1989 (Table 6.2) – and its evolution from stage 3 to stage 4 in the early part of this period has resulted in a substantial structural adjustment of its domestic economy as well as a shift towards higher value added activities of its firms. This is reflected in the decline of its *RCA(I)* in less technology intensive sectors from 1.45 in 1980 to 0.94 in 1989, whereas its *RCA(I)* in more technology intensive sectors has risen from O.91 to 1.07 over the same period. Examining Japan's share of total world

Table 6.12 Regression of the technological advantage of nations over the 1980s: six countries

	α	β	tα	tβ	R
US	−0.0455	1.0040	0.1731	3.6666**	0.7570 |B| > |R|
Japan	0.0372	1.0030	0.1767	5.0089***	0.8460 |B| > |R|
Germany	−0.0276	1.1156	0.1763	8.9206***	0.9430 |B| > |R|
Canada	0.4478	0.5246	1.9271*	2.0196*	0.5380
Austria	0.2671	0.7360	1.3506	3.4485***	0.7370
Australia	0.5324	0.4620	1.9911*	1.3922	0.4030

Notes: * Coefficient significantly different from zero at 10% level
** Coefficient significantly different from zero at 5% level
*** Coefficient significantly different from zero at 1% level
N = 12

manufacturing outward FDI, there has been a considerable increase in its share across both groups of industries. The largest growth has occurred in its share of world outward FDI in motor vehicles,[16] electrical equipment, metals and non-electrical equipment. Although the growth of outward direct investment has not been as great in Germany as in Japan, its share of outward FDI has increased substantially in textiles, rubber and plastics and other transportation equipment.

Part of the growth of the outward FDI from these two economies has been at the expense of the US multinationals, whose share of outward FDI has declined most markedly in paper products, non-electrical equipment, motor vehicles, electrical equipment and non-metallic mineral products. This is associated with the process of convergence – Japan and Germany are the countries which have 'caught up' with the US economically. As the US has slipped back in its share of outward FDI, its firms have lost market share in the industries in which they have traditionally led the way in the internationalisation of production as European and Japanese firms have increasingly become internationalised and more global.

Comparing the stability between *RPA* and international production, it is interesting to note that Japan and Germany have both been relatively stable in their pattern of technological advantage but have had unstable international production. However, the fact that, while the degree of specialisation in technological advantage for both has increased, the extent of specialisation in international production has risen for Germany but fallen for Japan, suggests that these two countries have followed different paths towards internationalisation. This may be explained partly by the benefits Germany accrues from being a core member of the EU; while Japan has had to invest in production facilities in the EU because of barriers to entry to its exports as well as costs arising from psychlogical and economic distance and fears of an imminent 'fortress Europe' (i.e. 'pull' factors[17]), German firms have had to make fewer investments that are import-substituting in nature, at least among European markets, utilising instead their domestic production facilities to supply these markets. This is an advantage that accrues to a lesser extent to Austria, with its close economic ties to Germany.

Australia and Canada, which have been seen to have experienced a narrowing specialisation of international production, are also the countries that have shown instability in their pattern of their *RPA*. This may be associated with their shift away from traditional industries based on natural resources, and towards technology intensive sectors in manufacturing. Indeed, their economies and the structure of their FDI have been seen to be moving away from the primary sector and towards manufacturing and services as their L advantages change, especially in the case of Canada, where the share of the primary sector in total outward and inward investment stock has declined from 9.93% to 6.47%, and 7.52% to 4.76% respectively between 1980 and 1989. Corresponding figures for Australia are from 19.31% to 19.24%, and from 22.25% to 15.05%. As firms that have previously had O advantages in natural-resource-based sectors diversify and develop competitive advantages in other sectors, this will lead to some instability in the industrial distribution of their technological advantages. It will also reflect in their international production – but only to an extent, since these firms will attempt to transfer their production in lower value added activities to countries whose L advantages are more suited to these industries.

In the case of exports, the industrial pattern of all six countries has remained stable over the period in question, and is significant at the 1% level. In the case of Australia and Japan, there has been a narrowing of specialisation, while in Austria, the US, Canada and Germany the industrial pattern of exports has broadened. We have previously hypothesised that the degree of specialisation of national exports should more closely mirror the degree of specialisation of technological advantage than would international production. We would therefore expect that the same countries that have exhibited stability in their industrial distribution patterns of technological advantage will show stability in their manufacturing exports. Comparing Tables 6.11 and 6.12, we find that this is generally true: all countries in our sample except Australia have exhibited stability in both their industrial pattern of exports and technological advantage. Interestingly, Australia's industrial pattern of exports has become more specialised. We also note from Table 6.2 that its share of OECD manufacturing exports has declined over the period in question.

The increasing specialisation of Japan's exports indicates the country's shift away from lower technology intensive sectors, which are relatively labour intensive, as the NIEs have become increasingly competitive in these sectors.

THE SECTORAL PATTERN OF SPECIALISATION OF FIRMS AND COUNTRIES

Hitherto we have examined the stability of the pattern of international production and exports of manufactured goods over the 1980s separately. Here we wish to determine the relationship between national exports and the international production of a country's firms. To what extent is the specialisation of a country's exports reflected in the specialisation of production of its firms in overseas locations? This is tested by means of the following regression:

$$SHODI_{it} = \alpha + \beta SHX_{it} + \varepsilon_i.$$

This test was conducted for both periods, and the results are tabulated in Tables 6.13 and 6.14. In the early 1980s, the international production of countries was positively (and significantly) correlated with the exports of their home country for Germany and Canada, suggesting that firms from these countries engage in outward FDI in the same industries in which their home economies are favoured. The relationship was found to be positive and insignificant in the case of Japan and Austria, while for the US and Australia there was a negative but insignificant relationship. In the case of the US, Japan, Canada and Germany, their MNEs were more specialised than their domestic operations. By the late 1980s the pattern had changed somewhat: Canada and the US were found to have a positive and significant relationship between the sectoral distribution of their international production and their home country exports, although the significance in the case of the US was at the 10% level. Japan, Germany and Austria had a positive but insignificant relationship. Australia continued to show a negative but insignificant relationship between international production and exports. In this period MNEs from all the countries except Austria were found to have a higher extent of specialisation than their domestic counterparts.

The case of the US is surprising in the first instance. The instability of the relationship between the industrial activity of US MNEs and US domestic firms over time suggests that the country's international production activities complemented its exports in 1980 but by 1990 were in similar sectors. Tables 6.10 and 6.11 suggest that the shift in industrial distribution took place in US overseas production and not in domestic production. Given the maturity of US MNEs and their high level of

Table 6.13 Regression of the international production of firms on the national share of exports, 1980

	α	β	$t\alpha$	$t\beta$	R
US	60.2122	−0.6385	5.0146***	−0.8634	0.2520 $\|B\| > \|R\|$
Japan	3.7866	0.5910	0.4746	0.9354	0.2710 $\|B\| > \|R\|$
Germany	−11.3286	1.3275	−2.0133*	3.7713***	0.7510 $\|B\| > \|R\|$
Canada	0.9032	0.9665	0.3398	2.2751**	0.5660 $\|B\| > \|R\|$
Austria	0.0360	0.0352	0.3352	0.6420	0.1900
Australia	0.5763	−0.0580	1.5910	−0.2926	0.0880

Notes: * Coefficient significantly different from zero at 10% level
** Coefficient significantly different from zero at 5% level
*** Coefficient significantly different from zero at 1% level
$N = 13$

Table 6.14 Regression of the international production of firms on the national share of exports, 1989

	α	β	$t\alpha$	$t\beta$	R
USA	20.5337	1.7214	1.5556	2.0915*	0.5330 $\|B\| > \|R\|$
Japan	5.8627	0.6643	0.9422	1.3354	0.3730 $\|B\| > \|R\|$
Germany	1.4298	0.7192	0.1162	0.9659	0.2800 $\|B\| > \|R\|$
Canada	−0.6798	1.3797	−0.2135	2.8831**	0.6560 $\|B\| > \|R\|$
Austria	−0.0016	0.0756	−0.0158	1.5369	0.4200
Australia	1.6100	−0.4088	2.0671*	−0.7761	0.2280 $\|B\| > \|R\|$

Notes: * Coefficient significantly different from zero at 10% level
** Coefficient significantly different from zero at 5% level
*** Coefficient significantly different from zero at 1% level
$N = 13$

internationalisation, it would seem that they have restructured their overseas production in response to the declining L advantages of the US – away from trade supportive and import substituting activities and towards supplying foreign markets through an efficiency seeking and regionally rationalised strategy as well as a means to acquire strategic assets.

This shift in industrial distribution may also have been motivated by the developments in the EU arising from increased economic integration. A recent UN (1993b) study suggests that the increase in investments by US firms resulting from 'EC 1992' came through the restructuring and consolidating of existing EC activities rather than major new investments. The case of Germany illustrates the point that the more internationalised the activity of firms, the more they can specialise in the areas in which they are the strongest (Cantwell 1989). Germany prior to the 1980s was relatively more dependent on exports than it was on outward FDI, compared with economically equivalent countries. However, during the 1980s this pattern began to change (see Table 6.2) as the costs of domestic production rose, forcing German manufacturers to seek foreign production sites. There are to some extent within the EU, as the benefits of integration have made intra-EU investments in rationalised production more viable. However, the largest benefactor of the growth of the outward investment by German firms has been the US, where production costs have been falling relative to those in Germany; as this has happened, the industrial distribution of German outward FDI has become more specialised, and is decreasingly a function of its home-country-specific characteristics. The case of Japan is similar, except that the growth of its outward direct investment predates that of Germany because of restrictions on its exports through voluntary trade restrictions, and hence its firms are at a higher level of internationalisation, explaining the lack of significance during both periods.

The industries in which Canada exports are significantly and positively correlated to those in which its firms engage in international production over both periods. The stability in the case of Canada is a function of the importance of the Canada–US free trade agreement; the US has been (and continues to be) Canada's most significant trading partner, and its importance as a destination of its outward FDI has increased, so this comes as no surprise. Australia, however, does not accrue any special benefits from close economic ties with its large markets, and, although like Canada its competitive advantage is in similar sectors, viz. low technology, mature and resource-based industries, it does not possess privileged access to large markets such as the EU or NAFTA, and is unable to compete with the Asian NIEs since these industries are generally labour intensive, despite its having a relatively higher productivity than these countries. Australia has been unable to make the adjustment towards more technology intensive sectors, partly because of the weakness of its industrial policy and national systems of innovation; although its business R&D expenditures have doubled as a percentage of GDP over this decade, they are still among the lowest of the industrialised countries, closer to that of Spain.

FDI AND EXPORTS: SUBSTITUTES OR COMPLEMENTS?

There is evidence to suggest that MNEs are more trade oriented than their uninational counterparts, and several works have confirmed that outward FDI and exports are complementary, especially in the case of the industrialised (and most internationalised) countries (e.g. Lipsey and Weiss 1981, Swedenborg 1979, 1985, Pearce 1990). However, some of these studies found that in certain industries there is a substitution effect.

The importance of the stage of internationalisation is significant from the perspective of this chapter. At early stages, FDI is made for trade supportive purposes, either as a means to acquire intermediate goods or to service customers, or to overcome barriers to trade, such as import substitution. At a later stage, FDI is a means of structural adjustment; as comparative advantage of the home countries declines owing to rising factor costs, they shift their production to seek lower factor costs elsewhere – this is what Kojima (1990) refers to as 'Japanese trade-oriented FDI'.

Up to this point, trade and outward FDI are substitutes. As firms acquire more advantages in higher value added activities in several locations, their O advantages are a function of several locations, and FDI and trade become increasingly complementary; their FDI activity no longer reflects their home country comparative advantage, and becomes increasingly complementary to their home exports. Essentially, we suggest that it is generally true that, at earlier stages of internationalisation of firms, exports and outward FDI are substitutes and are associated with the country-specific advantages of its home location, but as internationalisation proceeds, and the motives for investment become more complex, investment and exports are decreasingly a function of country-specific advantages, and the relationship between the two may be ambiguous because of the increasing complementary nature of the two. It should be noted that different industries of the same country may be at different stages of internationalisation.

A caveat needs to be noted here. Small countries are likely to engage in overseas production and exports to a greater extent than larger countries, and are more internationalised at an earlier stage of economic development. They are more likely to have a substitution effect, especially if they are involved in scale intensive manufacturing.

To examine the relationship between FDI and trade, we regress the following equation:

$$\Delta SHODI_i = \alpha + \beta(\Delta SHX_i) + \varepsilon_i,$$

where $\Delta SHODI$ is the change in the share of outward FDI over the decade, and ΔSHX is the change in the share of exports over the period. The results are given in Table 6.15. The relationship is positive and significant for Japan and Germany, positive but insignificant for the US and Australia, negative and significant for Austria and negative and insignificant for Canada. The results are puzzling in the case of small countries, but may be due to the specialisation of these countries in fewer sectors, especially in the more technology intensive sectors. From Tables 6.3–6.8 we see that, because of the high specialisation, their share of outward FDI is zero in several industries, and, although their exports share is low, it would nevertheless cause the correlation to be negative

Table 6.15 Correlation of the growth of share of international production and exports over the 1980s: six countries

US	0.3347
Japan	0.5963**
Germany	0.5054*
Canada	−0.4056
Austria	−0.6568**
Australia	0.0389

Notes: * Coefficient significantly different from zero at 10% level
** Coefficient significantly different from zero at 5% level
*** Coefficient significantly different from zero at 1% level

because of the relatively large proportion of these industries. In the case of Canada, if we exclude the sectors in which its outward FDI share is zero in both periods, there is a positive relationship between $\Delta SHODI$ and ΔSHX among the low technology intensive sectors, but a negative relationship in the two more technology intensive sectors in which it has outward investment: Chemicals and Petroleum products. These latter sectors are those in which the US firms possess considerable advantages. In Australia, the positive correlation is extremely weak at 0.039. On an industrial level, it has a positive relationship in only two sectors, both of which are low technology intensive: Food products (exports and outward FDI shares both declining) and Non-metallic mineral products (outward FDI and export shares both rising), while there is a substitution effect between FDI and exports in the others.

Although the observations made here are tentative at best, it would seem that, in industries in which a country's firms are competitive and the home country possesses L advantages, there is a complementary relationship between FDI and exports. This relationship also seems to be stronger among the most industrialised countries. However, what seems clear is that the extent to which its exports are complements or substitutes for FDI depends to a great extent on the advantages of its host countries.

EXPORTS AND FDI: THE RELATIONSHIP TO COUNTRY-SPECIFIC FACTORS

Our analysis up to now has examined the stability, extent of specialisation and interdependence between exports and FDI and the way these have changed for our sample countries over the 1980s. It has also been argued that among industrialised countries the industrial pattern and distribution of outward investment are weakly related to the pattern and distribution of the domestic production. On the other hand, while the pattern and industrial distribution of exports have been seen to be relatively stable to a greater extent than outward FDI, the pattern and distribution of export activities are increasingly influenced by the activities of MNEs, as an increasing proportion of trade is conducted intra-firm. We have mentioned that outward direct investment can either act as a substitute to exports or complement it. The extent to which either occurs depends on the motivation and nature of the FDI, which varies not just with the extent of internationalisation of its firms and the stage of development of the country, but also on the extent of the country-specific advantages of the home country. Clearly, such influences are also industry-specific, since certain industries are more amenable to FDI than others.

In this section we examine the influence of 'endogenous' and 'exogenous' country-specific advantages on the propensity to engage in outward direct investment and export activity. Our dependent variables are *RCA*(*I*) and *RCA*(*X*). The relationship between *RCA*(*X*) and the country advantages is hypothesised to be stronger than for *RCA*(*I*). We do not measure the importance of exogenous country-specific variables directly, but expect that if their influence is significant our selection of countries with varying extents of natural assets will reveal this by the way in which they group themselves.

We test the correlation between *RCA*(*I*) and *RCA*(*X*) against two proxies of country-specific advantages independently, although it is axiomatic that the influence of each of these variables does not explain the variation in the independent variable on its own, given the complexity involved. The propensity to engage in international economic activity is a function of all these factors, and their influence may well be multiplicative. However, once again, the small sample size prevents us from testing all but the most simple hypothesis through single factor correlations. Our two variables, described above, are *RPA* and trade ratio (*TRAT*). These variables are indicative of the L advantages of the country, and are highly associated with the influence of government policy. *RPA* is indicative of the national system of innovation associated with that industry in a particular country, as well as the level of the technological advantages. In other words, it proxies the country-specific created-asset-type O advantages, as well as the extent of location-specific infrastructure for the development of created assets, since *RPA* indicates the output of R&D facilities in an industry. As discussed earlier, it is an imperfect measure, especially since it assumes that all innovative activity is patentable. In the first place, as studies on the appropriation of innovative activity have pointed out,[18] firms may prefer not to patent their innovative output, preferring to rely on secrecy or protection through lead time instead. Second, innovation in low technology sectors may not be patented. Third, *RPA* is a better measure of the output of innovative activity than of the input (Soete 1987, Patel and Pavitt 1992), thereby making it at best a partial indicator of country-specific advantages; however, data on R&D on an industry level are generally unavailable. Fourth, although R&D of MNEs is often concentrated in their home country, with globalisation and regional and global integration, this is already changing. Firms are investing in other locations to acquire assets, and these may be transferred to their home country. Although this is not a widespread or significant practice, the growth of R&D activities by foreign MNEs in the US during the 1980s suggests that it is a potential concern.

We do not predict the sign of the correlation between the *RCA* indices and *RPA* – they may be negative in cases where the MNEs of that country either rely almost entirely on Oa advantages that are derived from their overseas activities, or are dependent on Ot advantages, as may be the case where production is concentrated in the lower technology intensive sector. Further, we do not expect them to be necessarily significant, for five reasons (apart from their biases, which have been discussed above). First, location advantages represent only part of the explanation of the propensity for countries to export or engage in FDI – for a complete explanation, one must include variables that measure the O advantages, as well as the I advantages. Second, we have already pointed out the significance of firm-specific advantages in determining the propensity of firms to engage in outward FDI. Third, these advantages may derive from the country-specific determinants of other countries in which the MNE has operations – the benefits of various other national systems of innovation. Fourth, the propensity to engage in outward FDI is influenced not just by the OLI configuration of the home country, but by the OLI configuration of the host country. Fifth, we have already argued that the Ot advantages of firms play a significant role. Keeping in mind the other reasons, even if these derived from country-specific determinants, they are not measured by the *RPA* index. The correlation of *RCA*(*X*) with *RPA* is expected to be higher than that of *RCA*(*I*) since exporting activities are more closely associated with country-specific advantages, but the correlations are not expected to be significant, given the importance of intra-firm trade.

TRAT is indicative of the general L advantages of the country – when *TRAT* has a high (low) value, it indicates that the country in question has a comparative (dis)advantage in that sector. However, it is also indicative of the effect of government policy on the organisation of domestic economic activity as well as on the openness of the economy to exports and inward direct investment; the ratio may also be high where tariff and non-tariff barriers influence the flow of imports. Obviously, the correlation is expected to be positive and significant with *RCA*(*X*), since *TRAT* is indicative of the location advantages that are particular to export activity. In the case of *RCA(I)*, the correlations are not expected to be significant, since policies and L advantages that affect trade do not necessarily influence outward FDI, and the influence of the organisation of domestic economic activity does not necessarily affect overseas production, except perhaps through its influence on intra-firm trade. It is possible that we have negative correlations between the variables, and we predict that these will conform to those countries for which we had negative correlations in Tables 6.13 and 6.14. Second, depending on the stage of internationalisation, the policies and the OLI characteristics of the host country, exports may either be substitutive or complementary to outward FDI, and this would vary by industry. As such, the extent to which the correlations are positive would depend on the relationship between the country's exports and its outward FDI. We expect that the correlations will mirror those in Tables 6.13 and 6.14. If so, we conclude that *TRAT* is a poor indicator of country-specific determinants of FDI.

The results are given in Table 6.16. In general, the relationship between *RCA(X)* and our locational variables is much stronger than that of *RCA(I)* and the country advantages, confirming our earlier observation.

Since exports and outward FDI are increasingly complementary, we would expect that countries that have a strong positive relationship between exports and outward FDI will have a positive relationship between *RCA(I)* and *TRAT* . The signs of the correlations should be broadly the same as those in Tables 6.13 and 6.14, which identify the countries with a significant positive correlation as Canada and Germany in 1980, and the US and Canada in 1989. This is confirmed by our correlations (Table 6.16). The sign associated with the US has changed over the period, and would suggest that US firms switched from investing overseas in industries for which the locational advantages were low, to investing in industries where the home locational advantages encouraged exports. This switch is in fact due partly to the increased intra-firm exports from the US *because* of its high level of internationalisation, a decline in imports that is due to the growth of inward FDI manufacturing activity, which was encouraged by the improving L advantages of the US relative to its major competitors.[19]

Although the correlation change over the 1980s for Japan was similar, it had different roots. First, Japan's outward investment prior to the 1980s was primarily in sectors where its O advantages were low, as were its exports. Second, Japan strongly discouraged manufactured imports prior to the 1980s, thereby causing the trade ratio in 1980 to be higher than otherwise might be the case. By the end of the decade, not only had imports increased substantially,[20] but Japanese MNEs had become more internationalised and their investments had increasingly rationalised, and

Table 6.16 Correlation of the *RCA*(*I*) and *RCA*(*X*) to indicators of country-specific advantages, 1980 and 1989

	Trade ratio (*TRAT*)		*RPA*	
	1980	*1989*	*1980*	*1989*
RCA(*I*)				
US	−0.1289	0.4326	0.2502	0.1223
Japan	−0.1577	0.2615	0.2663	0.3950
Germany	0.5331*	0.2110	0.3902	0.6381**
Canada	0.8296***	0.8187***	0.7491***	0.5747*
Austria	0.4173	0.3173	−0.0698	−0.0763
Australia	−0.0565	−0.1781	0.1912	0.0829
RCA(*X*)				
US	0.8893***	0.9069***	−0.4951	−0.1663
Japan	0.6318**	0.8912***	0.6431**	0.8289***
Germany	0.8358***	0.8179***	0.5719*	0.7675***
Canada	0.8862***	0.9149***	0.5431*	0.3500
Austria	0.8469***	0.7403***	−0.1196	0.4006
Australia	0.9902***	0.9537***	−0.0188	0.7073*

Notes: * Coefficient significantly different from zero at 10% level
** Coefficient significantly different from zero at 5% level
*** Coefficient significantly different from zero at 1% level

in similar sectors as their O advantages, thereby explaining the change of sign in the correlation.

As expected, the relationship between *RCA*(*X*) and *TRAT* is consistently positive and significant for both periods and all countries. The implication of the greater significance of *RCA*(*X*) than *RCA*(*I*) is relatively obvious, since *TRAT* provides a measure of the extent to which governments encourage the export activity of their firms through various micro and macro policy measures. We also conclude that country-specific determinants affecting exports are different from those influencing outward FDI.

In the case of *RCA*(*I*) and *RPA*, the results in Table 6.16 broadly agree with our expectations – a positive correlation is obtained for all the countries except Austria. The negative figures associated with Austria are due to the higher specialisation of outward FDI in fewer sectors than for other countries – when the correlations are run eliminating the sectors in which *RCA* is zero, a positive relation is found.[21] The fact that they are not significant but are positive for all countries except Canada in 1980 and 1989, and Germany in 1989, suggests several things. First, the competitive advantages of MNEs are not dependent only on the technological advantages associated with their home countries. Second, their competitive strengths derive from Ot advantages. Third, the 'endogenous' country-specific determinants such as national systems of innovation are an important but insufficient explanation for the outward investment activity of firms. It would seem that the technological activity of the home country is a necessary but not sufficient condition for competitive success of firms in exporting and outward FDI. The relationship between *RCA(X)* and *RPA* suggests a similar story.

If country-specific determinants were declining in significance as their MNEs became more internationalised, we would expect the correlation between *RCA(I)* and the independent variables to decline over time. This is not the case – for *RPA*, Japan and Germany have an increase in the correlation coefficient, while for *TRAT*, there is an increase in the correlation coefficient for the US and Japan. We must conclude that the country-specific determinants are becoming more important for some countries, and are declining for others. The groups of countries for which correlations are increasing or decreasing do not correspond to their groupings by market size (i.e. small *v.* large) or resource intensity (i.e. high *v.* low), indicating that 'exogenous' country-specific advantages are unimportant in determining their international production activities. We must conclude, albeit tentatively, given the small sample of countries, that 'endogenous' country-specific determinants such as government are playing an increasing role in determining the international production activities of firms.

Similarly, the correlation of *RCA(X)* and the independent variables is increasing over time – in the case of *TRAT* for all countries except Germany and Austria, and in the case of *RPA* for all countries except Canada. Once again, since this grouping does not reflect those export activities due to 'exogenous' determinants, we conclude that the role of 'endogenous' determinants is becoming increasingly important.

This admittedly simplistic analysis, though very tentative, suggests that 'endogenous' country-specific determinants are more important in influencing the export activities of firms' domestic production activities than their international production activity. The low significance of *RPA* on the dependent variables suggests that created-asset-type advantages of locations are not a sufficient explanation of the O advantages of MNEs or domestic firms. One explanation is that these firms develop their Oa advantages internally, via the acquisition and development of technology through its various overseas subsidiaries, thereby making their O advantages the function of various national systems of innovation. However, if that were the case, then we would expect the correlations to weaken over time, as firms became more internationalised, and the *RCA(X)*–*RPA* relationship to be much stronger than it is. Another explanation is that Oa advantages such as those *RPA* measures do not explain the O advantages on their own, but require the inclusion of firm-specific Ot advantages, which are not measured by *RPA*. However, such a discussion is highly speculative, because neither L advantages nor O advantages on their own explain the propensity to invest, nor are home country OLI characteristics sufficient in themselves to explain outward FDI. What we *can* say is that country-specific differences resulting from 'endogenous' country-specific determinants are playing an increasingly important role; but, although they are a necessary input to explain the propensity to invest overseas, they are not sufficient in themselves to explain outward FDI activity.

SUMMARY AND CONCLUSIONS

Although the results are tentative, this chapter has demonstrated that, while 'exogenous' country-specific determinants, such as size and traditional factor endowments, still influence the pattern of competitive advantages of firms from industrialised countries, their importance is declining, when analysis is restricted to industries that are created-asset-based, such as in the manufacturing sector. On the other hand, the role of 'endogenous' country-specific determinants such as those that are due to the influence of government is becoming more important.

However, an analysis such as the one conducted in this chapter may create more questions than it can answer, partly because of the aggregated nature of the data. We are restricted by the quality of comparable direct investment data across countries. The broad generalisations across the high technology intensive sectors are particularly unsatisfactory.

We have tried, albeit in a simplistic way, to allow for broad differences in the size of countries. Apart from the fact that smaller countries tend to be specialised in a few niche sectors, and have a relatively higher level of international economic activity than large countries, there seems to be little difference between the two groups. It has been noted that their activities tend to be concentrated in lower technology intensive industries, but this may have to do with the fact that the countries in our sample are at an earlier stage of the IDP than the large countries. As the analysis has highlighted, while 'exogenous' country-specific endowments determine the *kind* of created assets associated with a country, the *extent and quality* of created assets depend on the 'endogenous' country-specific determinants.

Over the 1980s, the countries that have converged economically on the US – Japan and Germany – have shown the greatest instability in their industrial distribution of international production, as their outward direct activity has matured. The growth of outward investment from these countries has moved away from a trade-supportive role to a trade-complementary role. Interestingly, the industrial distribution of export activity from all our countries has been shown to have been stable over the period in question, and to have become increasingly specialised. We have also found tentative evidence to suggest that the outward investment of firms from a country is in general in different sectors than national exports, and that their international production is increasingly more specialised than their export activity. However, another finding also reports that the growth of outward FDI is positively associated with the growth of exports, suggesting that exports are complementary to FDI, especially among the most industrialised and fastest-internationalising countries. If we take the last two points together, we may tentatively conclude that there has been increased intra-firm trade, but this may not necessarily be intra-industry, suggesting that exports and outward FDI are complementary in more ways than one.

The weakening relationship between export and international production, and the fact that the sectoral distribution of exports has remained stable while outward FDI has not, both point to the fact that the O advantages of firms from a particular location that engage in international production may not necessarily be the same as those of domestic firms, which by definition are more likely to reflect the home country's comparative advantages, given the fact that the sectoral distribution of technological advantages of these countries have been relatively stable over the decade.

We confirm this by examining the relationship between some country-specific advantages and the revealed comparative advantage of exports and international production, and find that, while the competitive advantage of domestic firms shows a relatively stronger relationship with these variables, the competitive advantage of its MNEs do not. However, the increased significance of intra-firm trade over the decade in question plays a significant role. Although one might expect the relationship between RCA indices and country-specific advantages to decline over time as the level of globalisation increases, this in fact is not the case for all countries. This points to the increasing significance of national systems of innovation and the importance of the organisation of economic activity, both of which are 'endogenous' country-specific advantages, and to a declining role of 'exogenous' country-specific advantages. Although one might be tempted to conclude that country-specific advantages are experiencing a resurgence as determinants of international economic activity, the data presented here are too weak to support such a conclusion. What we can conclude is that country-specific advantages are a necessary but insufficient factor to explain the international economic activities of countries. Also, the L advantages that determine the export activities of firms operating within a country are different from those influencing the international production activities of its firms. The fluctuation of the importance of country-specific determinants seems relatively independent of the extent of the home country's integration into the world economy, suggesting the importance of firm-specific factors in determining the international production activities, and the nature of the motivation of their outward investment.

Although the evidence here is weak, and is based on wide aggregative groupings of industries, taken together, it suggests that MNEs are increasingly relying on firm-specific advantages, and possibly on technological advantages (Ot advantages), rather than on those associated with their domestic, home country operations. Gradually too, as the level of integration rises and firms become increasingly globalised, domestic firms are being drawn away from traditional comparative advantages towards O advantages that are less specific to their location, as a result of growing cross-investments, intra-firm trade and strategic networks.

The differences between country-specific advantages that we have observed on the aggregate level may be minimal, but on a more detailed examination, the contrast may be greater. These contrasts, however small, are to an increasing extent government-induced. The specialisation of small countries in a few niche sectors may be a result of traditional comparative advantages, but their continuing competitiveness in some of these sectors, as well as in some of the high growth, high technology sectors, is not. The extent and nature of their international economic activities are also influenced by government policy and, sometimes, by the lack of it.

An important interaction between the 'endogenous' and 'exogenous' country-specific determinant needs to be highlighted. Market size can be affected through supranational government policy – when government policy is coordinated across countries to achieve economic integration such as the EC or NAFTA agreements, it effectively increases the market available to a country's firms, reducing the economic distance between a group of countries. The choice between exporting and outward FDI depends less on barriers to entry, and more on differences in other L advantages. This has benefited German firms, for example, relative to Japanese firms. Close economic ties that derive from historical trading relationships, often between geographically close countries, achieve this aim – for instance, the relationship between Germany and Austria, or New Zealand and Australia. Such *de facto* and *de jure* integration blurs the relationship between country-specific advantages and the international economic activity. Austria has no domestic motor vehicle industry, but has a growing export market share and technological advantages in this sector; because of its close economic ties with Germany, these advantages have 'spilled over' through inward investment by German firms.

To fully appreciate the nature of the relationship between 'endogenous' country-specific determinants and the international and domestic production activities of its firms, a much deeper analysis of the nature of the influence of government policy on the activities of firms at the micro and macro level needs to be undertaken, especially concerning the role of government in developing national systems of innovation and the organisation of economic activity required for the development of created assets. Further, it is important to include measures of the host country OLI characteristics to allow for the differences that may occur owing to the different motives for investment. This is undertaken to a degree in Chapter 7 for Japan and the US.

7

TRANSPACIFIC FDI: A FORTY-YEAR VIEW OF CHANGING COMPETITIVENESS

INTRODUCTION

The aim of this chapter is to examine and explain the growth and structure of transpacific direct investment (TPDI)[1] between Japan and the US over the past four decades. More specifically, it considers the changing configuration of the ownership, location and internalisation (OLI) variables facing Japanese firms with respect to their value added activities in the US, and those facing US firms with respect to their value added activities in Japan over the period 1945–90. Each stage of IDP brings with it a change in the composition of a country's absolute and comparative advantage (which might itself be modified by the inward and/or outward investment it attracted in a previous stage); and this, in turn, will affect the configuration of its future international investment patterns.

We intend to evaluate the efficacy of our theoretical framework in explaining the post Second World War interaction between US and Japanese MNE activity and the evolution of the direct investment activities of the US and Japan. In doing so, we intend to highlight the role of country-specific determinants in affecting the evolution of their international production activities. By examining the relative FDI positions and OLI configurations of the two countries we also hope to resolve several of the questions posed by previous chapters. To what extent, for example, has US investment in Japan helped to fashion the location-bound competitive advantages of the Japanese economy and/or the more transferable competitive advantages of Japanese firms? How far have changes in the cross-border exchange rates – particularly between the yen and the dollar – and the organisation of transpacific intermediate product markets affected the flow and form of Japanese investment into the US? To what extent have the activities and actions of the US and Japanese governments aided or inhibited the ability of their respective MNEs to compete in global markets and the willingness of foreign MNEs to invest in their countries? These are the kind of question that this chapter seeks to answer. In particular, its objectives are four-fold:

1 to depict how the investment interaction between Japan and the US has changed over time using the concept of the investment development path;
2 to make use of the eclectic paradigm to explain the changing balance of the OLI advantages of US and Japanese MNEs and the US and Japanese economies;
3 to distinguish between natural and created assets as factors affecting the O, L and I variables and their configuration; in particular, this chapter examines the role of government in the innovation and maintenance of created assets, and how this role might change at different stages of the investment development path;
4 to identify the different types of FDI in the context of TPDI over the last forty years; in doing so this chapter highlights the differences between the role of MNE activity in *exploiting* existing firm- or country-specific assets and in *acquiring* new assets.

UNDERLYING DIFFERENCES IN COUNTRY-SPECIFIC ADVANTAGES

We shall confine our attention to the post Second World War period. First, we offer some general observations about the interaction between FDI and the investment development path of Japan and the US, and the underlying reasons for the differences in the character of their direct investment patterns.

Since 1945, Japan has progressed through the first four stages of the investment development path. At the same time, the role of MNE activity in its development path has been quite unique, with outward direct investment from Japan exceeding and growing much faster than inward direct investment for almost the entire period. In the very early stages of the country's post-war development, there were three main reasons for this unusual interaction between MNE activity and the investment development path. The first was Japan's lack of domestic natural resources, which forced Japanese firms to seek access to these in foreign locations – and to do so at least partly by outward direct investment. The second reason was the critical and unique role played by the Japanese government in fostering outward investment, although behind and supporting that role were Japan's distinctive L characteristics, and particularly the need to acquire the resources in which the country was poorly endowed. The third reason was that, in spite of the wholesale devastation caused by the Second World War, Japan was able to retain a relatively sophisticated infrastructure, an educated and well trained workforce, a relatively well developed market structure and a mission oriented, well organised and authoritarian administration. Its previous accumulated experience in industrialisation provided Japanese firms with a valuable base of accumulated technology and well trained manpower (Nakamura 1981). At the same time, the presence of a domestic oligopolistic market structure in the form of well established networks of firms, the *zaibatsu* (which formed the basis of the *keiretsu* after the war), together with a restrictive government policy, discouraged the flow of inward direct investment.

In contrast to the Japanese situation, for the first part of the post-war period the US was in stage 4 of its investment development path, and enjoyed almost total economic and technical hegemony. Furthermore, it possessed two other important country-specific advantages that affected the character of its international investment activity. First, being relatively well endowed in natural resources, it had a less pressing need than Japan to engage in resource seeking FDI. Second, its domestic market size has always acted as a locational attraction to domestic and foreign firms, simultaneously discouraging outward investment and encouraging inward investment. This has meant that its net investment position has been lower on a per capita basis than for other industrial countries. Since the mid 1970s the US has been showing increasingly signs of being in stage 5 of the investment development path; that is to say, its rate of growth has stabilised or has been declining relative to that of its major competitors while its inward investment has grown faster than outward investment.

In the US, for both historical and cultural reasons, government policy has not played a significant role in the changes that have taken place, save for its decisive impact on defence and space activities and sporadic protectionist moves, such as voluntary export restraints and tariffs. In general, its role has been largely limited to macro-economic policy, through bilateral and multilateral negotiations for the removal of trade and investment barriers to its firms and their products, as well as currency devaluations. This contrasts with more activist Japanese macro-organisational intervention.

In the next section, we shall examine the evolution of TPDI in the framework of the investment development path. For each time period we shall first present the prevailing 'pull' factors that have attracted US outward direct investment to Japan as well as the 'push' factors that have led to the expansion of US MNE activity in Japan. This will provide the background for an examination of the evidence on the changes in the OLI variables that are consequent upon these facts. An identical analysis will then be conducted for Japanese outward direct investment in the US over the same period.

THE EVIDENCE[2]

1945–60: Japan's resource dependency: the US economic hegemony

(*i*) *US direct investment in Japan*

Background

Between 1950 and 1960, Japan's GNP per capita grew from $171 to $460. In the first stage of the post-war period, the L advantages of Japan and the O advantages of Japanese firms were insignificant. While Japan had progressed through the first two stages of its investment development path prior to the war, the country was now faced with a massive reconstruction task. Moreover, as a direct result of the war, Japan had been forced to surrender its natural-resource-rich colonies which had earlier supplied a considerable proportion of the raw materials for its domestic industries. Much of the country's plant capacity in light industry (a sector responsible for a substantial proportion of its pre-war export earnings) had been scrapped or destroyed, although its installed capacity in heavy and chemicals industry had increased.[3] Export trade had fallen by over 50% between 1940 and 1950, thereby curtailing severely the country's import earning capacity.

Until 1952, the Japanese post-war economy operated under the general supervision of the allied powers. More particularly, during this time a general economic framework was developed under the Dodge Plan,[4] the purpose of which was to encourage a free market economy not unlike that of the US, and far removed from the pre-war oligopolistic structure that relied heavily on state support. At the same time, to protect Japan's balance of payments position prior to full economic recovery, a Foreign Exchange Control Law was passed in 1949 which provided a mechanism to limit imports.[5] Inward investment, though generally welcomed, was also to be restricted so as not to inhibit the development of indigenous assets. Thus, the Foreign Investment Law of 1950 was used to limit foreign equity participation to those ventures 'which will contribute to the self support and sound development of the Japanese economy and to the improvements of the international balance of payments'.[6]

After full independence in 1952, an important change in Japanese economic policy occurred. Many of the laws and policies introduced in the previous seven years were re-interpreted so as to give more protection to indigenous firms. In preference to acquiring foreign technology via inbound direct investment, local firms were encouraged to engage in cross-border contractual agreements such as technology agreements to obtain new technology and management skills. Yoshida (1987) suggests that the foreign exchange controls provided the Ministry of International Trade and Industry (MITI) with the leverage it needed to influence the strategy and actions of Japanese firms. By restricting manufacturing imports, Japan's infant industries were guaranteed a domestic market and sufficient breathing space to upgrade their competitive assets *vis-à-vis* foreign firms. A similar situation existed in the resource intensive sectors such as the oil industry, where domestic firms were granted preferential treatment over joint ventures in obtaining import allocations. Where FDI was allowed, majority ownership and control was discouraged, except where it was impossible to obtain critical technology by other means. Foreign loans were generally preferred to equity investments. In 1956, equity acquisition by foreign firms in yen was allowed only if the investing firms were prepared to forgo the explicit right to remit profits and capital.[7]

Another important change to the pre-independence economic policy was the 1953 revision of the anti-monopoly law which authorised cartels and sanctioned retail price maintenance. The exclusion of foreign firms in these cartels effectively discriminated in favour of their domestic competitors. During this period, domestic industrial policy was directed to developing its post-war competence in light manufacturing sectors, as well as encouraging import substitution.

Thus, the policies designed to promote the O advantages of Japanese firms, while inhibiting foreign firms from exploiting their O advantages in Japan, resulted in subdued FDI inflows.

The considerable technological capabilities of US firms coupled with rising domestic production costs led to a rapid growth of US outbound direct investment in the post-war period. By the 1950s, domestic real wage costs were rising and there was a real shortage of US currency throughout the world. As a consequence, to service their foreign markets, US firms increasingly had to manufacture in foreign locations. One indication of this trend was that the US share of world exports accounted for by US firms fell between 1948 and 1960 from 23.9% to 17.2%, while the share of global outward direct investment accounted for by US MNEs between 1938 and 1960 increased from 27.7% to 48.3%. However, investment by US firms in Japan was limited despite their having absolute competitive advantages in most industrial activities.

The evidence

As might be expected of a country in the first stage of its investment development path, and whose government restricted inward investment, there was comparatively little US MNE activity in Japan prior to 1960. As Table 7.1 indicates, in 1950, when the first post-war census of US overseas assets was carried out, US direct investment in Japan was $19

Table 7.1 Growth of the US direct investment stake in Japan, 1950–90

	Total investment				*Manufacturing investment*			
	(1) *US$ (m)*	*(2)* *Annual increase (%)*	*(3)* *(1) as % of all US FDI*	*(4)* *(1) as % of GDP*	*(5)* *US$ (m)*	*(6)* *Annual increase (%)*	*(7)* *(5) as % of (1)*	*(8)* *(5) as % of GDP*
1950	19	—	0.16	0.134	5	—	26.32	0.035
1951	48	152.63	0.37	0.294	9	80.00	18.75	0.055
1952	75	56.25	0.51	0.434	13	44.44	17.33	0.075
1953	101	34.67	0.62	0.518	17	30.77	16.83	0.087
1954	112	10.89	0.64	0.517	22	29.41	19.64	0.102
1955	129	15.18	0.67	0.540	28	27.27	21.71	0.117
1956	140	8.53	0.62	0.519	35	25.00	25.00	0.130
1957	185	32.14	0.73	0.601	58	65.71	31.35	0.189
1958	181	−2.16	0.66	0.566	63	8.62	34.81	0.197
1959	209	15.47	0.70	0.582	69	9.52	33.01	0.192
1960	254	21.53	0.80	0.590	91	31.88	35.83	0.211
1961	302	18.90	0.87	0.567	103	13.19	34.11	0.194
1962	373	23.51	1.00	0.633	122	18.45	32.71	0.207
1963	472	26.54	1.16	0.695	145	18.85	30.72	0.214
1964	599	26.91	1.35	0.747	208	43.45	34.72	0.259
1965	676	12.85	1.37	0.746	276	32.69	40.83	0.305
1966	731	8.14	1.41	0.697	366	32.61	50.07	0.349
1967	834	14.09	1.47	0.678	442	20.77	53.00	0.359
1968	1,005	20.50	1.62	0.686	527	19.23	52.44	0.360
1969	1,226	21.99	1.80	0.707	645	22.39	52.61	0.372
1970	1,482	20.88	1.96	0.724	768	19.07	51.82	0.375
1971	1,913	29.08	2.31	0.825	978	27.34	51.12	0.422
1972	2,323	21.43	2.58	0.763	1,185	21.17	51.01	0.389
1973	2,671	14.98	2.64	0.646	1,399	18.06	52.38	0.338
1974	3,319	24.26	3.02	0.723	1,520	8.65	45.80	0.331
1975	3,339	0.60	2.69	0.669	1,557	2.43	46.63	0.312
1976	3,797	13.72	2.78	0.679	1,691	8.61	44.54	0.302
1977	4,593	20.96	3.15	0.669	1,968	16.38	42.85	0.286
1978	4,963	8.06	2.96	0.515	2,317	17.73	46.69	0.241
1979	6,208	25.09	3.32	0.622	2,728	17.74	43.94	0.273
1980	6,243	0.56	2.90	0.600	2,971	8.91	47.59	0.286
1981	6,755	8.20	2.98	0.579	3,236	8.92	47.91	0.277
1982	6,636	−1.76	3.20	0.613	3,232	−0.12	48.70	0.299
1983	7,661	15.45	3.70	0.649	3,915	21.13	51.10	0.332
1984	7,936	3.59	3.75	0.633	3,942	0.69	49.67	0.314
1985	9,235	16.37	4.01	0.696	4,584	16.29	49.64	0.346
1986	11,472	24.22	4.42	0.586	5,439	18.65	47.41	0.278
1987	14,671	27.89	4.67	0.617	8,107	49.05	55.26	0.341
1988	18,009	22.75	5.36	0.633	8,929	10.14	49.58	0.314
1989	18,488	2.66	5.00	0.652	9,721	8.87	52.58	0.343
1990	20,994	13.55	4.98	0.729	10,623	9.28	50.60	0.369

Source: US Department of Commerce, *Survey of Current Business*, various years

million or 0.16% of its total worldwide stake. The corresponding figures for manufacturing industry alone were $5 million and 0.13%. The comparative percentage figures of the US stake in West Germany, another war-ravaged nation, were 1.7% and 3.2% respectively.

By 1960, US direct investment in Japan had risen to $254 million or 0.80% of the total worldwide stake. The corresponding figures for manufacturing industry were $91 million and 0.76%, but much of this increase (35% of the increase in total investments) occurred in the period 1950–53, before the structural impediments to inward direct investment were introduced.[8] However, despite the introduction of restrictions on inward direct investment, US manufacturing investments continued to grow at a faster rate than investment in other sectors. Allowing for the case-by-case screening of inward direct investment, this would suggest first that the US manufacturing firms possessed O advantages not available to Japanese firms and therefore that the Japanese firms were unlikely to be able to compete directly with them; and second that the Japanese authorities considered such inward direct investment necessary for the development of the Japanese economy. Between 1952 and 1960, manufacturing as a percentage of the total US stake in Japan increased from 17.3% to 35.8%.

Table 7.1 further shows that the total US direct investment stock as a percentage of the GDP of Japan grew between 1953 and 1960 from 0.52% to 0.59%, whereas that of manufacturing investment rose from 0.09% to 0.21%. This latter figure would suggest that the competitive position of at least some US manufacturing firms improved over this period, although, over the same time, US exports as a percentage of Japanese GDP fell from 3.5% to 1.3%. The improvement in L advantages of supplying goods from a Japanese location is illustrated by the fact that, while US exports grew by a factor of 2, US direct investment in Japan grew by a factor of 3.4.

It is not difficult to imagine that, had Japanese government policy remained as it was before 1953, the US capital stake would have risen much faster. For example, the percentages of US capital stake in Germany for 1952 and 1960 are 0.73% and 3.1%; corresponding ratios for Japan are 0.43% and 0.79% respectively.

The subdued participation of US MNE's in the growth of the Japanese economy compared with that of its war-time ally Germany was due not so much to the natural L disadvantages of Japan, but to the country-specific controls that prevented US firms from exploiting their O advantages through hierarchies rather than markets. Government policy curtailed inward direct investment as a mode of inbound technology transfer, and encouraged in its stead non-equity participation such as licensing and technology agreements.

While the role of US firms was constrained, the presence of US firms was not insubstantial relative to that of other foreign firms. Of the 88 foreign controlled subsidiaries operating in Japan in December 1954, 63 were US owned. The increasing importance of all non-equity technological agreements relative to FDI can be gauged from the ratio of foreign direct investment stock to capitalised value of technology agreements, which in 1953 was 0.15; in 1954 this ratio had dropped to 0.13.[9] The corresponding ratios for technology agreements signed with US firms to US FDI stock decreased from 0.81 to 0.62. In 1954, of the 431 technological assistance contracts with foreign firms, 307 were with US firms; in terms of their capitalised value, they accounted for 62.1% of all technology agreements. Therefore, while the importance of the US as a source of technological capability is in no doubt, it is also clear that US firms possessing these advantages could not fully exploit them through FDI in Japan because of restrictions imposed by the Japanese government.

(*ii*) *Japanese direct investment in the US*

Background

In terms of the investment development path, the US was already at stage 4 – its outward investment flows exceeded its inward investment flows. Its GNP per capita was $1890 in 1950 and $2830 in 1960. At the end of the Second World War, the US was at the height of its technological and economic supremacy. Indeed, it was one of the only developed countries to survive with its industrial base not only intact, but strengthened. Its firms found themselves, not unsurprisingly, in the enviable position of having a competitive advantage in almost all industrial activities.

At the same time, given the relatively high cost of labour intensive manufacturing, the US was not an attractive location for direct investment by firms from developing countries, including Japan. Even though the US was well endowed with natural resources, the L advantages of the US for labour intensive investment (including resource seeking investments) were low, despite the fact that there were no restrictions on inward direct investment in the US. The affluence of the US market made it an attractive location for exports from foreign countries, and much of the FDI in the US was at this time in trade supportive activities.

As with inward investment, outward direct investment by Japanese firms was controlled by the Japanese government. The Foreign Exchange Control Law of 1949 laid down the guidelines and was implemented by a case-by-case screening. According to Ozawa (1989), the guidelines used for approving such investment were that it should be export supporting, or directed to securing natural resources vital to the Japanese economy. Moreover, it was required that the outcome of outbound FDI not be detrimental to the competitive position of Japanese firms in Japan; nor must it adversely affect domestic monetary policy. In other words, outward direct investment activity was intended to be supportive rather than complementary to the interests of domestic production. However, when it was approved, it was often protected by investment guarantee schemes through the Export–Import Bank of Japan, which had been set up in order to provide loans to overseas investors and to promote exports.

In these years, Japan's domestic economic development was geared towards re-establishing its competitive advantages in labour intensive, light manufacturing industries; indeed, these accounted for the bulk of its exports during this period, which grew substantially between 1950 and 1960 as Japan's share of total world exports increased from 1.5% to 3.6%. None the less, the government-induced O advantages of Japanese firms in manufacturing were largely of a location-specific kind, and they were generally insufficient to exploit through outward direct investment in developed countries such as the US. Much of the outward direct investment of Japanese firms in the 1950s was in other developing countries, especially Latin America, and was either resource seeking or, where large protected markets existed,[10] market seeking in nature.

The evidence

At the beginning of the period, Japan had negligible investments overseas, and none in the US. Table 7.2 shows that by 1959 Japanese direct investment in the US stood at $80 million,[11] which represented 0.016% of US GDP. This stake was entirely in non-manufacturing sectors such as financial services (20%) and trade (80%).[12] Its exports to the US as a percentage of its total exports increased from 2.2% in 1950 to 27.2% in 1960. This confirms that Japanese firms had begun to develop their own O-specific assets, although these were still much lower than those of US firms. Where O advantages existed, they were better exploited by exports than by FDI owing to the L disadvantages of producing in the US.

1960–72: The rapid growth of Japan: the US loses some of its hegemony

(*i*) *US direct investment in Japan*

Background

The years between 1961 and 1970 were the era of the National Income Doubling Plan.[13] During the duration of this plan, real GNP in Japan grew by 10.7% against a planned growth rate of 7.7%. The corresponding GNP growth rates for Germany and the US were 4.6% and 3.9%. By 1970, Japan had a GNP per capita in current dollars of $2593, 56% of that of the US and 61% of that of West Germany, although the total value of Japan's GNP was second only to that of the US.

For most of this second period, inward FDI continued to be restricted, and, with the exception of yen-based investments,[14] was subject to a case-by-case screening. However, the latter mode was not popular among foreign firms because such investments could be used only to buy new issues of stock; nor could the remittances of dividends be guaranteed. Nevertheless, these yen-based firms accounted for two-thirds of all majority owned subsidiaries established through 1963, when this form of inward direct investment was discontinued. However, beginning in 1967, and in response to international pressures,[15] the Japanese began

Table 7.2 Growth of Japanese direct investment stake in the US, 1950–90

	Total investment				*Manufacturing investment*			
	(1) US$ (*m*)	*(2)* *Annual increase* (%)	*(3)* *(1) as % of all US FDI*	*(4)* *(1) as % of GDP*	*(5)* US$ (*m*)	*(6)* *Annual increase* (%)	*(7)* *(5) as % of (1)*	*(8)* *(5) as a % of GDP*
1950	n.a.	n.a.	n.a.	n.a.	n.a.	n.a.	n.a.	n.a.
1958	n.a.	n.a.	n.a.	n.a.	n.a.	n.a.	n.a.	n.a.
1959	80	n.a.	1.21	0.016	n.a.	n.a.	n.a.	n.a.
1960	88	10.00	1.27	0.017	50	n.a.	56.82	0.010
1961	92	4.55	1.24	0.018	51	2.00	55.43	0.010
1962	112	21.74	1.47	0.020	51	0.00	45.54	0.009
1963	104	−7.14	1.31	0.017	55	7.84	52.88	0.009
1964	72	−30.77	0.86	0.011	54	−1.82	75.00	0.008
1965	118	63.89	1.34	0.017	56	3.70	47.46	0.008
1966	103	−12.71	1.14	0.014	60	7.14	58.25	0.008
1967	108	4.85	1.09	0.014	64	6.67	59.26	0.008
1968	181	67.59	1.67	0.021	65	1.56	35.91	0.007
1969	176	−2.76	1.49	0.019	67	3.08	38.07	0.007
1970	229	30.11	1.73	0.023	70	4.48	30.57	0.007
1971	−227	−199.13	−1.63	−0.021	76	8.57	−33.48	0.007
1972	−154	−32.16	−1.04	−0.013	72	−5.26	−46.75	0.006
1973	152	−198.70	0.74	0.012	141	95.83	92.76	0.011
1974	345	126.97	1.37	0.024	330	134.04	95.65	0.023
1975	591	71.30	2.14	0.038	325	−1.52	54.99	0.021
1976	1,178	99.32	3.83	0.069	304	−6.46	25.81	0.018
1977	1,755	48.98	5.07	0.092	332	9.21	18.92	0.017
1978	2,749	56.64	6.73	0.129	474	42.77	17.24	0.022
1979	3,493	27.06	6.41	0.147	696	46.84	19.93	0.029
1980	4,723	35.21	5.69	0.183	1,033	48.42	21.87	0.040
1981	7,697	62.97	7.08	0.257	1,321	27.88	17.16	0.044
1982	9,677	25.72	7.76	0.311	1,624	22.94	16.78	0.052
1983	11,336	17.14	8.27	0.338	1,605	−1.17	14.16	0.048
1984	16,044	41.53	9.75	0.431	2,460	53.27	15.33	0.066
1985	19,313	20.38	10.46	0.487	2,738	11.30	14.18	0.069
1986	26,824	38.89	12.17	0.640	3,578	30.68	13.34	0.085
1987	35,151	31.04	13.35	0.786	5,345	49.39	15.21	0.119
1988	51,126	45.45	16.24	1.065	11,065	107.02	21.64	0.231
1989	67,319	31.67	18.01	1.304	13,978	26.33	20.76	0.271
1990	83,498	24.03	20.68	1.515	15,169	8.52	18.17	0.275

Source: US Department of Commerce, *Survey of Current Business*, various years

the first of a series of liberalisation rounds which permitted majority foreign ownership of firms in selected sectors. Two groups of industries were identified, one in which 100% foreign participation was to be allowed, and the other in which it was to be restricted to 50%. By the time the fourth round of liberalisation took place in August 1971, seventy-seven sectors had been cleared for 100% foreign participation, and all but seven sectors were open to 50% foreign ownership. This gradual and stepwise removal of regulations was timed to coincide with the perceived improved competitiveness of the Japanese economy in the same sectors (Buckley *et al.* 1987). Minority ownership and joint ventures continued to be granted automatic approval. However, foreign acquisitions of Japanese firms were still restricted and required a case-by-case screening if they involved an equity stake greater than 10%. Not surprisingly, there was no large rush of inward MNE activity. The use of technology agreements remained the most important form of foreign involvement, and was further facilitated by the automatic approval of technology contracts of values not exceeding $50,000.

Japan's industrial policy during this stage shifted towards the development of its heavy manufacturing industries, especially chemicals and machinery, and away from metals and light manufactures. Although wage rates rose more quickly in Japan than in the US (163.0% compared with 28.7% between 1965 and 1970), labour productivity grew by 68.3% compared with 10.8% in the US. Over the same period,[16] unit costs in Japan remained highly competitive. The competitiveness of Japanese industry was also helped by the government pegging the yen at ¥360 to the US dollar. As such, Japanese L advantages were superior to those of the US in labour intensive manufacturing, but government policy continued to prevent US firms from exploiting their O advantages through direct investment.

The evidence

Table 7.1 sets out details of the growth of US direct investment in Japan. In 1961 this was $302 million, of which $103 million or 34.1% was in manufacturing. By 1972 it had risen to $2.3 billion, of which $1.2 billion or 51.0% was in manufacturing. This represented an annual average rate of growth of 55.8% in all sectors and 87.5% in manufacturing. The corresponding growth rates of the US capital stake over the same period in Germany were 36.6% and 34.9%. In 1961 the investment by US firms in Japan represented 0.9% of the total US direct investment stake, but by 1972 this had almost tripled to 2.6%. During the same period, the percentage of cumulative US direct investment stake in Germany doubled from 3.4% to 6.6%.

At the same time, the competitive advantages of U.S firms continued to earn them attractive profits. While comparable data are not available prior to 1967, the average rate of return on US investments in manufacturing for the period 1967–72 was about 21%, whereas the average rate of return for all US foreign direct investment in manufacturing for the same period averaged 15%.[17] This would suggest that, despite the restrictive policies of the Japanese government, Japan remained quite an attractive location to US MNEs.

Though limited,[18] data on a sectoral distribution of the US stake in Japanese manufacturing suggest that growth was not uniform across sectors. It was greatest in chemicals and machinery, and least in sectors such as metals, food and transportation. Interestingly, the revealed trading advantages of Japanese firms had grown during this period in chemicals and machinery, and declined in metals, food and light manufactures. This suggests that the O advantages of US firms were sufficiently superior to those of its Japanese competitors in at least some of the subsectors within these industries.

Table 7.1 also gives details of the rising importance of the US direct investment stake in the Japanese economy. During this period, the US stake in manufacturing as a percentage of Japanese GDP grew from 0.19% to 0.42%. These data confirm the superior O advantages of US affiliates over their domestic rivals or at least reveal that their activities were concentrated in the fastest growing sectors in the Japanese economy.

The extent to which local production by US firms replaced exports of US firms to Japan over this period provides us with an indication of the changing L advantages of Japan. Sales data of US affiliates in Japan are unavailable before 1966, but between 1967 and 1972 they increased by over three times, while imports from the US increased by a factor of 3.5. Table 7.3 presents a breakdown of the sales of US manufacturing affiliates in Japan, exports from the US and the ratio of the two broken down by industry. This ratio is seen to increase substantially over the period 1967–72 in the chemicals and non-electrical machinery industries. Moreover, while the sales of US affiliates in the electrical machinery industry also rose, exports from the US posted an even greater increase, from $23.1 million to $228 million. At least some of the increase in exports represent intra-firm exports due to the presence of US MNEs, and to the extent that this is the case, it is an indicator of their rising I advantages. However, such data, as well as those on the relative importance of technology agreements compared with FDI, another indicator of I advantages, are not available for this period.

This evidence would suggest that, whereas in the 1960s US MNEs possessed considerable O advantages over Japanese firms, the L and I advantages of Japan as a manufacturing base for US firms prevented these from being exploited through direct investment.

(ii) Japanese direct investment in the US

Background

While for much of the period, and in most sectors, the competitive prowess of US firms remained unsurpassed, Japanese firms were beginning to make inroads into US markets by the late 1960s. With a GNP per capita of $7115 in 1972, compared with $4570 for Japan, the US remained the most lucrative outlet for manufactured goods, and was therefore the objective of Japanese firms' export oriented strategy. Beginning in 1965, Japan's merchandise trade surplus with the US began to grow.

The US market was served primarily through exports from Japan, given the relatively high wage rates in the US,[19] and Japanese exports grew especially quickly in sectors in which they had a comparative advantage. Outbound MNE activity was mainly directed towards developing countries, especially in Asia. Capital exports continued to be discouraged by the Bank of Japan until 1969, when automatic approval

Table 7.3 Sales of US manufacturing affiliates in Japan and US exports to Japan, 1967–89

	All industries			*Total mfg*			*Food & kindred*			*Chemicals*			*Metals*			*Machinery except elect.*			*Electrical machinery*			*Transportation eqpt*		
	(A) Sales ($m)	(B) Exports ($m)	A/B	(A) Sales ($m)	(B) Exports ($m)	A/B	(A) Sales ($m)	(B) Exports ($m)	A/B	(A) Sales ($m)	(B) Exports ($m)	A/B	(A) Sales ($m)	(B) Exports ($m)	A/B	(A) Sales ($m)	(B) Exports ($m)	A/B	(A) Sales ($m)	(B) Exports ($m)	A/B	(A) Sales ($m)	(B) Exports ($m)	A/B
1967	2,520	2,635	0.96	944	771	1.22	63	487	0.13	357	227	1.57	1	86	0.01	395	305	1.30	52	23	2.25	2	89	0.02
1972	6,727	4,928	1.37	2,516	1,909	1.32	90	799	0.11	807	314	2.57	NSA	126	—	1,185	575	2.06	147	228	0.64	20	447	0.04
1977	13,232	10,419	1.27	3,132	2,757	1.14	NSA	2,516	—	725	975	0.74	58	153	0.38	1,532	855	1.79	163	453	0.36	3	371	0.01
1982	25,788	20,367	1.27	5,880	13,279	0.44	648	3,938	0.16	1,659	2,556	0.65	108	782	0.14	2,300	1,055	2.18	536	1,595	0.34	4	1,067	0.00
1985	28,018	21,603	1.30	10,011	15,148	0.66	NSA	4,394	—	2,318	2,849	0.81	165	624	0.26	NSA	1,440	—	991	2,348	0.42	NSA	1,713	—
1986	34,378	22,891	1.50	13,518	16,548	0.82	NSA	4,463	—	3,339	3,047	1.10	244	576	0.42	NSA	1,448	—	1,347	2,631	0.51	NSA	2,135	—
1987	42,416	26,906	1.58	17,268	19,370	0.89	NSA	5,484	—	4,282	3,366	1.27	291	774	0.38	NSA	1,468	—	1,747	3,316	0.53	NSA	2,283	—
1988	53,382	36,048	1.48	21,525	26,673	0.81	NSA	6,814	—	4,489	3,934	1.14	272	1,400	0.19	NSA	2,254	—	2,302	4,657	0.49	NSA	2,911	—
1989	58,083	42,752	1.36	22,434	32,067	0.70	1,809	7,447	0.24	4,130	4,664	0.89	312	2,044	0.15	NSA	2,693	—	2,681	5,775	0.46	146	2,993	0.05

Source: US Department of Commerce, *Survey of Current Business*, various years, and UN *Commodity Trade Statistics*, various years

was granted, initially to finance small (less than $200,000) projects. By 1971, however, the ceiling on automatic approvals was eliminated. This was prompted both by the growing current account surpluses, and by trade disputes with the US, which led to voluntary export restraints (VERs) in steel and synthetic textiles towards the end of the period.

In the early part of the period, Japanese *sogo sosha* were responsible for most of the trade supportive FDI (sales outlets, service facilities) in the US, as they strove to promote Japan's manufactured exports, as well as to secure vital imports such as capital goods, foodstuffs, coal, lumber and pulp. Exports had shifted in this period from light industrial production (such as textiles, sporting goods, toys) to a more diversified pattern, with technology-based exports such as motor cycles, cameras and cars becoming increasingly important (Ozawa 1979). The restructuring of exports was accompanied by a change in the ownership of, and motivation for, some of the newer FDI. For example, independently of the trading companies, some technology-based Japanese firms began to set up foreign facilities to acquire or strengthen their domestic O advantages, as well as to seek low cost inputs (such as industrial chemicals and soybeans).[20] None the less, such strategic asset seeking investments were the exception rather than the rule; for example, according to Yoshida (1987), only twenty-two Japanese manufacturing affiliates were established in the US before 1971.

The evidence

As Table 7.2 shows, total Japanese direct investment in the US in 1961 was only $92 million, of which $51 million was in manufacturing. While comparable figures are not available,[21] it is estimated that this accounted for about a third of total Japanese outward direct investment. In the years that followed, Japan's FDI was directed mainly towards Asia and Latin America. These two areas alone accounted for more than two-thirds of FDI outflows from Japan (Takeuchi 1990). While investments in Latin America were of a market seeking kind designed to overcome import restrictions, those directed to East Asian countries were more export oriented.[22] By 1970, the total stock of Japanese direct investment in the US was only about a quarter of total Japanese stock of FDI worldwide, valued at $229 million, of which $70 million was in manufacturing. Over the previous decade, the annual average rate of growth of such investment had been 16.5% overall and 4.1% in manufacturing.

Therefore the relative importance of the US as a location for outward direct investment had diminished over this period. But the state of Japanese O advantages relative to those of its indigenous competitors in the US market can be ascertained from the following facts:

1 The Japanese direct investment stake in manufacturing as a percentage of total FDI in the US actually *decreased* during this period from 1.85% to just under 1%.
2 While no data are available for sales of Japanese affiliates in the US during this period, the ratio of the cumulative investment stake of Japanese firms in the US to US GDP also decreased over this period, from 0.010% in 1961 to 0.006% in 1972.
3 At the same time, as Table 7.4 shows, the ratio of US manufacturing investments in Japan to Japanese manufacturing investments in the US increased, from 2.02 in 1961 to a peak of 16.5 in 1972. This point is underlined by the fact that both the total FDI by US MNEs and the total inward direct investment into the US rose between 1967 and 1973, although the ratio between the two decreased from 5.7 to 4.9.
4 Japanese exports to the US grew eight-fold between 1960 and 1972, while as a percentage of US GDP they increased from 2.5% to 2.9% during this interval.

These data clearly suggest that the Japanese competitive position with respect to its rivals was weak during the 1960s, and that in general the US economy was outpacing the growth of these Japanese affiliates.

Moreover, it would seem that any O advantages possessed by Japanese firms *vis-à-vis* their foreign competitors were more likely to be exploited through exports than by FDI. But in what industries were these competitive advantages developing? Taking the share of particular sectors in total exports provides us with some clues. For example, the share of textiles as a percentage of total Japanese exports dropped from its 1955 peak of 37.3% to 9% in 1970. The share of steel also fell, from its peak of 34.2% in 1960 to 14.7% in 1970.[23] By contrast, Japanese exports to the US grew rapidly in transportation equipment and fabricated metals, followed by chemicals and non-electrical machinery. Taking a revealed comparative advantage (RCA) index based on a ratio of total exports to total imports, the RCA index of the Japanese food and metals industry fell respectively from 0.47 and 6.98 in 1962 to 0.19 and 3.87 in 1972. By contrast, the ratio increased for machinery, transportation and chemical sectors.

Data on trade in technology are sparse. However, Japanese figures for 1974 suggest that the ratio of royalty and licensing fees paid to Japanese firms by foreigners to those received from Japanese firms on a worldwide basis was 0.35. Taking the same ratio for technology payments to and receipts from North America over the same period, the figure is 0.06. North America accounted for 66.9% of the total flows payments and 12% of the receipts (Sekiguchi 1979).

Table 7.4 Ratio of US direct investment stake in Japan to Japanese investment in the US, 1950–90

	Total investment		*Manufacturing investment*	
	Inward (*I*)	*Outward* (O)(*I*)/(*O*)	*Inward* (*I*)	*Outward* (*O*)(*I*)/(*O*)
1950	19	n.a.n.a.	5	n.a.n.a.
1958	181	n.a.n.a.	63	n.a.n.a.
1959	209	802.61	69	n.a.n.a.
1960	254	882.89	91	501.82
1961	302	923.28	103	512.02
1962	373	1123.33	122	512.39
1963	472	1044.54	145	552.64
1964	599	728.32	208	543.85
1965	676	1185.73	276	564.93
1966	731	1037.10	366	606.10
1967	834	1087.72	442	646.91
1968	1,005	1815.55	527	658.11
1969	1,226	1766.97	645	679.63
1970	1,482	2296.47	768	7010.97
1971	1,913	− 227n.a.	978	7612.87
1972	2,323	− 154n.a.	1,185	7216.46
1973	2,671	15217.57	1,399	1419.92
1974	3,319	3459.62	1,520	3304.61
1975	3,339	5915.65	1,557	3254.79
1976	3,797	1,1783.22	1,691	3045.56
1977	4,593	1,7552.62	1,968	3325.93
1978	4,963	2,7491.81	2,317	4744.89
1979	6,208	3,4931.78	2,728	6963.92
1980	6,243	4,7231.32	2,971	1,0332.88
1981	6,755	7,6970.88	3,236	1,3212.45
1982	6,636	9,6770.69	3,232	1,6241.99
1983	7,661	11,3360.68	3,915	1,6052.44
1984	7,936	16,0440.49	3,942	2,4601.60
1985	9,235	19,3130.48	4,584	2,7381.67
1986	11,472	26,8240.43	5,439	3,5781.52
1987	15,664	35,1510.45	8,107	5,3451.52
1988	18,009	51,1260.35	8,929	11,0650.81
1989	18,488	67,3190.27	9,721	13,9780.70
1990	20,994	83,4980.25	10,623	15,1690.70

Source: US Department of Commerce, *Survey of Current Business*, various years

1973–82: Elementary Japanese multinationalism: declining US competitive advantages

(i) US direct investment in Japan

Background

The period between 1972 and 1982 marked Japan's passage through the third stage of its investment development path. There was a gradual decrease in the rate of growth of inward direct investment to Japan as domestic firms began to compete successfully with MNEs from countries further along the development path.

During stage 3, the growth in GNP experienced by Japan in the second stage of the investment development path decelerated, although it still remained higher than that of the US or Germany; the average growth rates for 1973–82 were 4.5% for Japan,[24] 2.8% for Germany and 2.9% for the US. The GNP per capita for Japan and the US grew from $3230 and $6410 in 1973 to $10,280 and $13,620 in 1982.

There were various changes in the attractions of Japan as a manufacturing base during this period. These were brought about mainly by the restructuring of resource allocation in the Japanese economy and a series of exogenous events, which resulted in a change in the status of Japan as a host country.

The two most important exogenous events of the 1970s were the devaluation and floating of the dollar and the oil crisis. The first was responsible for the sharp rise in the value of the yen to ¥308/$1 at the end of 1971, from ¥360/$1 where it had been pegged for the post-war period. This was followed by the floating of the yen in 1973. The net result of these events was an appreciation of the yen against the dollar of about 35% by the summer of 1973(Ozawa 1979: 16). This further increased the cost of manufacturing in Japan. The yen continued to appreciate until October 1978, when it reached ¥170/$1. This represented an appreciation of about 40% from its January 1977 value. After this, the dollar strengthened *vis-à-vis* the yen for the rest of this period.[25]

Simultaneously with the rise in the yen, the Japanese government embarked on a programme of R&D and education and training which was intended to provide its industries with the necessary human and physical capabilities to upgrade their value added activities. At the same time, as the L advantages of Japanese resources and the O advantages of Japanese firms became more competitive, the restrictions on inward FDI were gradually relaxed. By the fifth stage of liberalisation in 1973, the government had removed the 50% ceiling on foreign participation in certain sectors, and reduced the list of restricted industries to agriculture, forestry and fishing, mining, oil, leather manufacturing and the retail trade (Sekiguchi 1979).

However, despite some liberalisation of restrictions on inward investment, a host of non tariff barriers (NTBs) continued (Ozawa 1989). Some of these pertained to investment related trade issues in service sectors, while others were institutional barriers, such as unequal treatment in standards and approvals, complex import clearance procedures and unequal treatment of foreign and domestic companies.[26] Effective from March 1980, the government abolished the Foreign Investment Law and the Foreign Exchange Control Law, thereby removing formal capital controls and allowing MNEs to invest without licensing applications.

US firms continued to invest in foreign production facilities, particularly in high technology industries and differentiated consumer goods (Dunning 1989). There was also an increasing emphasis on the European Community (EC) as a host region. Historically, US MNEs have always had a substantial presence in several European countries, and some of the new investment represented a higher degree of internationalisation as they adapted their motives from market seeking to a rationalised production. Despite the growing competitiveness of European firms and the rising value of currencies in these countries, the potential of the evolving Single Market outweighed these considerations, and as such the EC represented the largest destination for US direct investment during this period.

The largest inflow of US direct investment to Japan was from the motor vehicle manufacturers, which took substantial (albeit minority) stakes in several Japanese car firms. The purpose of these investments was not so much to exploit their own O advantages but to secure an offshore source of components and cars. The subsequent six-fold increase in stock led to an almost equal increase in US imports from these affiliates (Encarnation 1992). Although with US investment in other industrialised host countries' mergers and acquisitions accounted for a growing share of new investments, this mode of growth was relatively unimportant in Japan. This was initially due to the restrictions placed on such activities, but even after the liberalisation of regulations the US recorded only eight acquisitions in Japan between 1979 and 1983, compared with 169 in the UK and 53 in Germany (Encarnation 1992).

The evidence

The US direct investment stake in Japan experienced a decelerating growth between 1972 and 1982. Total US direct investment grew from $2.67 billion in 1973 to $6.63 billion in 1982, a growth rate of 15.8%. Manufacturing investment grew at the lower rate of 13.1%. The share of manufacturing investments as a proportion of the total US investments fell from 52.4% to 48.7% (see Table 7.1), in spite of a more liberal attitude

by the Japanese authorities to inbound MNE activity. This slowing down reflected not only a deterioration in the L advantages of Japan, but also the decline in the O advantages of US affiliates relative to Japanese firms in a number of industries.
Some evidence in support of the above points include the following:

1 There was a gradual deceleration of the rate of growth of the US direct investment stake in Japan. However, US direct investment in Japan as a percentage of total US direct investment increased from 2.64% to 3.20% over this period. This contrasts with a relative decline of the US direct investment stake in the EC as a whole.[27] In the case of Germany in particular, the US direct investment stake experienced a marginal decrease as a percentage of all US outward direct investment.
2 The percentage of the investment stake directed towards manufacturing, as given in Table 7.1, slipped from 52.4% to a low of 42.8% in 1977 before recovering somewhat by 1992 to 48.7%.
3 The US capital stake as a percentage of Japanese GDP fell slightly, from 0.72% in 1973 to 0.67 in 1977 and 0.61% in 1982. US exports as a proportion of Japanese GDP fell from 2.2% in 1973 to 1.5% in 1978 before returning to 2.2% in 1982.
4 The ratio of US manufacturing direct investment in Japan to Japanese manufacturing direct investment in the US began to decrease from its high point of 16.5 in 1972 to 1.99 in 1982 (Table 7.4).
5 The US manufacturing direct investment stake as a percentage of Japanese GDP fell from 0.42% to 0.30%. US manufactured exports also experienced a slowing of growth, recording a rate of 19.8% over the period 1967–72 to 7.6% over the next five years.
6 The average rate of return on Japanese direct investment stake between 1973 and 1982 was about 14%, whereas in the five years prior to that it was 17%.
7 The growth rate of sales of US manufacturing subsidiaries in Japan increased at the rate of 4.9% over the period 1972 -77, and 17.5% between 1977 and 1982, much less than that between 1967 and 1972, during which the annual growth rate was 33.3%.

Taken together, these facts suggest a decline in the O advantages of US MNEs operating in Japan. These figures also reflect the appreciation of the yen, which reduced the attractiveness of Japan as a location for overseas production. An indication of this declining L advantage is provided by the falling ratio of sales of Japanese affiliates of US firms to the exports of the US to Japan. As illustrated in Table 7.3, this ratio decreased from 1972 to 1982, falling from 1.37 to 1.27 overall, and from 1.32 to 0.44 in manufacturing. On a sectoral level, this ratio declined in

Table 7.5 Ratio between royalties and fees received from and paid to affiliated firms in Japan and US to those received from non-affiliated firms, 1972–90

	Receipts from Japan by US parents				*Payments to Japan by foreign firms*			
	Affiliated (1)	*Unaffiliated* (2)	*Total* (1) + (2)	*Ratio* (1)/(2)	*Affiliated* (3)	Unaffiliated (4)	*Total* (3) + (4)	*Ratio* (3)/(4)
1972	114	240	354	0.48	1	6	7	0.17
1977	300	289	589	1.04	−38	15	−23	NC
1980	413	354	767	1.17	156	−19	137	NC
1981	413	379	792	1.09	39	89	128	0.44
1982	302	494	796	0.61	−172	37	−135	NC
1983	387	500	887	0.77	−154	38	−116	NC
1984	394	524	918	0.75	9	53	62	0.17
1985	476	576	1,052	0.83	111	24	135	4.63
1986	715	632	1,347	1.13	168	114	282	1.47
1987	1,080	723	1,803	1.49	185	88	273	2.10
1988	1,399	1,022	2,421	1.37	241	123	364	1.96
1989	1,480	1,044	2,524	1.42	299	129	428	2.32
1990	1,653	1,205	2,858	1.37	349	184	533	1.90

Source: US Department of Commerce, *Survey of Current Business*, various years.
Notes: Royalties and fees given are net. Negative numbers indicate that receipts of royalties and fees of US affiliates from their Japanese parents exceeded payments to Japanese parents in that year
NC = Not calculable

chemicals, electrical machinery and transport equipment, but grew in food, metal products and non-electrical machinery.

It might be hypothesised that the reason for the fall in the rate of increase of US FDI in Japan was that US firms were using external markets for the transfer of technology. In fact the opposite seemed to be the case. One measure of the extent to which US firms were internalising the exports of their proprietary skills and technology to Japan is the ratio of royalties and fees received from affiliates of US firms to those received from non-affiliate firms. Some details are set out in Table 7.5. The hypothesis is that, the higher the net hierarchical costs of organising cross-border transactions, the higher the ratio should be. However, this ratio increased from 0.48 in 1972 to 1.09 in 1981. This suggests that, although the overall significance of US FDI had fallen and the relative attractions of its O advantages had dipped in relation to their previous status, the modality of exploiting these advantages had shifted towards hierarchies and away from external markets.

(*ii*) *Japanese direct investment in the US*

Background

US GNP per capita grew $6410 to $13,620 during this period. The US was still at stage 4 of its investment development path, and continued to be the target of Japanese exports, although direct investment activity by Japanese MNEs remained in its nascent stage.

While the removal of restrictions that began in 1971 eventually led to the abolition of case-by-case screening of outward direct investment, the Japanese government still discouraged it wherever it was thought likely to adversely affect the Japanese economy and the balance of payments in particular. However, with the floating of the yen and a strong balance of payments surplus, Japan's policy was redirected to reduce government controls, and both the laws that restricted outward direct investment – the Foreign Exchange Control Law and the Foreign Capital Law – were revised in 1979[28] to allow near-complete freedom in outbound MNE activity (see Yoshida 1987: 124–8).

Developments in the international economy also affected the growth pattern of Japanese investments abroad. The change in the exchange rate regime encouraged FDI, as did the oil crisis of the mid 1970s. This second 'shock' encouraged firms to transfer energy intensive industries to locations where energy was abundant. Coupled with increasing international reserves, Japan began to induce firms that were not already undertaking FDI to do so by offering them subsidised loans. This directly led to new FDI flows to petroleum-rich locations such as the Middle East and Indonesia.

The growth of outward direct investment occurred for a number of other reasons. First, Japanese firms had further developed their O advantages. Second, their indigenous production costs were rising relative to those of the countries to which they were exporting. Third, although the market for Japanese goods in the US and Europe was rapidly growing, the rate of penetration by Japanese exporters into those markets, and away from domestic producers, eventually led to the imposition of various forms of trade constraints, including VERs. Fourth, the Japanese yen continued to appreciate.

In the context of this study, it is relevant to note that the O-specific advantages that enabled Japanese firms first to penetrate foreign markets were not so much the result of significant product innovations, but rather modifications of otherwise fairly standardised products and techniques which, to begin with at least, were adapted primarily with the Japanese market in view. They were in large part of two types (Dunning 1993c).

First, there were those to do with the tangible technological advantages of Japanese firms and associated with patentable products and process innovation. These include product modifications peculiar to the Japanese market such as the development and manufacture of compact and fuel efficient cars which were *de rigeur* in a country where space and fuel were at a premium. After the oil crisis of 1973, the demand for such vehicles increased in the US. The revealed patenting advantages (*RPA*)[29] of Japanese firms, compared with US and European firms, have been documented by Cantwell and Hodson (1991), and indicate that during the earlier part of this period Japanese firms' advantages were largely in relatively standardised technology.[30]

Second, there were ownership advantages, which reduce the transaction costs of value added activity associated with more efficient production processes and organisational methods. Examples of such advantages include superior management techniques, just-in-time delivery, leaner production, quality control circles and the ability to improve the efficiency of intermediate product markets.[31]

Japanese MNEs had created distinct O advantages in the production of fairly standardised products that were relatively mature by the use of superior design, quality consistency and efficient working methods. In addition, the availability of support services and commercial infrastructure (often supplied by government), coupled with aggressive marketing techniques and the rigorous demands of Japanese consumers, offered the cutting edge for Japanese firms to succeed in overseas markets. In fact, one estimate suggests that only about 3% of Japan's cost advantage in the manufacture of small cars at this time was due to superior technology, the rest being derived from these production and organisational skills.[32] These kinds of O-specific assets tend to take longer to diffuse across national boundaries than do technological advantages (Kogut 1993), while their efficient use often requires them to be 'internalised' within the transferring company, and controlled by centralised decision taking (Dunning 1993b).

The trade friction between the US and Japan in the late 1970s may explain the increase in outward direct investment by Japanese firms towards the end of the period, regardless of the changing nature of the L advantages of the US. Shishido (1989) refers to this shift towards US production as the setting up of 'survival centres' to reduce trade friction and to counteract import restrictions. With the rising value of the yen against the dollar, this situation was affected by the relatively faster rate of economic growth of Japan compared with that of the United States. Thus, as the yen appreciated against the dollar, the attractiveness of manufacturing sites in the US increased relative to those in Japan.

While Japanese MNEs continued to exhibit a preference for greenfield investments in the US – especially where they possessed distinctive O advantages – merger and acquisition activity began to grow in the 1970s. Such activity provided Japanese firms with a speedy access to the US market, as well as to a source of complementary assets. In 1974, for example, there were twelve major acquisitions undertaken by Japanese firms compared with just ten by German firms (Encarnation 1992).

Finally, the 1970s saw the beginning of strategic asset acquiring FDI that was directed towards R&D activity and less towards manufacturing.[33] Such firms would tend not to be highly capitalised. Companies such as Sony, Kyocera International and Toyo Bearings were all motivated to manufacture in the US to tap technology and research skills that were being developed in that country (Ozawa 1979: 118). However, these investments were the exception rather than the rule. The primary Japanese motive for FDI continued to be the sustenance and control of transpacific trade.

The evidence

The Japanese manufacturing investment stake in the US in 1973 was $141 million. This represented just 1.7% of the total manufacturing FDI stock in the US. There was, however, considerable Japanese participation in such sectors as banking and commerce, where Japanese FDI accounted for almost a quarter of all inbound investment. The US accounted for almost 68% of Japanese worldwide investment in the tertiary sector.[34] By 1982, Japanese manufacturing investments were $1.6 billion, a five-fold increase from 1973. Exports to the US, on the other hand, remained at the 25% level of all Japanese exports over this period (Yoshida 1987).

By 1982, the stake of Japanese manufacturing outward direct investment in the US as a percentage of US GDP had increased five-fold from its 1973 value. As Table 7.2 highlights, this increase is further underscored by the fact that, between 1975 and 1977, the ratio fell before returning and exceeding its 1974 level. The rate of growth between 1978 and 1982 was 36.3% compared with 23.9% between 1973 and 1977. This post 1978 growth was most significant in the food, machinery and transportation industries.[35] It may be hypothesised that the sharp increase in Japanese investments in the US between 1972 and 1974 was a result of changes in the world economy, rather than a sudden improvement in the O advantages of Japanese firms. The fact that the ratio subsequently declined implies that Japanese firms grew at a slower pace than the US economy as a whole in the mid 1970s and picked up only towards the end of the decade. What were the reasons for this? In examining the relationship between changes in exchange rates and the number of Japanese affiliates established in the US per year, Yoshida (1987) confirmed that the number of Japanese affiliated manufacturing plants surged shortly after the exchange rate hit a trough (i.e. a weaker US dollar and a stronger yen) in 1973, 1978, 1981 and 1983. This would suggest that, while the improving O advantages of Japanese firms may have accounted for some of the growth of investment in the US, the changing L advantages of the US were a pivotal consideration, particularly the various protectionist measures introduced by the US government.

During this period, therefore, Japanese direct investment in the US was, for the most part, due to pull factors associated with the trade friction between the two countries. Those firms that did invest to supply markets had difficulty in optimally utilising their O advantages in the US, whereas other firms invested to acquire technology. Therefore, it is not surprising that the rate of return of Japanese investment in manufacturing was consistently negative since 1975 (except for 1978 and 1979) in the US, despite an increase in the value of its investment stock.[36]

But what of the changing L advantages of the US relative to Japan? Demand for Japanese products continued to grow at sometimes phenomenal rates. While this demand was partly met by an increased output from Japanese affiliates, its main source was Japanese imports. For example, US imports from Japan of electrical machinery increased by a factor of almost 10 between 1980 and 1985, while sales of Japanese affiliates in the US increased three-fold.[37] Table 7.6 gives details of the ratio of sales of Japanese affiliates in the US to manufacturing exports from Japan. While comparable data are not available on sales until 1977, it can be seen that between 1977 and 1982 this ratio increased in almost all other manufacturing sectors, but particularly in food products, chemicals and non-electrical machinery.

Royalties and fees paid to Japanese firms by US based firms were also on the increase. According to US Department of Commerce data, in 1972 just 1% of all royalties and fees paid by all US based firms were to

Table 7.6 Sales of Japanese manufacturing affiliates in the US and Japanese exports to the US, 1977–89

	All industries			*Total mfg*			*Food & kindred*			*Chemicals*		
	(A) Sales ($bn)	(B) *Exports ($bn)*	*A/B*	*(A) Sales ($bn)*	(B) *Exports ($bn)*	*A/B*	*(A) Sales ($bn)*	(B) *Exports ($bn)*	*A/B*	*(A) Sales ($bn)*	(B) *Exports ($bn)*	*A/B*
1977	50.80	18.90	2.69	2.26	18.66	0.12	0.28	0.24	1.17	0.12	0.49	0.24
1980	84.20	32.96	2.55	3.99	32.50	0.12	0.46	0.30	1.53	0.38	0.75	0.51
1982	106.70	39.92	2.67	5.20	39.26	0.13	0.57	0.32	1.78	0.44	0.92	0.48
1985	152.10	72.38	2.10	11.19	71.40	0.16	0.65	0.52	1.25	0.61	1.48	0.41
1986	116.60	85.45	1.36	11.95	84.36	0.14	NSA	0.52	—	NSA	1.87	—
1987	182.30	88.07	2.07	14.00	86.91	0.16	0.61	0.47	1.30	1.35	2.23	0.61
1988	225.30	93.16	2.42	24.75	91.78	0.27	1.00	0.39	2.55	2.73	2.26	1.21
1989	267.01	97.11	2.75	39.26	95.66	0.41	1.64	0.34	4.80	3.80	2.50	1.52

	Metals			*Machinery except elect.*			*Electrical machinery*			*Transportation eqpt*		
	(A) Sales ($bn)	(B) *Exports ($bn)*	*A/B*	*(A) Sales ($bn)*	(B) *Exports ($bn)*	*A/B*	*(A) Sales ($bn)*	(B) *Exports ($bn)*	*A/B*	*(A) Sales ($bn)*	(B) *Exports ($bn)*	*A/B*
1977	0.65	3.44	0.19	0.32	2.00	0.16	0.18	3.15	0.06	NSA	5.55	—
1980	1.07	4.91	0.22	0.52	6.20	0.08	0.68	2.85	0.24	NSA	13.20	—
1982	1.16	5.64	0.21	1.00	3.55	0.28	0.92	9.27	0.10	NSA	16.20	—
1985	4.93	5.50	0.90	1.19	7.36	0.16	1.86	22.26	0.08	0.63	25.17	0.03
1986	3.08	4.64	0.66	1.81	8.87	0.20	1.68	26.06	0.06	NSA	32.52	—
1987	3.54	4.44	0.80	2.38	10.11	0.24	1.89	26.79	0.07	NSA	32.54	—
1988	5.20	5.09	1.02	3.22	11.84	0.27	3.09	19.46	0.16	2.96	30.26	0.10
1989	7.31	4.85	1.51	6.10	14.01	0.44	4.13	21.65	0.29	7.35	30.82	0.24

Source: US Department of Commerce, Survey of Current Business, various years, and *UN Commodity Trade Statistics*, various years
Note: NSA = data not separately available or industry breakdown suppressed

affiliated firms in Japan and only 4% were paid to unaffiliated firms. By 1981 these figures were 9% and 30% respectively. Table 7.5 gives the ratio of fees paid to affiliated Japanese firms to those paid to unaffiliated Japanese firms by US affiliates. This ratio is seen to increase from 0.17 to 0.44 between 1972 and 1981. This gives some support to the hypothesis that there was an increasing propensity of Japanese firms to internalise the US market for their O advantages rather than to use external markets. While the data on intra-firm royalties and fees may be distorted by transfer pricing, the fact that 30% of all royalties and fees paid to unaffiliated foreigners by US based companies were directed to Japan points to the growing strength of Japanese firms in technology intensive sectors. The low percentage of internalised flows of technology is consistent with the actions of MNEs investing in unfamiliar territories – but ones in which there are reasonable endogenous supply capabilities – in the early stages of internationalisation.

1982 – mid 1990s: Japan enters stage 4: the US moves to stage 5

(i) US direct investment in Japan

Background

In the 1980s, Japan entered stage 4 of its investment development path. Between 1983 and 1989, its GNP per capita increased from $9953 to $23,443, overtaking that of the US in the process. The growth of Japan's outward direct investment continued to outpace that of its inward direct investment, although the latter was considerably less restricted by government intervention. Through bilateral negotiations, many of the non-tariff barriers that affected US manufacturing firms had been either dismantled, or substantially reduced.[38] At the same time, the continuing rising value of the yen has made FDI in Japan relatively more expensive.

While the size and character of Japanese markets in the 1980s have made them extremely lucrative for foreign firms, the O advantages of Japanese firms have developed quite considerably, and particularly in some of the sectors, e.g. semiconductors, colour TVs and cars, in which US firms had traditional strengths. These facts notwithstanding, the presence of US MNEs in Japan continues to grow. By 1989, for example, FDI from the US accounted for 50.5% of total FDI in Japan (MITI 1990b). Considerable investment activity occurred in the chemicals industry, an area in which US firms retained considerable O advantages, and this followed on the heels of increased demand for US exports of goods and technology, especially pharmaceuticals.[39]

Manufacturing investments by US MNEs in Japan in the 1980s were prompted partly to gain access to the Japanese market, partly to acquire new assets and partly to gain an insight into Japanese technological capabilities. The direction of both types of investment essentially reflected the restructuring of the Japanese economy towards higher value added and research intensive activities. This restructuring has been coordinated through a mix of closely controlled and government-initiated educational, industrial and social strategies, although the direct interventionism of the 1960s and 1970s was now beginning to be replaced by a market facilitating and 'signalling' role (Porter 1990: 409).

As the O advantages of Japanese firms have increased, so too has the infrastructure needed to support them. This is shown by the existence of extensive research and development facilities (and the skilled manpower needed to run them) of Japanese firms in high value added sectors in which US firms had earlier held a dominant position. The features of the Japanese R&D infrastructure are multifaceted. There is a large national R&D expenditure that represents a sustained commitment to R&D by both the private and the public sectors. As a percentage of GDP, such expenditure has grown from 2.0% of GDP in 1975 to 3.1% in 1991. Corresponding figures for the US are 2.3% and 2.7%. While the share of private R&D of total R&D expenditures in the two countries was similar (70.9% for Japan and 69.2% for the US), real annual compound growth in business R&D expenditure between 1983 and 1991 was 9.0% for Japan and 2.3% for the US (World Economic Forum and IMEDE 1993). Not surprisingly, there has been considerable growth in R&D activities: the number of R&D personnel per 1000 labour force for Japan, Germany and the US in 1991 was 14.1, 14.1, and 7.7 respectively (World Economic Forum and IMEDE 1993).

The development of infrastructural support is exemplified by the creation of industrial zones catering exclusively to corporate R&D facilities such as Tsukuba Science City. These are aimed at encouraging the clustering of R&D activities (Japan Update 1990). Unlike earlier stages of development, the Japanese government has been providing incentive schemes to encourage affiliates of foreign firms to participate. This infrastructure, combined with the strong O advantages of firms in Japan, acts as a powerful magnet to research oriented firms, so much so that by 1989 no fewer than 156 foreign enterprises had R&D facilities in Japan (Ozawa 1989).

The L advantages of Japan have also changed as a consequence of the structural impediments talks between Japan and the US in the late 1970s and mid 1980s,[40] which were aimed at redressing the growing trade imbalances between the two countries. These resulted in several agreements covering various industries, including telecommunications and semiconductors, to increase the access to the Japanese markets of foreign companies. But as Encarnation (1992) notes, the subsequent increase in inward direct investment would not have occurred had US firms not possessed considerable O advantages in these areas. The growth of US direct investment in Japan during this period was, however, not helped by the decline of the dollar against most major currencies including the yen. Overall, the overseas activities of US MNEs increased at a slower rate than outward FDI from other home countries in this period. For example, the stock of US direct investment as a percentage of the total world stock of investment decreased from 42.5% to 30.5% between 1980 and 1988, whereas that of Japan increased from 3.8% to 9.8% over the same period.[41] *Inter alia,* this reflects the increasing competitiveness of MNEs from other countries (including Japan), as well as the increasing L attractions of the US as a host country for FDI. This latter phenomenon has also helped the competitiveness of US exports; for example, between 1983 and 1989 US exports to all countries grew at an annual rate of 13.6%, while those to Japan grew at 17.6%.

The US entered stage 5 of its investment development path during this period. This was starkly shown by the fall in the ratio of its total outward direct investment to total inward direct investment from 2.60 to 1.04 between 1980 and 1990.[42] More particularly, US based firms were faced with increasing competition from firms from other industrialised countries in both foreign and domestic markets, which had the effect of accelerating outward but decelerating inward investment. The motivation for, and location of, FDI by US firms also changed. Increasingly it was directed to the other countries of the Triad (UNCTC 1991). Increasingly too, it was allocated to high technology and R&D intensive sectors. Increasingly it took the form of mergers and acquisitions; and increasingly it was geared towards restructuring existing value added activities, or acquiring new assets to protect or strengthen the regional or global competitiveness of the investing firms

The evidence

US outward direct investment in Japan increased from $7.7 billion in 1983 to $21 billion in 1990, an annual average growth rate of 24.9%. As a percentage of total US outward direct investment, investment in Japan grew from 3.7% to 5.0%. However, in 1990 its total value still remained only about one-third of that in the UK, and three-quarters of that in Germany.

The US manufacturing capital stake in Japan grew from $3.9 billion in 1983 to $10.6 billion in 1990, an annual growth rate of 24.2%. This represented 6.3% of the total US stake in manufacturing in 1990, up from 4.1% in 1983. The percentage of manufacturing investment as a share of total US direct investment in Japan was maintained around the 50% level.

The sectors that experienced the greatest growth were transportation, electrical machinery, chemicals and fabricated metal products. This is a curious combination of industries in that they include some in which the US had a competitive advantage (sectors of electrical machinery such as computers, transportation and chemicals) and others in which Japan had a competitive advantage (fabricated metal products and electrical machinery). This would suggest that, in the 1980s, US firms were exploiting existing competitive advantages in Japan and also seeking to acquire new competitive advantages.

For the previous period, we observed a possible decreasing O advantage of US firms compared with Japanese firms. In this period, the following facts indicate the state of US competitiveness:

1 Although comparable figures are not available, US outward direct investment in Japan as a proportion of total inward direct investment in Japan appears to have been maintained at about 50% of total inward direct investment over this period. However, the corresponding percentages were 70% in 1974, and 83% in 1960.
2 Compared with their indigenous competitors, US affiliates appeared to make little inroad into Japanese markets in the 1980s. Table 7.1 sets out the ratio of US capital stake to the Japanese GDP, and shows that, while this increased from 0.65% in 1983 to 0.70% in 1985, the year of the Plaza Accord, by 1989 it had fallen back again to 0.65%. The corresponding proportions of US manufacturing investments to Japanese GDP for the same years are 0.33%, 0.35% and 0.34%. Preliminary figures for 1990 indicate that both ratios were higher than their 1985 level, 0.73% for total US investments in Japan, and 0.37% for manufacturing investments. This suggests a possible regeneration of US MNEs O advantages, although at least part of this growth is due to an appreciation of the dollar.
3 The ratio of US manufacturing direct investment stake in Japan to Japanese manufacturing direct investment in the US decreased from 2.44 in 1983 to 0.70 in 1990 (Table 7.3). *Ceteris paribus*, this would reflect a noticeable improvement in the O advantages of Japanese firms *vis-à-vis* US firms, and/or a strong reduction in the L advantages of Japan, relative to the US, as a manufacturing base.
4 Actual capital expenditures of US affiliates doubled between 1985 and 1989, while plans for 1990 and 1991 are for an average increase of about 14% (Mataloni 1990). Capital expenditures of US affiliates have been demonstrating steady growth, growing at a rate of 22.8% over the period 1985–89, whereas the equivalent rate for all developed countries was 7.7% (Mataloni 1990). The implication of these data is that, despite point 3 above, Japan is becoming a more attractive base for outward direct investment by US firms. The reason for this is the above

average profits which can be earned in Japan. During the period 1980–88, for example, the rate of return of US direct investment in manufacturing in Japan was 20%, much higher than the rate of return of US manufacturing outward direct investment in all countries, which was 13%.[43]

These data imply several things. First, they suggest that the decline in US competitive advantages may have been arrested in certain sectors which have enabled the US MNEs to better compete with Japanese companies on the latter's own turf. Popular and academic literature abounds with anecdotal evidence of the competitive pressures on US firms both to reduce costs and to relearn the organisation and production technology skills so successfully applied by Japanese firms. In the car sector in particular, US firms have widely adapted Japanese systems of quality control, work methods, cost-saving techniques and organisational technology;[44] although in other sectors, e.g. digital high definition television and biotechnology, they have more than held their own in international markets.

Turning next to the advantages of Japan as a production base, as Table 7.3 indicates, although the ratio of sales of manufactures of US subsidiaries to US exports of manufactures rose rapidly from 0.49 in 1982 to 0.89 in 1986, by 1989 it had dropped back to 0.70. On a sectoral level, all industries on which data are available showed a similar initial rapid growth, before dropping to ratios closer to their 1982 levels. This was due to three factors. First, several large US MNEs invested heavily in Japan in the wake of the trade agreements and in response to the structural impediments initiative during the early part of this period. Second, such investments may have led to an increase in intra-firm US exports, which typically lag FDI. Encarnation (1992), for example, notes that intra-firm US exports accounted for one-seventh of all US exports to Japan in 1988, three times their share in 1982. Third, the spurt of export growth may also be due to changes in the exchange rate which made US exports more competitive.

Having outlined the L advantages of Japan, the question that begs answering is this: given the strong O advantages of Japanese firms, would this not deter inward investment? The answer is 'Yes' – as far as the exploitation of traditional O advantages is concerned. Firms producing created asset intensive products will *require* such an infrastructure as a necessary condition for investing. This is confirmed by data on the revealed patentry advantages (RPAs) of Japan in the foreign research activities of its MNEs. Japan's RPA as a location for R&D activities has remained greater than 1 in several industries and has increased most dramatically in agricultural chemicals, telecommunications and motor vehicles (Cantwell and Hodson 1991).

Overall, one may hypothesise that these data suggest an improvement in the L advantages in Japan facing US firms, and/or an improvement in the O advantages of US firms, in at least some sectors of industrial activity. However, as Lawrence (1992) points out, much of the growth of the US stake in Japan in the 1980s was through the reinvested earnings of existing firms rather than through capital inflows from new investors, from which he inferred that there still remain (perceived) obstacles to first time investment activities by foreign firms in Japan.

What of the I advantages of US firms in exploiting their O advantages in Japan? As Table 7.5 shows, the ratio of royalties and fees received by US firms from affiliated firms in Japan to those received from unaffiliated firms rose steadily from 0.61 in 1982 to 1.37 in 1990. Over the same period, the ratio decreased in the rest of the world from 3.97 to 3.63. Clearly, the use of hierarchial transactions by US firms selling their technology to Japan was increasingly favoured relative to its use in other countries.

(*ii*) *Japanese direct investment in the US*

Background

Between 1983 and 1990, the GNP per capita of the US rose from $14,150 to $19,870. This represented a growth rate of 6.5% compared with a corresponding growth rate for Japan of 15.3%. The erosion of O advantages of US firms that had begun in the late 1960s and continued in the 1970s slowed down, and in some sectors was reversed in the 1980s. However, the O advantages of firms from other countries (especially the Triad countries) continued to grow, as did the extent of their overseas operations. Much of this investment was directed to the US market: between 1980 and 1989, the share of world stock of inward direct investment in the US increased from 16.5% to 28.6% (US Department of Commerce 1991), and partly because of this, the US began to experience a chronic balance of payments problem of extraordinary proportions by the early 1980s. This was further exacerbated by the strength of the US dollar at this time. These changes represented not only an increasing economic interdependence between the EC and the US, but also the increasing convergence of patterns of FDI and domestic economic structure among the Triad countries. Indeed, the growth of inward investment into the US has been shown to be positively related to the relative GNP growth of the US, and especially so in the case of Japanese inward investment (Ray 1989).

The Plaza Accord, which led to the devaluation of the US dollar against the currencies of the G-7 countries, came as a shot in the arm for US industry. It also had a significant effect on the exports of the major trading partners of the US. The value of the dollar against the yen fell by 29.4% between 1985 and 1986[45] and by a further 15% in the following year. Indeed, by 1988, and converted at the exchange rate of the time, the hourly wage in manufacturing industry in Japan was estimated to be $11.41 compared to $10.18 in the US and $10.44 in Germany (Keizai Koho Center 1991). The circumvention of VERs, which in the last period were an important motivation for Japanese manufacturing investment in the US, ceased to be a prime factor in the late 1980s.

Partly as a result of these changes, Japanese exports to the US were seriously jeopardised. Japanese firms immediately responded by raising domestic productivity through enhanced automation, by moving to higher value added segments and by undertaking global rationalised production. The extent to which Japanese firms have undertaken rationalised production is much less than that of their US or European counterparts. This, in part, reflects the relatively early stage of their internationalisation and in part the nature of their O advantages, which until recently have been based on organisation skills and other intangible assets, which take longer to transfer, and are more likely to require greater central control over their application (Dunning 1993c). The O advantages of Japanese firms prior to the 1980s had been based more on the efficient organisation of existing technologies than on their ability to produce new technologies; i.e. they were weak in the innovation of new technology, but were world leaders in its management and application.

None the less, in the 1980s the US still possessed competitive advantages in certain sectors such as pharmaceuticals, software, electrical machinery and computers. The significant portion of Japanese FDI had hitherto been knowledge seeking and market seeking. This has continued to the present day; however, whereas in the 1970s the investment had been primarily *defensive*, e.g. in response to protectionism, in the last decade it has become increasingly *offensive*, and directed to sectors in which Japanese firms have strong O advantages.

The evidence

The Japanese direct investment stock in the US between 1983 and 1990 grew from $11.3 billion to $83.5 billion, an annual average rate of 90.9% compared with 33.7% for that from the EC. Not surprisingly, the Japanese share of total FDI stock in the US increased from 8.2% in 1983 to 20.7% in 1990. The growth of Japanese manufacturing investment stock in the US since 1986 has exhibited a dramatic annual average growth of 81%, compared with 41% between 1983 and 1986. As a percentage of the stock of total manufacturing FDI in the US, such investment rose from 3.5% in 1983 to 9.5% in 1990. The sectors that recorded the greatest gains were fabricated metals and machinery, and these sectors were responsible for

20.2% and 28.7% of the total new investment respectively. That these industries were growing is not surprising, for it is these that especially benefit from economies of common governance. They are also the same industries in which exports by Japan had earlier been increasing most dramatically – and were now losing ground owing to the rising value of the yen.[46]

Table 7.4 shows that the ratio of the stock of US manufacturing investment in Japan to that of Japanese manufacturing investment in the US markedly fell from 2.44 to 0.57 between 1983 and 1989. For the first time in 1988, Japan had more invested in manufacturing in the US than the other way round. More than anything else, these data reflect the contrast between the changing configuration of OLI advantages facing Japanese firms and the Japanese economy compared with those facing US firms and the US economy. In a transpacific context, Japanese outward direct investment in the US clearly outpaced US inward investment in Japan. On a worldwide basis and across all sectors, the ratio of Japanese outward direct investment to inward direct investment *increased* from 3.5 in 1974 to 16.8 in 1989, while the corresponding ratio for the US over the same period *decreased* from 4.4 to 0.9 (MITI 1990b).

Given the distinct changes in the L advantages facing Japanese firms in the US, it is interesting to observe the ratio of Japanese investment stake as a percentage of US GDP. Table 7.2 shows that this ratio grew from 0.34% in 1983 to 1.52% in 1990. The ratio of Japanese manufacturing direct investment stake to GDP also increased, from 0.05% in 1983 to 0.28% in 1990. These data confirm that Japanese firms increased their O-specific advantages relative to their US counterparts. However, it is also worth noting that the growth in Japanese markets in the US was concentrated in the faster growing sectors.

The 1980s marked a redirection in the motives for FDI of all firms, and especially those investing in the Triad, away from the US and from market and natural resource seeking, towards efficiency-enhancing and the acquisition of critical and competitiveness-enhancing created assets. Firms from other industrialised countries had begun to 'catch up' with US firms in their technological capabilities, and were trying to sustain or advance their global markets. As a consequence, they began to restructure their US investments to embrace high value added activities, especially in areas where US firms have traditionally had a competitive advantage. Japanese firms had hitherto preferred to be involved in the US through technology agreements or greenfield investments (in which the Japanese firm developed its own technology but used the US infrastructure). In the 1980's, however, joint ventures, strategic alliances and mergers and acquisitions became the preferred mode of entry. These modes of investment have the advantage of reducing the high fixed costs and lengthy development times associated with innovation in high technology industries and in developing new markets. Between 1986 and 1989, the volume of Japanese acquisitions of US companies increased five-fold, to $13.7 billion. In 1989, 187 deals were concluded, of which the largest ten accounted for almost 60% of the total value of these investments. In contrast, 88 deals were concluded in 1986.[47]

Another aspect of Japanese investment needs to be mentioned. It is a well known feature of the internationalisation process of market seeking investment that investments are first made in the final stages of the value added chain and gradually deepen as vertical integration occurs. Alternatively (or in addition), other foreign firms may set up to engage in supplying operations. Part of the growth of Japanese direct investment in the US has been as a direct result of the Japanese affiliates of major companies developing backward linkages, to ensure a steady supply of inputs for their manufacturing operations. Often, such firms have encouraged suppliers from their home market to make direct investments in the US so as to continue an established relationship (and these firms are often affiliated in some way to one another).[48] This has resulted in the agglomeration of suppliers which have set up operations around particular major manufacturers, and may have to do with Japanese firms' O advantages in process technology (such as just-in-time delivery) with which the Japanese suppliers are already familiar. While the US Department of Commerce does not report intra-firm trade, a MITI (1990a) report suggests that approximately 30.1% of all inputs were purchased from US based members of the same *keiretsu*.

Part of the increase in Japanese manufacturing investments in the US was most certainly at the expense of its manufacturing exports to the US. However, it is important to remember that strategic asset acquiring FDI is not substitutable for exports. Therefore the changing sales to export ratio will reflect both the L advantages to *exploit* the O advantages of Japanese domestic firms and the L advantages to *acquire* foreign O advantages. From Table 7.6, which gives the ratio of sales of Japanese affiliates to exports from Japan, we see that this ratio increased between 1982 and 1989 in fabricated metals from 0.21 to 1.51, in non-electrical machinery from 0.28 to 0.44 and in chemicals from 0.48 to 1.52. The ratio in food and kindred products grew from 1.78 to 4.8, whereas the ratio for all manufacturing rose from 0.13 to 0.41. This clearly implies that the L advantages of supplying these goods made by Japanese firms from a US location increased substantially over this period. The ratio of sales to exports in electrical machinery fell from 0.1 in 1982 to 0.07 in 1987 despite the tripling of FDI over this period, while exports increased by a factor of 8. In 1988 this ratio picked up to 0.15, and by 1989 it stood at 0.29. In transportation equipment, the ratio increased from 0.03 in 1985 to 0.24 in 1989. These data also suggest that the L advantages of Japan as a production base for these manufactures were generally superior to those of the US until 1987. However, as Japanese firms learnt how to exploit their O advantages in foreign locations efficiently, and as the yen appreciated, the L advantages of the US have been increasing even in electrical machinery, an industry in which the Japanese have had a technological dominance over the previous two decades.[49] Whether this trend will continue is a matter of conjecture, although it is possible that with new waves of protectionism, as well as the appreciating yen, this will most likely be the case.

Until the mid 1980s, Japanese firms obtained most of their payments for technology sales to the US from arm's-length transactions. In 1981, for example, the ratio of royalties and fees paid by affiliated firms in the US to those paid by unaffiliated firms in the US to Japan was 0.44; by 1990 this ratio had risen to 1.9, which suggests a marked increase in the propensity of Japanese firms to internalise the market for their technological advantages in the US (Table 7.5). The worldwide ratio for all payments of royalties and fees by affiliated firms to those paid by all unaffiliated firms increased from 1.44 in 1981 to 1.58 in 1990, indicating that internal and external transactions of intermediate services of Japanese firms had reached the level of those of the more internationalised operations of European MNEs in a relatively short period of time.[50] Since intra-firm transactions tend to predominate in high technology sectors as well as in those subject to economies of scale and scope, these data provide an interesting insight into the changing nature of Japanese production in the US.

SUMMARY AND CONCLUSIONS

The purpose of this chapter has been to apply the concept of the investment development path to explain the level and structure of international direct investment flows between the US and Japan over the post Second World War period. In doing so, it has confirmed the importance of country-specific factors in influencing the OLI configuration of MNEs, or potential MNEs, and has also demonstrated the ways in which the O-specific advantages of firms at one period may affect, or be affected by, the L-specific advantages of countries at another period of time.

In making a clear distinction between natural and created assets, this chapter has argued that, in the post-war period, it is the innovation and efficient use of the second kind of assets that pre-eminently have determined the trajectory of an industrialised or industrialising country's investment development path. In particular, we have sought to explain why the recent level and pattern of Japanese outward and inward direct investment flows have been so different from that of its US counterparts – although in the early 1990s there has been some suggestion that they are converging. Because of differences in their L-specific endowments and also their initial positions on the investment development path, the propensity of Japanese firms to internationalise their value added activities has been several steps behind that of US MNEs. At the same time, the sectoral distribution of their respective competitive advantages has reflected their comparative abilities to create and exploit particular kinds of O-specific assets.

While the Japanese international direct investment position in the last forty years has moved from stage 2 to stage 4 – and to the beginnings of stage 5 – of the IDP, the US position has waivered between stages 4 and 5. At the same time, for reasons explained in this chapter, the trajectory of the Japanese path has been quite unique, in that for most of the period the amount of inward direct investment has been much lower than one would have expected for an industrialising (and, later, industrialised) country and, indeed, much less than that which occurred in the earlier stages of US industrial development. This is partly determined by the 'exogenous' country-specific factors of Japan versus the US – while Japan is natural resource-deficient, the US is well endowed in natural resources. This chapter in particular has emphasised that government policy (endogenous factors) has played a decisive role among countries whose competitive advantages rest more on the created than the natural assets they possess.

This chapter has further illustrated the ways in which the competitive (or O) advantages of firms both affect and are affected by the competitive (or L) advantages of countries, and also how each influences the ways in which resources and capabilities are organised across national markets.

The role of government as a factor affecting both the structure of a country's international direct investment position at a given moment of time and the way it changes over a period of time has been a central theme of this volume. Indeed, the role of government in influencing the competitive advantages of its firms and locationally bound assets may itself be considered as a critical L-specific advantage (or disadvantage). In the context of transpacific investment flows, we have sought to contrast a holisticly managed Japanese economy and an American economy in which – except for the defence and space sectors – governments have preferred only to intervene to counteract structural distortions.

Such differences in the systemic roles of governments reflect a host of historical and cultural country-specific characteristics, and also the fact that in Japan the relative significance of created to natural assets is so much higher than in the US. There is also little disagreement among scholars that the trajectory of Japan's investment development path – and particularly in the earlier part of the post-war period – has been strongly influenced and closely monitored by the Japanese government, even though the policies pursued have been broadly consistent with the (dynamic) market forces. This chapter has also shown how the nature and direction of the Japanese government's involvement have changed as the economy has become both more advanced and more internationalised.

We have also emphasised the importance of strategic asset acquiring FDI. Over the past decade, an increasing proportion of FDI – both of Japanese and US origin – has been undertaken to *acquire* O-specific advantages rather than to *exploit* such advantages. Clearly, such investment is likely to be directed to countries that are home to firms that possess complementary assets to those already possessed by the acquiring firms. To that degree, then, a country that attracts more investment than it exports, i.e. is a net inward investor, might be doing so from a position of economic strength rather than weakness – a situation that was not countenanced in the initial framing of the investment development path.

In conclusion, we believe that the prospects of TPDI in the 1990s are mixed. There can be little doubt that outward direct investment in Japan is currently well below that which one would expect in a country of that income level and industrial structure; and there is a tremendous potential for more US MNE activity in Japan. On the other hand, the prospects for Japanese investment in the US continue to remain favourable, albeit perhaps at a reduced greenfield rate. Most certainly, the higher costs of entry by greenfield foreign investors into the Japanese production and marketing systems, *vis-à-vis* those into its US counterpart, seem unlikely to be much reduced in the next decade. If a speedy breakthrough is to occur, it must surely be through a M&A route. Here, if the conclusion of strategic alliances is anything to go by, the portends are not at all encouraging, as the rate of increase in new alliances concluded between US and Japanese firms over the period 1985–89 compared with the previous five years is well below that concluded between US and European firms, or that within Europe or the US.

At the same time, one cannot help but believe that, just as there are both economic and political pressures for Japan to do more to open its markets to US imports, so the pressures will mount for Japan to follow similar principles as the US, with respect to the extent to which it allows its own firms to be taken over or merged with foreign firms. If such an event should occur, US and European firms could regain some of their earlier global competitive advantages, one might well expect to see Japan entering the fifth stage of its investment development path by the late 1990s, and, rather belatedly, for inward direct investment to rise much more markedly than outward direct investment.

8

SUMMARY, CONCLUSIONS AND POLICY IMPLICATIONS

The central aim of this monograph has been to examine the relationship between industrial development and foreign direct investment activities, and the interaction between MNE activity and economic structure. The issue of economic structure has been evaluated from at least two perspectives. First, we were concerned with the changing structure of the world economy as a whole, and with the dynamics of the relationship between industrial development and the extent of FDI activities across countries from an aggregative development perspective. The explicit hypothesis here is that there exists a systematic relationship between these two issues. Second, we evaluated the concurrent (and interrelated) evolutionary processes behind economic growth and MNE activity, and assessed how these evolutionary forces impact on the economic structure of individual economies in the industrialised world.

The argument that the structure and level of development of a particular economy are related to its inward FDI activity as well as its outward FDI activity is in itself not new. Indeed, our theoretical perspective is based on the work of Dunning (1981a, 1988a) on the investment development path (IDP). The emphasis in this volume has been on the dynamic aspects of the relationship, particularly with regard to the industrialised countries. However, the 'new' version of the IDP presented in Chapter 2 is peculiar in that it can be viewed as two separate and distinctive analytical frameworks.

The first framework is concerned with the process of economic growth and how it interacts with FDI activity, emphasising the evolutionary and path-dependent nature of the two as well as their interdependence. In other words, the extent and nature of FDI activities, as well as the economic structure associated with a given country at a given point in time, are a function of their FDI and economic structure in previous periods. Additionally, the role of government is emphasised as a prime catalyst in determining the nature of the evolution and interaction of FDI activities. It is no accident that this approach mirrors that taken by scholars of 'new' growth theories. Technological accumulation and the central role of innovation in economic growth represent an important common element between our theoretical approach and that of both the evolutionary economists and the neo-Schumpeterians. We regard technology as being endogenous to growth, and as the primary determinant of ownership advantages of firms.

We make a clear distinction between *natural* assets and *created* assets. The balance between the level of natural and created assets of a country essentially determines their economic structure. The nature of their comparative advantages helps determine the nature of the firm-specific assets of the firms operating in a given environment. The inter-temporal dynamics that lead to shifts in the economic structure are strongly associated with the process of technological accumulation and the development of firms' competences, as well as with the role of governments in facilitating industrial development and economic growth through policy implementation and development. As economies evolve, the importance of created assets increases, while the role of natural assets declines.

The second framework developed here represents a stages-of-growth approach to the first framework. The dynamics of growth and FDI are used to explain the inter-temporal changes in FDI and economic development and, when introduced to create a dynamic version of the investment development path, provide a clearer explanation of both 'how' and 'why' FDI activities change with economic development. A novel feature of the dynamic IDP is the introduction of a *fifth* stage, which focuses on the changing relationship between FDI and economic structure of the industrialised countries. This fifth stage reflects the changes in the world economy associated with the process of globalisation and economic 'catch-up' and convergence that is occurring among and between these countries. Since the economic structures of industrialised countries are created-asset-based, and the O advantages of their firms are firm-specific, and have increasingly geographically spread production activities, their O advantages are decreasingly a function of their home-country-specific characteristics and their factor endowments.

Chapters 3 and 4 examined the stages-of-growth framework for a sample of countries at different stages of the IDP using a cross-sectional approach. We utilised this type of approach as a proxy for longitudinal analysis. Although cross-sectional analysis represents a static analysis of a dynamic phenomenon and conceals country-specific differences, the results indicate that the changes in the world economy arising from a convergence among the industrialised countries and a 'falling-behind' of most of the developing countries are reflected in the extent of their FDI activity. There continues to be a relatively strong relationship between FDI activity and economic development. Furthermore, the results confirm that the significance of natural assets (such as natural resources) declines as countries develop, while the significance of created assets (such as innovatory capability) increases. The results also signal that, relative to developing countries, firm-specific factors play a much more significant role than country-specific ones as determinants of inward and outward FDI activity by industrialised countries.

However, our use of cross-sectional analysis requires the aggregation of data which conceal differences between countries. First, the actual investment development path of every country is idiosyncratic given different national contexts, factor endowments and national systems of innovation. Since we have indicated that the nature of the dynamics between FDI and economic structure is partly path-dependent, important differences are concealed by the use of a stages-of-growth approach. Second, it allows us to understand only the *extent* of FDI and broad changes in economic structure. If we are to evaluate how changes in economic structure within a given country relate to their FDI activity, we need to understand the *nature* of FDI and economic structural changes among and between sectors.

The rest of the monograph, therefore, concentrated on understanding the dynamics between FDI and economic structure by focusing on a comparison of individual industrialised countries. The importance of understanding the dynamic nature of FDI and economic structure among the industrialised countries is highlighted by the fact that an increasing proportion of FDI is directed from industrialised countries to other industrialised countries, while their economies have been seen to have similar economic structures, consumer tastes and homogeneous factor endowments. This 'regionalisation' among the countries of the Triad is particularly interesting when it is noted that the growth rates of FDI activity have outstripped their domestic growth rates, and that the L advantages of locations, and the O advantages of their firms, in so far as created assets are concerned, are becoming broadly similar as they become increasingly integrated. This is by no means unrelated to the evolution of their MNEs, which have become increasingly globalised through hierarchies that act as networks, seeking complementary assets through their network of affiliates, both to exploit their O advantages and to acquire them. In a sense, therefore, these countries are experiencing *de facto* integration. Such a trend would be further enhanced by *de jure* integration efforts such as NAFTA and the EU. As such, the competitive advantages of the MNEs from these countries reflect not just the competitive advantages of the home country, but, to an increasing extent, those of their various host countries, as their O advantages become more firm-specific.

The effects of globalisation on the FDI activities in the Triad were the focus of Chapter 5. If the role of traditional supply factors is declining and their income levels and economic structure are becoming similar, why not the sectoral pattern of the inward and outward FDI? In other words, country-specific factors should in fact decline to insignificance as a determinant of FDI activity. The economies of these countries are increasingly based on created assets. We attempt to distinguish between 'exogenous' country-specific factors, which are a function of their natural assets, and which are path-dependent and becoming increasingly homogeneous over time across countries, and 'endogenous' country-specific factors, which are government-policy-based, such as national systems of innovation, and which are heterogeneous across countries. This suggests a paradox. Increasing economic convergence should lead to homogeneity of both economic structure and FDI activities; on the other hand, given that created assets are path-dependent, and that each country is idiosyncratic and is endowed with a different configuration of natural assets, their FDI activities should continue to reflect these differences. Some of the evidence reviewed in Chapter 5 indicates that such a paradox exists, and that outward and inward FDI of the industrialised countries still reflect both 'endogenous' and 'exogenous' country-specific characteristics.

Chapter 6 has attempted to resolve this paradox, arguing that the 'exogenous' country-specific factors, such as traditional factor endowments and market size, while determining the *kind* of competitive advantages associated with its firms, play a decreasingly important role in determining the FDI and trading activities of these firms. On the other hand, 'endogenous' country-specific factors, which are influenced by the policies of governments (such as technology, trade and education policies), determine the *extent* and *quality* of these competitive advantages in created assets, and are of increasing significance as determinants of the competitive advantage of a country's firms and their international economic activity. Indeed, we have attempted to argue that the role of government may itself be regarded as a critical location-specific advantage.

This theme is further explored through some quantitative analysis regarding the changing pattern of manufacturing exports and outward FDI and their relationship to country-specific factors. The results broadly confirm these propositions. One surprising finding is that the ownership advantages of firms engaged in exports may be different from those engaged in outward FDI. Also, the structure of the exports of the countries studied has remained stable over the 1980s, but has become increasingly specialised, while their outward FDI has been unstable and is more specialised than their exporting activities. The analysis suggests that overall, while the path-dependent, natural-asset-based country-specific variables are declining in importance, they still play an important role in determining the nature and extent of outward FDI. On the other hand, they remain significant in determining the exporting activities of their domestic firms. Given the high extent of intra-firm trade noted in the literature, and the fact that the growth of exports is positively related to the growth of outward FDI, this may be because these two groups of firms do not overlap, with the exporting firms being largely uninational in nature. Another possible (and more plausible) explanation for this phenomenon may lie in product life cycle theory: MNEs may prefer to export different goods from those that they produce overseas through outward FDI activity. In other words, while MNEs are increasingly engaged in intra-firm trade, they are not necessarily engaged in intra-industry trade, and have increasingly rationalised their production activity. Differences in country size do not play a significant role except that small countries tend to be specialised in fewer sectors but are relatively more internationalised, suggesting that *de facto* and *de jure* integration has considerably minimised the limitations associated with achieving economies of scale. The results indicate a very obvious but easily overlooked fact: *homogeneous does not mean identical.* We elucidate. Much has been written about the fact that the industrialised countries have become increasingly homogeneous in their consumption patterns and in terms of their income levels. The increasing role of MNE activity through both international production and exports among these countries is partly credited for this process. Proponents of globalisation have argued that the growth of intra-Triad MNE activity has led to a further blurring of country-specific differences as MNEs are able to exploit their international production activities through global rationalisation. What we are suggesting is that, although these countries are indeed broadly similar in terms of their economic structure, they are as yet by no means identical.

The results in Chapter 6 are only very tentative in nature, given the paucity of data on FDI. Also, by examining exports, outward FDI and home-country-specific factors, we have examined only one side of a complex equation. Chapter 7 addressed these weaknesses by conducting a qualitative analysis of bilateral changes in FDI activity and economic structure between Japan and the US for a forty-year period. This analysis permitted us to distinguish between the different (and changing) motives for outward and inward FDI. It also highlighted the role of government in facilitating the innovation and maintenance of created assets, and how this role has changed over time and with industrial development. The contrast between the US and Japan is particularly interesting because of the two very different approaches the respective governments have taken to manage economic growth.

However, we must add a cautionary note. The evidence examined here is of a tentative and exploratory nature, given the limitations associated with studying a complex phenomenon on an aggregate level. It would be an exercise in futility to offer an exhaustive list of limitations and qualifications with an analysis that covers a wealth of complex phenomena. None the less, with a view to being objective, we highlight some of the more significant issues. First, there are distinct difficulties associated with evaluating the macro phenomena of economic structure against the activities of MNEs, which are essentially a micro phenomenon. With the growing extent of firm-specific advantages, these difficulties are exacerbated.

Second, the extent to which internationalisation has occurred varies across industries and firms, and is a function of a myriad of variables, only some of which have been examined here. For instance, we have not fully examined the role of technology accumulation, which is essentially a firm-specific phenomenon, and the importance of technological trajectories, which is an industry-specific phenomenon. Another important issue, referred to only in passing, is the influence of governments on the organisation of economic activity.

Third, the growth of alternative forms of overseas value added activity such as strategic alliances needs to be taken into account. Given that the MNEs from the industrialised countries are increasingly focused towards high technology sectors, this is especially important. As suggested elsewhere, strategic alliances have become an important means by which MNEs from industrialised countries have begun to engage in cross-border activities since the 1980s. The evidence suggests that there is an increasing preference for Triad-based MNEs to utilise non-equity-based cooperative agreements in preference to equity-based agreements (such as joint ventures) in their intra-Triad partnering activities in these sectors (Hagedoorn and Narula 1994), although this preference does not extend to those undertaken between Triad-based firms and developing countries: Freeman and Hagedoorn (1994) suggest that between 1980 and 1989 almost 70% of strategic technology partnering agreements between Triad firms and developing country firms were equity based, while for intra-Triad agreements it was less than 50%. Such agreements are naturally not reflected in the FDI data, and, since well over 95% of all strategic alliances are intra-Triad in scope (Freeman and Hagedoorn 1994), the use of FDI data for industrialised countries without allowing for the growth of strategic alliances may make the results questionable. The use of strategic alliances represents a quasi-hierarchical mode of international economic activity, and represents a middle road which firms are increasingly exploiting. To ignore the growth of strategic alliances is akin to the myopic view of the neo-classical school in ignoring FDI.

In order to do justice to such a broad array of issues, a wealth of information is needed on the nature of activities of firms, both domestic and multinational, and this represents a task that requires resources of far greater magnitude than are at our disposal. One of the most important restrictions is the availability of FDI data. Data are not available in sufficient detail on the industrial distribution of MNE activity for sufficient countries, or over a long enough period. The quality and comparability of FDI data can also be called into question. The definition of FDI varies by country, and reflects government estimates. Investments made are often not reported, and stock figures represent historical estimates that do not always include reinvested profits and capital flows to and from third countries.

Given these limitations, with great caution, we venture to suggest that the fifth stage is still in the making; the process of economic integration that is currently occurring among industrialised countries has led to a considerable adjustment and has increased cross-investment. Such global readjustment in patterns and nature of FDI activity *may* lead to a slowing of FDI activity after an initial turbulent period, once firms have achieved rationalised production and countries have become increasingly interdependent through the activities of such MNEs, but it is safe to say that, by the early 1990s at least, this has not occurred. Although there are some significant exceptions, few MNEs are engaged in international production activities on a globally rationalised basis. Many still base much of their high value added activity in their home countries, which dominate their production and strategic decisions.

POLICY IMPLICATIONS

There are at least two reasons why a study such as this may be significant in terms of policy implications. First, from the point of view of developing countries, it is germane to identify why FDI inflows have declined. The growing share of direct investment capital concentrated among industrialised countries has severe implications for developing countries, a large number of whom have over the past decade or so moved away from import substituting regimes towards more open, export oriented regimes. Their development strategies are (often explicitly) increasingly reliant on the inward flow of foreign direct investment as a source of both capital and technology. Technology spillovers and capital are both necessary inputs for economic development, especially in less developed economies which are caught in the vicious cycle of poverty. With FDI increasingly flowing among the industrialised countries, this has caused a divergence, as developing countries, with the exception of the newly industrialising economies (NIEs), are experiencing slowing growth, further impairing their ability to 'catch up' with the industrialised world. It therefore becomes increasingly germane to understand the reasons behind the growth of FDI activity among the industrialised countries, and their increasing preference to invest intra-Triad.

Second, it is important to understand how industrial development and the foreign direct investment interact, given the process of globalisation and its influence the process of economic growth. This has important policy implications for industrialised and developing countries alike. With the increasing significance of international economic activity relative to their purely domestic activity, it has become paramount to understand the extent to which governments are able to maintain and strengthen the competitiveness of their firms and the economic structure of their own economies by utilising both inward and outward FDI. Given that policy makers are able to influence only their domestic environment, the extent to which country-specific characteristics determine the extent and structure of international economic activity is central to understanding whether and how they are able to control their economic growth. These two issues are clearly related.

It seems very obvious that one of the major implications of this study is the importance of created assets in determining the competitiveness of countries and their firms. It should by now be evident that the process whereby created assets evolve over time is a double-edged sword. On the one hand, it determines the locational advantages of countries, the kinds of economic structure they possess and the competitive advantages of their firms. The growth of inward FDI and the kinds of potential spillovers that this will provide for a given location are influenced by these issues. On the other hand, the nature of created assets also determines the extent to which spillovers will benefit the country and its firms. This is akin to the 'technological congruence' and 'social capability' argument initially put forward by Abramovitz (1990). Not only must the country possess locational advantages in terms of the availability of infrastructural facilities and skilled human capital to attract higher value added MNE activity, but domestic firms must be in a position to interact with the subsidiary if the country is to achieve economic growth because of it.

Let us assume for the moment that the governments take a hands-off approach to economic growth. The ability of domestic firms to interact successfully with MNEs is determined by their own technological competences, which are both cumulative and localised, and a function of their past technological competences. Its localised nature is implicit from its path-dependent nature, and is a function of the country's natural and created assets in past periods. A country that, in its early stages of development, had a comparative (or absolute) advantage in, say, petroleum extraction is more likely to be home to domestic firms engaged in this industry. The technological trajectory of domestic firms would, *ceteris paribus*, remain in this and related areas over time. Such firms may be unable to benefit from the establishment of a MNE subsidiary engaged in the electronics industry, unless it was engaged in labour intensive activity that did not require skilled manpower. The path dependency of a firm's competitive advantages renders it extremely difficult and costly for countries to move towards new and unrelated sectors.

This is not to say that countries are permanently constrained by their past competitive and comparative advantages. As we have highlighted in this monograph, path dependency is a feature of the 'exogenous' country-specific characteristics that are associated with a country's factor endowments. This is not the case with its 'endogenous' country-specific factors, which are determined primarily by governments. We have also emphasised the role of government in facilitating the innovation and maintenance of created assets, and the fact that they become increasingly important in determining the extent and quality of the created assets of countries and the competitive advantages of its firms. Indeed, the significance of government policy applies not just to industrialised countries, but to developing countries as well. It can also be argued that the success of the NIEs through 'late industrialisation' may be due to the central role of government (see for instance Amsden 1989, 1991 and Wade 1988, 1990). Governments are able to influence the technological trajectories of domestic firms through economic, technological and innovation policies associated with national systems of innovation (see for instance Lundvall 1992 and Nelson 1993), and by addressing infrastructural issues and market imperfections in a systematic way.

To take but one example, countries that are constrained by small market size generally tend to be short of natural resources, and their firms are limited in the scope of their production activities since local market conditions do not provide economies of scale, as in Belgium, the Netherlands, Taiwan and Singapore. If such countries' advantages were purely path-dependent, the competitive advantages of their firms and the locational advantages of the countries would be in industries that were characterised by a low minimum efficient scale. Instead, these limitations have been overcome by governments to a certain extent by two means: firstly, through an explicit attempt to reduce the disadvantage through an expansion of their *de facto* market size by encouraging rapid internationalisation of their economies, by means of exports and outward FDI; second, through fostering innovation by domestic firms in particular sectors that are amenable to internationalisation, and developing country-specific created assets such as the availability of skilled manpower and infrastructural support facilities to attract inward FDI in these same sectors.

Overcoming such exogenous limitations also argues for the importance of supranational government policy in reducing market imperfections across borders through *de jure* economic integration agreements such as NAFTA and the EU. Most successful small countries are more highly internationalised than larger countries, and have achieved *de facto* integration (in an economic sense) with countries that have larger market sizes.

The completion of the Uruguay round and the establishment of the World Trade Organisation also represent important supranational agreements that will increase international economic activity and the homogeneity of markets as international market imperfections are addressed.

The essential point here is that created assets are determined by technology, and it is easily overlooked that technology is much more than products and processes, *but includes the knowledge to engage in transactions efficiently, whether intra-firm or intra-market.* What we are trying to emphasise is that governments also need to act as 'facilitators', with a primary intention of reducing market imperfections that relate to the organisation of economic activity, in terms of coordinating and promoting the relative efficiency of inter- and intra-firm transactions. To the extent that the activities of firms are increasingly international, this requires a more global perspective than a national one. It is almost impossible for countries to function in isolation, and the struggle against globalisation and international market forces is a futile one which utilises resources that could more efficiently be used in promoting the development of created assets and the efficiency of firms. It is imperative that governments appreciate that infrastructural development, national systems of innovation and the fostering of efficiency in the organisation of economic activity represent related and interdependent issues in developing competitiveness. Russia represents an example of an economy that has considerable levels of technological capability and a relatively well developed infrastructure, but where there is systemic market failure in the efficiency of its inter- and intra-firm markets.

It is important to stress that government policy towards FDI cannot be considered in isolation from trade policy. The growth of intra-firm trade, and the extent to which FDI is both trade-complementary and trade substituting, require that policy makers take a holistic approach. In the industrialised countries and in technology intensive goods especially, the role of firm-specific advantages is becoming increasingly important. This is enhanced by the international nature of the operations of MNEs. It is no longer sufficient for a country to have a comparative advantage in a given sector: it must have an absolute advantage. As Dosi *et al.* (1990) have suggested, as absolute advantages shift within a globalised economy, market shares adjust. Differences in the competitive advantages of firms (which translate to absolute advantages on a country level) decide the flow of trade and FDI. However, unlike exports, outward FDI is not always indicative of competitive advantages of the MNEs: there is increasing use of FDI to acquire assets, as well as to exploit the existing assets of the MNEs. This represents a means to promote the competitiveness of an economy by exposing domestic firms to other national contexts and environments, thereby also allowing the firm to avoid the constraints associated with developing technological capabilities suited solely to its home market. MNEs from the developing countries such as Thailand, Indonesia, Taiwan, India and China, to name but a few, are increasingly engaging in FDI activity overseas with the active support of their home governments to acquire technological assets and competences in overseas locations with the intention of improving their competitive position.

APPENDIX 1

Correlation Matrices of Regression Coefficients (Chapter 4)

Equation 1

	Constant	*TI*	*GFCFPOP*	*XP*	*PATPER*	*HCPOP*	*RELDEMD*
Constant	1.0000						
TI	0.2819	1.0000					
GFCFPOP	−0.3953	−0.5825	1.0000				
XP	−0.7797	−0.3046	0.4880	1.0000			
PATPER	−0.4758	−0.7086	0.1969	0.3442	1.0000		
HCPOP	−0.3867	0.0729	−0.3929	−0.0718	0.2304	1.0000	
RELDEMD	−0.3370	0.1478	−0.1118	−0.0065	0.0379	0.2427	1.0000

Equation 2

	Constant	*GFCFPOP*	*XP*	*PATPER*	*HCPOP*
Constant	1.0000				
GFCFPOP	−0.4130	1.0000			
XP	−0.3948	0.0378	1.0000		
PATPER	−0.5404	−0.1248	0.2330	1.0000	
HCPOP	−0.6553	−0.0878	−0.1303	0.3506	1.0000

Equation 3

	Constant	*GFCFPOP*	*XP*	*MP*	*PATPER*	*HCPOP*
Constant	1.0000					
GFCFPOP	−0.3450	1.0000				
XP	−0.6647	0.4539	1.000			
MP	−0.7116	0.1388	0.1498	1.0000		
PATPER	−0.2032	−0.3641	0.0878	0.0228	1.0000	
HCPOP	−0.2439	−0.5153	−0.1973	0.1255	0.3074	1.0000

Equation 4

	Constant	*GFCFPOP*	*XP*	*PATPER*	*HCPOP*	*RELDEMD*
Constant	1.0000					
GFCFPOP	−0.3936	1.0000				
XP	−0.3675	0.1139	1.0000			
PATPER	−0.5393	−0.1134	0.2303	1.0000		
HCPOP	−0.5507	−0.2142	−0.2810	0.2707	1.0000	
RELDEMD	0.0234	0.2526	0.3137	0.0292	−0.5722	1.0000

APPENDIX 2 ISIC

ISIC REVISION 2 (Chapter 6)

Industrial breakdown

Agriculture, etc.	1000
Mining, etc.	2000
Total manufacturing	3000
Less technology intensive	31 + 32 + 34 + 36 + 37 + 381
Food, beverages & tobacco	31
Textiles, leather & clothing	32
Paper, printing	34
Non-metallic mineral products	36
Metals & metal products	37, 381
More technology intensive	36 + 37 + 382 + 383 + 384 + 35
Coal, petroleum products	353, 354
Chemicals	351, 352
Rubber & plastics	355, 356
Mechanical equipment	382
Electrical equipment	383
Motor vehicles	3843
Other transportation equipment	3841, 3842, 3844, 3845, 3849
Other manufacturing (wood, instruments)	33, 385, 39

NOTES

1 INTRODUCTION

1 The relationship between technological accumulation and FDI has been examined by Cantwell (1989, 1991), Dunning and Cantwell (1989), Dunning (1988b), Cantwell and Tolentino (1990) and Narula (1993).

2 See, for example, Abramovitz (1986 and 1990), Baumol (1986), Alam (1991 and 1992), Dowrick (1992), Dowrick and Nguyen (1989), Dowrick and Gemmell (1991), Verspagen (1993).

2 THE DYNAMICS OF FDI AND ECONOMIC GROWTH

1 For this reason, Ozawa (1995) has coined the alternative concept, 'technology development path'.

2 The nature of this interaction has been examined by Agarwal and Ramaswami (1992) on how it affects the firms choice of entry mode.

3 While we are concerned with the dynamic nature of the OLI variables, factor endowments that affect geographical distribution of location-specific advantages may be regarded as evolving gradually and therefore, over a short time period, may be viewed as static.

4 Defined as the difference in the stock of its inward and outward direct investment. Note that when the former exceeds the latter net investment position will be negative.

5 Among others, Cantwell (1989), Tolentino (1993), Cantwell and Tolentino (1990), Lall (1983 and 1990), UN (1993a).

6 Technological capability may be regarded as the collection of largely human skills necessary to efficiently utilise tangible resources at the disposal of a firm over time. These skills, which are to a great degree non-codifiable in nature, can be related to technical, managerial, entrepreneurial or marketing know-how. See Lall (1990) for a clear exposition on this issue. The existence of national technological capability as opposed to firm-level technological capability is a more complex issue. As Lall (1990) points out, it is not simply the sum of individual firm capabilities, although there is likely to be some synergy between individual capabilities. Instead, it is more practical to speak of ***national capabilities in particular industries***.

7 This issue is explored further in Narula (1993) while the influence of technology accumulation on FDI is dealt with in greater depth in Cantwell (1989).

8 It is to be noted that inward investment activity generally precedes outward investment activity.

9 The role of country-specific characteristics in determining the extent and pattern of FDI is discussed more fully in Dunning (1981b: chapter 4).
10 Although the actual amount of investment will almost certainly continue to rise.
11 Refer to the definition of TNC as put forward by Bartlett and Ghoshal (1989).
12 See the article by Reich (1990) for a succinct discussion on this issue.
13 Kogut (1991) and others have suggested that organisational- and cultural-based assets, not to mention the strategies and administration of governments, may not be transferable. This, depending on the transaction costs associated with the creation and deployment of the assets, could lead a country to having a permanently positive (or negative) net outward investment position compared with its competitors in stage 5. Also it is possible that the macro-organisational strategy of governments may deliberately encourage (discourage) outward or inward investment.
14 Indeed, GDP per capita has been used as a technology endowment indicator. Aquino (1981) in an analysis to examine changes in comparative advantage over time compares the use of GDP per capita against a more sophisticated technology endowment index, and finds that the results were not substantially different.

3 A CROSS-SECTIONAL TEST OF THE IDP

1 We assume that by arranging countries by GNP per capita, all countries with income levels greater than or equal to that of Italy's are industrialised countries.
2 An alternative would be to take flow data for 1968–75. However, data on pre-1970 flow data are limited.
3 A possible solution to the bias introduced by the use of the US dollar is the use of a basket of currencies such as the ECU.
4 In such circumstances, it is recommended to use Whites estimator. However, for small sample sizes Whites estimator is significantly biased.
5 Its inclusion does not affect the significance of our β values, but reduces the R^2 value to 0.347

4 NATURAL AND CREATED ASSETS AS DETERMINANTS OF FDI

1 These countries are: Bangladesh, China, India, Taiwan, Philippines, Malaysia, Korea, Indonesia, Sri Lanka, Thailand, Pakistan, Hong Kong, Japan, Canada, Australia, New Zealand, Fiji, Papua New Guinea, Nigeria, South Africa, Brazil, Equador, Venezuela, Mexico, US, Spain, Portugal, UK, France, Germany, Netherlands, Denmark, Norway, Finland, Sweden, Austria, Belgium, Italy, Turkey, Switzerland.
2 *Sources*: Unesco *Statistical Yearbook*, 1991, and United Nations *Statistical Yearbook*, various issues. There are certain limitations of patents as a measure of innovative activity; see Chapter 6 for a discussion of these limitations.
3 The use of this variable as an indicator of ownership advantages can only be made with the assumption that there is efficient usage of knowledge capital, viz. that the supply of skilled personnel is equal to or less than the demand for this resource. This is not always true in the case of developing countries, where a considerable amount of investment is in the primary

sector, which tends to be labour intensive. Furthermore, firms must internalise the use of such human capital if it is to be regarded as a measure of ownership advantages, an unrealistic assumption, especially in developing countries. For this reason, *HCPOP* is not a good measure of firm-specific technological capability, especially in the case of less developed countries.

4 *Source*: Unesco *Statistical Yearbook*, 1991.

5 *Source*: *World Development Report*, various issues.

6 Dunning (1980) examines a relative market size variable and finds that it is a significant determinant of FDI.

7 Obviously, this assumption is a simplification of reality. The optimal market size varies by industry and capital intensity; therefore this assumption requires two further assumptions: that most of the FDI is in manufacturing (which generally requires large markets to achieve economies of scale) and that the capital–output ratios across countries are the same.

8 Private consumption figures are taken in current prices. *Source*: IMF, *International Financial Statistics Yearbook*, 1991.

9 It can also be argued that two extra variables were used for equation 1, and additional variables tend to increase the R^2 value. However, the magnitude of the increase and the high significance of the variables in equation 1, make this argument weak.

10 See, for example, Wells (1983), Lall (1983), Kumar and McLeod (1981), Narula (1991), UN (1993a), Tolentino (1993).

11 See, for example, Lecraw (1977), Agrawal (1981), Khan (1987), Narula (1991).

12 Which caused an increase in the share of primary imports in 1975 and 1979 for non-OPEC countries.

5 GLOBALISATION, HOMOGENEITY AMONG INDUSTRIALISED COUNTRIES AND DIFFERENCES IN FDI PATTERNS

1 Lall (1990: 25–30) uses the phrase 'national technological competence'.

2 And indeed, over MNEs from other countries.

3 As suggested by the international product cycle theory (Vernon 1966). This may occur either because of the expiry of a patent, or because new technology by rival firms makes the technology obsolete in that market.

4 In the case of certain service sector industries, such natural assets can be internalised and can lead to the development of firm-specific created assets, and thus can be considered to be ownership advantages. However, this issue is not explored in detail here, as it is beyond the scope of the present work.

5 Therefore, they are more likely to reach the fifth stage of the IDP at an earlier level of per capita income.

6 It is important to note that the relationship between size and the propensity to undertake outward investment is not necessarily linear: the marginal propensity to invest is a decreasing function of the domestic market.

7 Such as might be associated with economic integration.

8 See for instance Wade (1988, 1990). A similar approach is also taken by the proponents of the 'late industrialisation' hypothesis such as Amsden (1989, 1991) and Hikino and Amsden (1994). These issues are examined in greater detail in Chapters 6 and 7 as well as in the various country studies in Dunning and Narula (1995b).

9 Growth rates in Tables 5.1 and 5.2 do not include data from 1967. This is

because the period before 1971, at which time the system of fixed exchange rates was eliminated, may have introduced a significant bias into results converted to US dollars from over- or under-valued exchange rates before their floating, and indeed may have acted to discourage FDI before this period.

10 It should be noted that all growth rates are based on market prices, and therefore GDP growth rates cannot be compared among themselves due to different inflation rates. Nevertheless, if we make the not unreasonable assumption that an equivalent inflation rate is inherent in the FDI growth rates, such rates can provide us with an indicator of the relative growth rate when compared for an individual country.

11 The convergence hypothesis is explored by several scholars including Abramovitz (1986,1990), Baumol (1986), Dollar and Wolff (1988), Dowrick and Nguyen (1989), Dowrick and Gemmell (1991) and Verspagen (1993).

12 This observation needs to be qualified. This overall high growth for developing countries, by virtue of its generalisation, conceals important differences within the group. Dowrick (1992) has demonstrated that the poorest developing countries are growing more slowly than the middle income countries. In other words, there is a divergence between these groups of countries, suggesting that the poorer countries are 'falling behind'. In terms of the IDP, these countries would be at stage 1 and 2. Dowrick also shows that the newly industrialised economies (stage 3 countries) are among the only economies that are catching up. This result is confirmed by Verspagen (1993) using a different sample. Indeed, data on FDI outflows from the IMF indicate that the four Asian NICs accounted for 57.6% of total outward flows from non-oil developing countries over the period 1980–90, and for 83% over 1988–90.

13 The UK was the exception, where outward FDI accounted for 25% of GNP.

14 These countries are Singapore, Mexico, Brazil, China, Hong Kong, Malaysia, Egypt, Argentina, Thailand, Taiwan.

15 The extent to which this occurred would depend on its level of internationalisation.

16 The largest tertiary outward direct investors in the developing countries are the US and Japan with 31.5% and 35.4% respectively.

6 COUNTRY-SPECIFIC FACTORS, TRADE AND FDI PATTERNS OVER THE 1980s

1 See for example, Patel and Pavitt (1992).

2 Unless it acquires these through strategic asset acquiring investments.

3 See Freeman and Lundvall (1988).

4 On an absolute scale – although the expenditure on R&D as a percentage of GDP of, say, Sweden is higher than that of the US (3% *v.* 2.6%), in absolute terms its R&D expenditures are just 3.9% that of the US (Freeman and Hagedoorn 1992).

5 The case of Japan and the US are examined in some detail in Chapter 7.

6 Of course, these countries also have access to a similar pool of technology, given their common cultural context (and hence social capability) and their history of trading activities. Innovations in most of the industrialised countries have generally diffused between these countries in a relatively short order. As such, they have implicitly enjoyed a similar level of

technological capabilities that has facilitated the assimilation of most subsequent waves of innovations. Of course, as Abramovitz and David (1994) point out, not all countries have the same ability to exploit technology spillovers given the path-dependent (and localised) nature of technological capabilities (see also Perez and Soete 1988).

7 Cantwell and Sanna Randaccio (1993).

8 For a succinct discussion of the relation between multinationality and firm growth see Cantwell and Sanna Randaccio (1993).

9 This point has been made much of by Kojima (1973, 1990).

10 Such an argument assumes that FDI and trade are not substitutes, as would be the case with import substituting FDI. However, such an assumption is realistic for industrialised countries since tariff barriers to manufactured exports are almost negligible. Although it is often argued that the presence of non-tariff barriers may restrict export activity, their efficacy is a matter of much debate.

11 Such a study is conducted for the case of the US and Japan in Chapter 7.

12 The cluster analysis technique is a K-means procedure into 6 groups and 50 iterations. This method splits a set of objects into a selected number of groups by maximising between relative-cluster variation to within-cluster variation.

13 I wish to acknowledge the assistance of Bart Verspagen of MERIT in providing me with the data for several of these variables.

14 See for instance Pearce and Singh (1992), Patel and Pavitt (1991), Freeman and Hagedoorn (1992), Dunning and Narula (1995a).

15 See Chapter 2 and Chapter 5.

16 It should be noted that the dramatic growth in its share of investment in motor vehicles – from 0 to 10.65 – may be due to a change in classification. Japanese data on outward investment record a very high value for investment in other transportation equipment in 1980 and zero for motor vehicles. In 1989, the data suggest the reverse. Correspondingly, *RCA*(*I*) and share of world outward FDI suggest that Japan had no advantage in motor vehicles but a very high advantage in 'other transportation equipment'. This is clearly not the case, as there is anecdotal evidence as well as data on inward investment from host countries that suggest that at least some of the outward FDI stocks attributed to 'other transportation equipment' in 1980 were actually 'motor vehicles'.

17 See Narula and Gugler (1991).

18 See Levin *et al.* (1987) and Mansfield and Wagner (1981).

19 See Chapter 7 for a detailed analysis of this trend.

20 Between 1980 and 1991, the share of manufactured goods in total imports increased from 22.8% to 50.8%.

21 For 1980 *RCA*(*I*) R = 0.2734; for 1989, R = 0.8235 (1%).

7 TRANSPACIFIC FDI: A FORTY-YEAR VIEW OF CHANGING COMPETITIVENESS

1 Defined as production in Japan financed by US direct investment and production in the US financed by Japanese direct investment.

2 FDI figures used throughout this section are based on US Department of Commerce data, and unless otherwise indicated are stock figures on an historical cost basis.

3 Nakamura (1981: 16–17).

4 Developed and implemented by Joseph Dodge, an American economist.

5 Yoshida (1987) points out that, although responsibility for foreign exchange controls had been transferred to the Japanese government in 1949, it had the approval of the Allies.

6 Excerpt from the Foreign Investment Law of 1950 (US Dept of Commerce 1956).

7 Sekiguchi (1979: 10). Encarnation (1992) notes that this mode of investment was allowed during the occupation to pre-war investors. Remittance of principal was not permitted during the occupation, and was limited to 20% per year from 1952.

8 From 1950 to 1953, investments grew at an annual average rate of 107.9%, compared with the 1954–60 period, when growth tapered off to 15.3%. The corresponding figures for manufacturing direct investment are 60% and 44.8%.

9 US Department of Commerce (1956: 1–1), based on data provided by the Japanese Ministry of Finance (MOF). Capitalised value of technology agreements were calculated by the MOF on the basis of a 5% interest rate and individual tenure of contracts.

10 Such as Brazil, where an import substitution programme had been instituted.

11 Although directly comparable data are not available, estimates are that this accounted for about 6%–7% of its total worldwide stake.

12 US Department of Commerce (1982).

13 It is interesting to note that, between 1952 and 1972, this and all other plans underestimated GNP growth. There were five long-term economic plans instituted, and they were not plans in the normal sense but five- to ten-year economic forecasts which overlapped (Japan Economic Institute of America 1984).

14 Although takeovers through this mode were screened.

15 Especially after Japan joined the OECD in 1964 (Sekiguchi 1979).

16 Sekiguchi (1979: 104).

17 Based on Department of Commerce data.

18 Disaggregated data before 1966 are available only on an intermittent basis.

19 Hourly wage rates in manufacturing increased between 1965 and 1970 from $0.52 to $1.06, whereas in the US they increased from $2.61 to $3.36. Labour productivity was also lower (Sekiguchi 1979: 104).

20 Ozawa (1979: 117–21) presents several examples of these investments.

21 Comparisons are difficult given the different basis for estimation used by official US and Japanese government agencies, and the figures are used here with some caution.

22 Figures for sales of Japanese foreign subsidiaries indicate that Latin American manufacturing subsidiaries exported less than 20% of their output, whereas for Asian subsidiaries the figure was closer to 50%, half of which was exported to Japan (Sekiguchi 1979).

23 Although the share of steel began to recover in the 1970s, it is possible that the undervalued yen at the time made exports of Japanese steel uncompetitive on the world market.

24 The 1973–77 plan had forecast a growth rate of 9.44% and 6 + % for the 1976–82 plan.

25 Although it hit a trough again in 1981.

26 See Saxonhouse and Stern (1989) for an exhaustive analysis of NTBs.

27 The UK was an exception: it grew in importance from 10.9% of total US direct investment stake to 13.2% by 1982.

28 Although the revision became effective in December 1980.

29 Revealed patentry advantage measures comparative advantages in innovative activity, and is defined as the share of US patents taken out by foreigners and attributable to research in the country in question in a given industry, relative to its total share of US patents taken out by foreigners. Therefore this index varies around one, with those locations (and firms from that country) that have a *RPA* of greater than 1 as being relatively advantaged in that sector. For further details see Cantwell (1989).

30 Over the period 1969–77, Japan had a *RPA* of over 1 in sectors such as metallurgical production, construction equipment, motor vehicles, non-metallic minerals, electrical equipment and professional instruments (Cantwell and Hodson 1991: 146–7).

31 Institute of Social Science (1990), Kogut (1991) and Dunning (1993b).

32 *New York Times*, 1 April 1983.

33 It is to be noted that the trend towards investment in R&D intensive sectors during this period applies not just to Japanese investment, but to all inward investment into the US (Kim and Lyn 1987). The difference between Japanese FDI and FDI from other (mainly European) countries is that Japanese firms primarily invested to acquire O advantages, not utilise them.

34 Prior to 1974, changes in parents' claims on their US affiliates resulting from capital gains and losses were treated as valuation adjustments to the year end direct investment position (US Department of Commerce 1984a). Figures for total direct investment stock are particularly inaccurate because of the large intercompany account outflows associated with the Japanese trading firms' activities in the US.

35 Department of Commerce data during this period had transportation machinery under the main heading of other manufacturing, which included other items such as instruments, glass, stoneware and textiles.

36 It is also possible that this may be as a result of transfer pricing practices, given the close relationship between Japanese manufacturing enterprises and the trading houses. Compared with the profitability of the former, the rate of return on trade-related Japanese direct investment has throughout the period been very healthy (*Survey of Current Business*, various years).

37 During the period 1977–80 electrical machinery manufacturing sales increased by a factor of about 4, while imports dropped slightly, perhaps compensated for by local production.

38 Most of the restrictions that are currently being negotiated affect US exports of primary products, and NTBs that inhibit FDI in non-manufacturing sectors.

39 For example, Encarnation (1992) has estimated that between 1978 and 1982 over half of the drugs approved by the Japanese government were manufactured using foreign technology.

40 Although these negotiations are still continuing, some of the most significant agreements made regarding market access to Japan for US goods date back to the mid 1980s.

41 Department of Commerce, unpublished data.

42 In 1989 this ratio had fallen to slightly below 1.

43 Based on Department of Commerce data. This is calculated by dividing net income (after US income taxes) by the average of the beginning- and end-of-year direct investment positions.

44 See especially Ouchi (1981), Destouzos *et al.* (1989), Christopher (1986) and Suzaki (1987).

45 IMF data, using period averages.

46 Porter (1990) identifies the clusters of competitive industries in the Japanese economy as being: transportation equipment, office machinery, consumer electronics, fabricated metal products and computing equipment.

47 UNCTC, unpublished data.

48 More than 25% of the total sales in Japan are accounted for by the six *keiretsu* or corporate groups. Within each *keiretsu* firms are linked through webs of interlocking directorates and shareholdings. There are estimated to be some 12,000 firms that make up the six *keiretsu* (Imai 1990).

49 The revealed patentry advantage (RPA) of Japan in electrical equipment was 1.24 during the 1969–77 period and 1.21 in the 1978–86 period, whereas that of the US has stayed constant at 1.03 (Cantwell and Hodson 1991).

50 The same ratio on payments of royalties and fees for EC firms increased from 0.98 in 1982 to 1.66 in 1990.

BIBLIOGRAPHY

Abd-el-Rahman, K. (1991) 'Firms competitive and national comparative advantages as joint determinants of trade composition', *Weltwirtschaftliches Archiv* 127(1): 83–97.

Abramovitz, M. (1986) 'Catching up, forging ahead, and falling behind', *Journal of Economic History* 46: 385–406.

—— (1990) 'The catch-up factor in postwar economic growth', *Economic Inquiry* 28: 1–18.

Abramovitz, M. and David, P. (1994) *Convergence and Deferred Catch-up: Productivity Leadership and the Waning of American Exceptionalism*, MERIT Working Paper Series no. 94–027, Maastricht.

Afriyie, K. (1992) 'Enhancing FDI and value-added production in developing economies: governments, MNEs and development agencies', *International Trade Journal* 7(1): 85–109.

Agarwal, S. and Ramaswami, S. (1992) 'Choice of foreign entry mode: impact of ownership, location and internationalisation factors', *Journal of International Business Studies* 23: 1–27.

Agrawal, R. (1981) 'Third World multinationals: Indian experience', in K. Kumar and M. McLeod (eds), *Multinationals from Developing Countries*, Lexington, Mass.: Lexington Books, 115–32.

Ahoroni, Y. and Hirsch, S. (1993) *Enhancing the Competitive Advantage of Developing Countries in Technology Intensive Industries: A Conceptual Scheme and Policy Implications*, Copenhagen: Copenhagen Business School Working Paper no. 1–93.

Alam, M. (1989) *Governments and Markets in Economic Development*, New York: Praeger Publishers.

—— (1991) 'Convergence tendencies: some time-series results', *Southern Economic Journal*, 57: 841–7.

—— (1992) 'Convergence in developed countries: an empirical investigation', *Weltwirtschaftliches Archiv* 128(2): 189–201.

Alam, M. and Naseer, A. (1992) 'Convergence and polarisation: testing for an inverted-u relation between growth rates and GDP per capita', *Applied Economics* 24: 363–6.

Amsden, A. (1989) *Asias Next Giant*, New York: Oxford University Press.

—— (1991) 'Diffusion of development: the late industrialization model and greater East Asia', *American Economic Review* 81: 282–6.

Aquino, A. (1981) 'Changes over time in the pattern of comparative advantage of manufactured goods', *European Economic Review* 15: 41–62.

Archibuigi, D. and Pianta, M. (1992) *The Technological Specialization of Advanced Countries*, Dordrecht: Kluwer Academic Publishers.

BIBLIOGRAPHY

Archibuigi, D. and Pianta, M. (1993) 'Patterns of specialisation and growth of innovative activities in advanced countries', in K. Hughes (ed.), *European Competitiveness*, Cambridge: Cambridge University Press, 105–32.

Ariff, M. (1989) 'TRIMs: a north-south divide or a non-issue?' *World Economy*, September: 347–60.

Balassa, B. (1977) 'A "stages approach" to comparative advantage', paper presented at the Fifth World Congress of the International Economic Association, Tokyo.

—— (1980) 'The process of industrial development and alternative development strategies', *Essays in International Finance* no. 141 (December).

Bank of Japan (1955) *Japanese Industry*, Tokyo: Foreign Capital Research Society.

Bartlett, C. and Ghoshal, S. (1989) *Managing across Borders*, Boston: Harvard Business School Press.

Baumol, W. (1986) 'Productivity growth, convergence, and welfare: what the long-run data show', *American Economic Review* 76: 1072–85.

Baumol, W. and Wolff, E. (1988) 'Productivity growth, convergence, and welfare: reply', *American Economic Review* 78: 1155–9.

Bellak, C. (1993a) 'A model of structural change and outward investors', mimeo, Vienna.

—— (1993b) 'A note on the Austrian "diamond"', *Management International Review* (special issue), 2/93: 109–18.

Blomstrom, M. (1984) *The Forms of Foreign Investment by Swedish Firms*, Stockholm: Industrial Institute for Economic and Social Research.

—— (1990) 'Competitiveness of firms and countries', in J.H. Dunning, B. Kogut and M. Blomstrom, *Globalization of Firms and the Competitiveness of Nations*, Lund: Lund University Press

Buckley, P., Mirza, H. and Sparkes, J. (1987) 'Direct foreign investment in Japan as a means of market entry: the case of European firms', *Journal of Marketing Management* 2: 241–58.

Business Week (1989) 'The Rx for Japan's drug companies', *American Business Week*, 20 November.

Cantwell, J. (1987) 'The reorganization of European industries after integration: selected evidence on the role of multinational enterprise activities', *Journal of Common Market Studies* 26(2): 25–48

—— (1989) *Technological Innovation and Multinational Corporations*, Oxford: Basil Blackwell.

—— (1991) 'The theory of technological competence and its application to international production', in D. McFetridge (ed.), *Foreign Investment, Technology and Economic Growth*, Calgary: University of Calgary Press.

Cantwell, J. and Hodson, C. (1991) 'Global R&D and UK competitiveness', in M. Casson (ed.), *Global Research Strategy and International Competitiveness*, Oxford: Basil Blackwell.

Cantwell, J. and Sanna Randaccio, F. (1990) 'The growth of multinationals and the catching up effect', *Economic Notes* 19: 1–23.

Cantwell, J. and Sanna Randaccio, F. (1993) 'Multinationality and firm growth', *Weltwirtschaftliches Archiv* 129(2): 275–99.

Cantwell, J. and Tolentino, P. (1990) *Technological Accumulation and Third World Multinationals*, University of Reading Discussion Paper in International Investment and Business Studies no. 139, May.

Chenery, H. (1979) *Structural Change and Development Policy*, New York: Oxford University Press.

Chenery, H. and Taylor, L. (1968) 'Development patterns: among countries and over time', *Review of Economics and Statistics* 50(4): 391–416.
Chenery, H., Robinson, S. and Syrquin, M. (1986) *Industrialization and Growth*, Washington: World Bank.
Chesnais, F. (1992) 'National systems of innovation, foreign direct investment and the operations of multinational enterprises', in B. Lundvall (ed.), *National Systems of Innovation: Towards a Theory of Innovation and Interactive Learning*, London: Pinter Publishers.
Christopher, R. (1986) *Second to None*, New York: Crown Publishers.
Clegg, J. (1987) *Multinational Enterprises and World Competition*, London: Macmillan Press.
Contractor, F. (1990) *Do Government Policies towards Foreign Investment Matter?* Rutgers Graduate School of Management Working Paper Series no. 90–15, July.
Culem, C. (1988) 'The locational determinants of direct investments among industrialized countries', *European Economic Review* 32: 885–904.
Dalum, B. (1992) 'Export specialisation, structural competitiveness and national systems of innovation', in B. Lundvall (ed.), *National Systems of Innovation: Towards a Theory of Innovation and Interactive Learning*, London: Pinter Publishers.
Daniels, P. (1993) 'Research and development, human capital and trade performance in technology-intensive manufactures: a cross-country analysis', *Research Policy* 22: 207–41.
De Long, J.B. (1988) 'Productivity growth, convergence, and welfare: comment', *American Economic Review* 78: 1138–53.
Destouzos, M., Lester, R. and Solow, R. (1989) *Made in America*, Cambridge, Mass.: MIT Press.
Dollar, D. and Wolf, E. (1988) 'Convergence in industry labour productivity among advanced economies, 1963–1982', *Review of Economics and Statistics* 70: 549–53.
Dosi, G., Pavitt, K. and Soete, L. (1990) *The Economics of Technical Change and International Trade*, New York: Harvester Wheatsheaf.
Dowrick, S. (1992) 'Technological catch up and diverging incomes: patterns of economic growth 1960–88', *Economic Journal* 102: 600–10.
—— (1993) 'Investment and resource allocation as sources of long run growth', paper presented at the conference on Catching Up, Forging Ahead and Falling Behind, Oslo, May.
Dowrick, S. and Gemmell, N. (1991) 'Industrialisation, catching up and economic growth: a comparative study across the world's capitalist economies', *Economic Journal* 101: 263–75.
Dowrick, S. and Nguyen, D. (1989) 'OECD comparative economic growth 1950–1985: catch-up and convergence', *Economic Journal* 79: 1010–30.
Dunning, J.H. (1980) 'Toward an eclectic theory of international production: some empirical tests', *Journal of International Business Studies* 11(1): 9–31.
—— (1981a) 'Explaining the international direct investment position of countries: towards a dynamic or developmental approach', *Weltwirtschaftliches Archiv* 119: 30–64.
—— (1981b) *International Production and the Multinational Enterprise*, London: George Allen and Unwin.
—— (1988a) *Explaining International Production*, London: Unwin Hyman.
—— (1988b) *Multinationals, Technology and Competitiveness*, London: Unwin Hyman.

—— (1990a) *The Changing Dynamics of International Production: Some Firm and Country-specific Influences*, Rutgers Graduate School of Management Working Paper Series.

—— (1990b) 'Globalization of firms and the competitiveness of countries', in J.H. Dunning, B. Kogut and M. Blomstrom, *Globalization of Firms and the Competitiveness of Nations*, Lund: Lund University Press.

—— (1991) 'Governments and multinational enterprises: from confrontation to co-operation?' *Journal of International Studies* 20: 225–44.

—— (1992a) 'Transatlantic foreign direct investment and European integration: the record assessed', *International Economic Journal* 6(1): 59–81.

—— (1992b) 'The competitive advantages of countries and the activities of transnational corporations', *Transnational Corporations* 1(1): 135–68.

—— (1992c) 'The global economy, domestic governance, strategies and transnational corporations: interactions and policy implications', *Transnational Corporations* 1(3): 7–45.

—— (1993a) *Multinational Enterprises and the Global Economy*, Wokingham, Berks.: Addison-Wesley.

—— (1993b) *Global Business: The Challenge of the 1990's*, London and New York: Routledge.

—— (1993c) 'The governance of Japanese and US manufacturing affiliates in the UK: some country-specific differences', in B. Kogut (ed.), *Country Competitiveness: Technology and the Organizing of Work*, Oxford: Oxford University Press.

—— (1993d) 'Globalization: the challenge for economic regimes', mimeo, Rutgers University.

Dunning, J.H. and Buckley, P. (1977) 'International production and alternative models of trade', *Manchester School of Economic and Social Studies* 45: 392–403.

Dunning, J.H. and Cantwell, J. (1989) 'The changing role of multinational enterprises in the international creation, transfer and diffusion of technology', in F. Arcangeli, P. David and G. Dosi (eds), *Technology Diffusion and Economic Growth: International and National Policy Perspectives*, Oxford: Oxford University Press.

Dunning, J.H. and Cantwell, J. (1991) 'MNEs, technology and competitiveness of European industries', in G. Faulhaber and G. Tamburini (eds), *European Economic Integration*, Boston: Kluwer Academic Publishers.

Dunning, J.H. and Narula, R. (1994) 'Transpacific direct investment and the investment development path: the record assessed', *Essays in International Business* no. 10 (May).

Dunning, J.H. and Narula, R. (1995a) 'The R&D activities of foreign firms in the US', *International Studies in Management and Organization* 25: 39–73.

Dunning, J.H. and Narula, R. (1995b) *Foreign Direct Investment and Governments: Catalyst for Economic Restructuring*, London: Routledge.

Dunning, J.H. and Rugman, A. (1985) 'The influence of Hymer's dissertation on theory of foreign direct investment', *American Economic Review* 75: 228–32.

Durkheim, E. (1964) *The Division of Labour in Society*, New York: The Free Press.

Encarnation, D. (1992) *Rivals beyond Trade*, Ithaca, NY: Cornell University Press.

Freeman, C. and Hagedoorn, J. (1992) *Globalization of Technology*, Maastricht, MERIT Working Paper Series no. 92–103.

Freeman, C. and Hagedoorn, J. (1994) 'Catching up or falling behind: patterns in international interfirm technology partnering', *World Development* 22: 771–80.

Freeman, C. and Lundvall, B. (1988) *Small Countries Facing the Technological Revolution*, London: Pinter Publishers.

Fujita, M. (1988) 'The rise of Japanese TNCs', *The CTC Reporter*, no. 26: 13–14.

Globerman, S. and Dean, J. (1990) 'Recent trends in intra-industry trade and their implications for future trade liberalization', *Weltwirtschaftliches Archiv* 126(1): 25–49.

Gray, H.P. (1980) 'The theory of international trade among manufacturing nations', *Weltwirshaftliches Archiv* 118: 447–70.

—— (1982) 'Macroeconomic theories of foreign direct investment: an assessment', in A. Rugman (ed.), *New Theories of the Multinational Enterprise*, London: Croom Helm.

—— (1992) 'The interface between the theories of international trade and production', in P. Buckley and M. Casson (eds), *Multinational Enterprises in the World Economy: Essays in Honour of John H. Dunning*, Aldershot: Edward Elgar, 41–53.

Greenaway, D. (1987) 'Intra-industry trade, intra-firm trade and European integration: evidence, gains and policy aspects', *Journal of Common Market Studies* 26(2): 153–72.

Guerrieri, P. (1991) 'Technology and international trade performance in the most advanced countries', mimeo, University of California, Berkeley.

—— (1992) 'Technological and trade competition: the changing positions of the United States, Japan, and Germany', in M. Harris and Moore, G. (eds), *Linking Trade and Technology Policies*, Washington: National Academy Press, 29–59.

Gugler, P. (1991) *Les Alliances strategiques transnationales*, Fribourg: Editions Universitaires.

Hagedoorn, J. and Narula, R. (1994) *Choosing Modes of Governance for Strategic Technology Partnering: International and Sectoral Differences*, Maastricht: MERIT Working Paper Series no. 94–025.

Hagedoorn, J. and Schakenraad, J. (1991) 'The internationalisation of the economy, global strategies and strategic technology alliances', *Nouvelles de la science et des technologies* 9: 29–41.

Hamalainen, T. (1993) 'The evolving role of government in economic organization', mimeo, Rutgers University, Newark, NJ.

Hikino, T. and Amsden, A. (1994) 'Staying behind, stumbling back, sneaking up and soaring ahead: late industrialisation in historical perspective', in W. Baumol, R. Nelson and E. Wolff (eds), *Convergence and Productivity: Cross Country Studies and Historical Evidence*, New York: Oxford University Press, 285–315.

Hirsch, S. and Meshulach, A. (1991) *Towards a Unified Theory of Internationalization*, Business and Economic Studies on European Integration Working Paper no. 10–91, Copenhagen, Institute of International Economics and Management.

Imai, K. (1990) 'The legitimacy of Japan's corporate groups', *Economic Eye*, autumn: 16–22.

Institute of Social Science (1990) *Local Production of Japanese Automobile and Electronics Firms in the United States*, Institute of Social Science, University of Tokyo Research Report no. 23, March.

Ito, K. and Pucik, V. (1993) 'R&D spending, domestic competition, and export performance of Japanese manufacturing firms', *Strategic Management Journal* 14: 61–75.

Japan Economic Institute of America (1984) *Japan's Industrial Policies*, Washington: Japan Economic Institute of America.

Japan Update (1990) 'Direct investments in Japan: new developments', *Japan Update* (Tokyo, Keizai Koho Center), winter.

Jones, K. (1990) 'The FAC dilemma: surviving middle age in Japan', *McKinsey Quarterly*, winter: 13–30.

Julius, D. (1990) *Global Companies and Public Policy*, New York: Council on Foreign Relations Press.

—— (1991) *Foreign Direct Investment: The Neglected Twin of Trade*, Occasional Papers no. 33, Washington: Group of Thirty.

Katseli, L. (1992) 'Foreign direct investment and trade interlinkages in the 1990s: experience and prospects of developing countries', in *Globalisation and Developing Countries: United Nations Symposium in the Hague, Background Papers*, New York: United Nations.

Kezai Koho Center (1986, 1990, 1991, 1992) *Japan: An International Comparison*, Tokyo: Kezai Koho Center.

Khan, K. (ed.) (1987) *Multinationals of the South*, London: Francis Pinter.

Kim, W. and Lyn, E. (1987) 'Foreign direct investment theories, entry barriers, and reverse investment in US manufacturing industries', *Journal of International Business Studies* 18: 53–66.

Kobrin, S. (1976) 'The environmental determinants of foreign direct investment: an ex post analysis', *Journal of International Business Studies* 6: 29–42.

Kogut, B. (1983) 'Foreign direct investment as a sequential process', in C. Kindleberger and D. Audresch (eds), *The Multinational Corporation in the 1980s*, Cambridge, Mass.: MIT Press.

—— (1991) 'Country capabilities and the permeability of borders', *Strategic Management Journal* 12: 33–47.

—— (1993) *Country Competitiveness: Technology and the Organizing of Work*, Oxford: Oxford University Press.

Kojima, K. (1973) 'A macro-economic approach to foreign direct investment', *Hitosubashi Journal of Economics* 14: 1–21.

—— (1990) *Japanese Direct Investment Abroad*, Tokyo: International Christian University.

Kojima, K. and Ozawa, T. (1984) 'Micro and macro economic models of foreign direct investment: towards a synthesis', *Hitosubashi Journal of Economics* 25: 1–20.

Koopman, T. and Montias, J (1971) 'On the description and comparison of economic systems', in A. Eckstein (ed.), *Comparison of Economic Systems*, Berkeley: University of California Press.

Kravis, I and Lipsey, R. (1989) *Technological Characteristics of Industries and the Competitiveness of the US and its Multinational Firms*, National Bureau of Economic Research Working Paper Series no. 2933, Cambridge, Mass.

Krugman, P. (1987) 'Is free trade passé?' *Economic Perspectives* 1(2): 131–44.

—— (1992) 'Technology and international competition: a historical perspective', in M. Harris and G. Moore (eds), *Linking Trade and Technology Policies*, Washington: National Academy Press, 13–28.

Kumar, K. and McLeod, M. (eds) (1981) *Multinationals from Developing Countries*, Lexington, Mass.: Lexington Books.

Kumar, N. (1990) *Multinational Enterprises in India*, London: Routledge.
Lall, S. (1983) *Third World Multinationals*, Chichester: John Wiley.
—— (1990) *Building Industrial Competitiveness in Developing Countries*, Paris: OECD.
Larre, B. and Torres, R. (1991) 'Is convergence a spontaneous process? The experience of Spain, Portugal and Greece', *OECD Economic Studies* no. 16: 169–98.
Lawrence, R. (1992) *Why is Foreign Direct Investment in Japan So Low?* Paper presented to the National Bureau of Economic Research Conference on Foreign Direct Investment, 15 May 1992.
Lecraw, D. (1977) 'Direct investment by firms from less developed countries', *Oxford Economic Papers* 29: 442–57.
—— (1981) 'Internationalisation of firms from LDCs: evidence from the ASEAN region', in K. Kumar and G. McLeod (eds), *Multinationals from Developing Countries*, Lexington, Mass.: Lexington Books.
—— (1991) 'Factors influencing FDI by TNCs in host developing countries: a preliminary report', in P. Buckley and J. Clegg (eds), *Multinational Enterprises in Less Developed Countries*, London: Macmillan, 163–80.
—— (1993) 'Outward direct investment by Indonesian firms: motivation and effects', *Journal of International Business Studies* 24: 589–600.
Levin, R., Klevorick, A., Nelson, R. and Winter S. (1987) 'Appropriating the returns from industrial research and development', *Brookings Papers on Economics Activity* no. 3: 783–820.
Linder, S. (1961) *An Essay on Trade and Transformation*, London: John Wiley.
Lipsey, R. and Weiss, M. (1981) 'Foreign production and exports in manufacturing industries', *Review of Economics and Statistics* 63: 488–94.
Lockwood, W. (1954) *The Economic Development of Japan*, Princeton: Princeton University Press.
Lundvall, B. (1992) *National Systems of Innovation: Towards a Theory of Innovation and Interactive Learning*, London: Pinter Publishers.
Maddison, A. (1982) *Phases in Capitalist Development*, Oxford: Oxford University Press.
Magee, S.P. (1977) 'Multinational corporations, the industry technology cycle and development', *Journal of World Trade Law* 2(4): 297–321.
Mansfield, E. and Wagner, S. (1981) 'Imitation costs and patents: an empirical study', *The Economic Journal* 91: 907–18.
Mason, M. (1987) 'FDI and Japanese economic development, 1899–1931', *Business and Economic History* 16: 93–107.
Mataloni, R. (1990) 'Capital expenditures by majority-owned foreign affiliates of US companies', *Survey of Current Business*, March: 21–32.
Ministry of International Trade and Industry (MITI) (1990a) *1987 Survey of Overseas Activities of Japanese Enterprises*, International Business Affairs Division, March (in Japanese).
—— (1990b) *Charts and Tables related to Foreign Direct Investment in Japan*, International Business Affairs Division, September.
Mirza, H. (1986) *Multinationals and the Growth of the Singapore Economy*, New York: St Martins' Press.
Moulton, H.G. (1931) *Japan: An Economic and Financial Appraisal*, Washington: Brookings Institution.
Nakamura, T. (1981) *The Postwar Japanese Economy*, Tokyo: University of Tokyo Press.

Narula, R. (1991) *The Role of Developing Country Multinationals in the Acquisition of Industrial Technology in Nigeria: A Pilot Study*, Rutgers Graduate School of Management Working Paper Series no. 91–14.

Narula, R. (1993) 'Technology, international business and Porter's "diamond": synthesising a dynamic competitive development model', *Management International Review* 33(2): 85–107.

Narula, R. and Gugler, P (1991) *Japanese Direct Investment in Europe: Structure and Trends in the Manufacturing Industry*, Business and Economic Studies on European Integration Working Paper no. 19–91, Institute of International Economics and Management, Copenhagen.

Nelson, R. (1993) *National Innovation Systems: A Comparative Study*, Oxford: Oxford University Press.

Nelson, R. and Winter, S. (1982) *An Evolutionary Theory of Economic Change*, Cambridge, Mass.: Belknap Press.

Norman, G. and Dunning, J.H. (1983) 'Intra-industry foreign direct investment: its rationale and trade effects', *Weltwirtschaftliches Archiv* 120: 522–40.

OECD (1989) *OECD Country Studies: Japan*, Paris: OECD.

—— (1991) *OECD in Figures*, Paris: OECD.

O'Hearn, D. (1990) 'TNCs, intervening mechanisms and economic growth in Ireland: a longitudinal test and extension of the Bornschier model', *World Development* 18: 417–29.

Oriental Economist (1956) 'Japan's overseas investments', *The Oriental Economist* 24: 589–91.

Ouchi, W.(1981) *Theory Z*, Reading, Mass.: Addison-Wesley.

Owen, R.F. (1982) 'Inter-industry determinants of foreign direct investment', in A. Rugman (ed.), *New Theories of the Multinational Enterprise*, London: Croom Helm.

Ozawa, T. (1979) *Multinationalism, Japanese Style*, Princeton: Princeton University Press.

—— (1985) 'Japan', in J.H Dunning (ed.), *Multinational Enterprises, Economic Structure and International Competitiveness*, Chichester: John Wiley.

—— (1989) 'Japan's "strategic" policy toward outward direct investment', mimeo, Fort Collins, Colorado.

—— (1992) 'Foreign direct investment and economic development', *Transnational Corporations* 1(1): 27–54.

—— (1995) 'Japan: the macro-IDP, meso-IDPs, and the technology development path', in J. Dunning and R. Narula (eds), *Foreign Direct Investment and Government: Catalyst for Economic Restructuring*, London: Routledge.

Papanastassiou, M. and Pearce, R. (1990) *Host Country Characteristics and the Sourcing Behaviour of the UK Manufacturing Industry*, University of Reading Discussion Papers in International Investment and Business Studies, series B, vol. 2, no. 140.

Patel, P. and Pavitt, K. (1991) 'Large firms in the production of world technology: an important case of non-globalization', *Journal of International Business Studies* 22: 1–21.

Patel, P. and Pavitt, K. (1992) 'The innovative performance of the world's largest firms: some new evidence', *Economic Innovation and New Technologies* 2: 91–102.

Pavitt, K. (1988) 'International patterns of technological accumulation', in N. Hood and J. Vahlne (eds), *Strategies in Global Competition*, London: Croom Helm, 126–57.

Pearce, R. (1990) *Overseas Production and Exporting Performance: Some Further*

Investigations, University of Reading Discussion Papers in International Investment and Business Studies no. 135.

Pearce, R. and Singh, S. (1992) *Globalising Research and Development*, London: Macmillan.

Perez, C. and Soete, L. (1988) 'Catching up in technology: entry barriers and windows of opportunity' in G. Dosi, C. Freeman, R. Nelson, G. Silverberg and L. Soete (eds), *Technical Change and Economic Theory*, London: Pinter Publishers.

Porter, M.E. (1990) *The Competitive Advantage of Nations*, New York: The Free Press.

Ranis, G. (1976) 'The multinational corporation as an instrument of development', in D. Apter and L. Goodman (eds), *The Multinational Corporation and Social Change*, New York: Praeger Publishers.

Ray, E.J. (1989) 'The determinants of foreign direct investment in the United States, 1979–85', in R. Feenstra (ed.), *Trade Policies for International Competitiveness*, Chicago: University of Chicago.

Reich, R. (1990) 'Who is us?' *Harvard Business Review* 68: 53–64.

Rostow, W. (1971) *The Stages of Economic Growth*, 2nd edn, Cambridge: Cambridge University Press.

—— (1990) *Theorists of Economic Growth from David Hume to the Present*, New York: Oxford University Press.

Rugman, A. (1987) *Outward Bound Canadian Direct Investment in the United States*, Washington: C.T. Howe Institute and National Planning Association.

Sakamoto, H. (1989) 'Japanese outward and inward foreign direct investment', *The CTC Reporter*, no. 27 (spring): 64–8.

Saxonhouse, G. and Stern, R. (1989) 'An analytical survey of formal and informal barriers to international trade and investment in the United States, Canada, and Japan', in R. Stern (ed.), *Trade and Investment Relations among the United States, Canada, and Japan*, Chicago: University of Chicago Press, 293–364.

Sazanami, Y. (1989) 'Trade and investment patterns and barriers in the United States, Canada, and Japan', in R. Stern (ed.), *Trade and Investment Relations among the United States, Canada, and Japan*, Chicago: University of Chicago Press, 90–140.

Sekiguchi, S. (1979) *Japanese Direct Foreign Investment*, Montclair, NJ: Osmun.

Shishido, T. (1989) 'Capital transfers from Japan to the United States: a means of avoiding trade friction', in R. Sato and J. Nelson (eds), *Beyond Trade Friction*, Cambridge: Cambridge University Press.

Soete, L. (1987) 'The impact of technological innovation on international trade patterns: the evidence reconsidered', *Research Policy* 16: 101–30.

—— (1988) 'Technical change and international implications for small countries', in C. Freeman and B. Lundvall (eds), *Small Countries Facing the Technological Revolution*, London: Pinter Publishers, 98–110.

Soete, L. and Verspagen, B. (1992) *Competing for Growth: The Dynamics of Technology Gaps. Condivergence and Imovation*, Maastricht, MERIT Working Paper series no. 92–024.

Stevens, B. and Andrieu, M. (1991) 'Trade, investment and technology in a changing international environment', in *Trade, Technology and Investment in the 1990s*, Paris: OECD.

Suzaki, K. (1987) *The New Manufacturing Challenge*, New York: The Free Press.

Swedenborg, B. (1979) *The Multinational Operations of Swedish Firms*, Stockholm: Industrial Institute for Economic and Social Research.

—— (1985) 'Sweden', in J.H. Dunning (ed.), *Multinational Enterprises, Economic*

Structure and International Competitiveness, Chichester and New York: John Wiley and Sons.

Takeuchi, K. (1990) *Does Japanese Direct Foreign Investment Provide Japanese Imports from Developing Countries?* Washington: World Bank Working Paper Series no. 458.

Tolentino, P.E. (1987) *The Global Shift in International Production: The Growth of Multinational Enterprises from Developing Countries*, PhD dissertation, University of Reading.

—— (1993) *Technological Innovation and Third World Multinationals*, London: Routledge.

UNCTAD (1994) *World Investment Report 1994*, New York: United Nations.

UNCTC (1990) *Regional Economic Integration and Transnational Corporations in the 1990s: Europe 1992, North America, and Developing Countries*, New York: United Nations.

—— (1991) *World Investment Report 1991*, New York: United Nations.

United Nations (1992a) *World Investment Report 1992*, New York: United Nations.

—— (1992b) *World Investment Directory, Vol. I*, New York: United Nations.

—— (1993a) *Transnational Corporations from Developing Countries: Impact on Home Countries*, New York: United Nations.

—— (1993b) *From the Common Market to EC 92*, New York: United Nations.

—— (1993c) *The Transnationalisation of Service Industries*, New York: United Nations.

—— (1993d) *World Investment Report 1993*, New York: United Nations.

—— (1993e) *World Investment Directory, Vol. III*, New York: United Nations.

US Department of Commerce (1953) *Direct Private Foreign Investments of the United States: Census of 1950*, Washington: Office of Business Economics.

—— (1956) *Investment in Japan*, Washington: Bureau of Economic Analysis.

—— (1960) *US Business Investments in Foreign Countries: A Supplement to the Survey of Current Business*, Washington: Office of Business Economics.

—— (1981) *US Direct Investment Abroad: 1977 Benchmark Survey*, Washington: Bureau of Economic Analysis.

—— (1984a) *Foreign Direct Investment in the United States, 1950–1979*, Washington: Bureau of Economic Analysis.

—— (1984b) *US Direct Investment Abroad: 1982 Benchmark Survey*, Washington: Bureau of Economic Analysis.

—— (1988) *International Direct Investment: Global Trends and the US Role*, Washington: Bureau of Economic Analysis.

—— (1989) *Foreign Direct Investment in the United States: US Businesses Acquired or Established by Foreign Direct Investors, 1980–1986*, Washington: Bureau of Economic Analysis, July.

—— (1991) *Foreign Direct Investment in the United States*, Washington: Bureau of Economic Analysis, August.

Vernon, R. (1966) 'International investment and international trade in the product cycle', *Quarterly Journal of Economics* 80: 190–207.

Verspagen, B. (1993) *Uneven Growth Between Interdependent Economies*, Avebury: Aldershot.

Veugelers, R. (1991) 'Locational determinants and ranking of host countries: an empirical assessment', *Kyklos* 44(3): 363–82.

Wade, R. (1988) 'The role of government in overcoming market failure in Taiwan, Republic of Korea and Japan', in H. Hughes (ed.), *Achieving Industrialiation in East Asia*, Cambridge: Cambridge University Press.

—— (1990) *Economic Theory and the Role of Government in East Asian Industrialization*, Princeton: Princeton University Press.

Wakelin, K. (1995) 'Empirical studies on the relationship between trade and innovation', unpublished PhD dissertation, European University Institute, Florence.

Walsh, V. (1988) 'Technology and competitiveness of small countries: a review', in C. Freeman and B. Lundvall (eds), *Small Countries Facing the Technological Revolution*, London: Pinter Publishers, 37–66.

Wells, L.T. (1983) *Third World Multinationals*, Cambridge, Mass.: MIT press.

World Bank (various dates) *The World Development Report*, Oxford: Oxford University Press.

World Economic Forum and IMEDE (1993) *World Competitiveness Report*, Geneva: World Economic Forum.

Yoshida, M. (1987) *Japanese Direct Manufacturing Investment in the United States*, New York: Praeger.

INDEX